War or Peace?

STEVEN L. BURG

War or Peace?

Nationalism, Democracy, and American Foreign Policy in Post-Communist Europe

A Twentieth Century Fund Book

NEW YORK UNIVERSITY PRESS
New York and London

NEW YORK UNIVERSITY PRESS
New York and London

Library of Congress Cataloging-in-Publication Data
Burg, Steven L., 1950–
War or peace : nationalism, democracy, and American foreign policy in post-communist Europe / Steven L. Burg.
p. cm.
"A Twentieth Century Fund book."
Includes bibliographical references and index.
ISBN 0-8147-1270-3 (alk. paper)
1. Europe, Eastern—politics and government—1989–
2. Nationalism—Europe, Eastern. 3. Democracy. 4. Yugoslav War, 1991– 5. United States—Foreign relations—Europe, Eastern
6. Europe, Eastern—Foreign relations—United States. 7. Europe—Politics and government—1989– I. Title.
DJK51.B867 1966
320.94′09171′7—dc20 96-32744
CIP

New York University Press books are printed on acid-free paper, and their binding materials are chosen for strength and durability.

Manufactured in the United States of America

10 9 8 7 6 5 4 3 2 1

for

SARAH SAMANTHA

and

DAVID GRAHAM

CONTENTS

TABLES AND MAPS

FOREWORD

The swift spring thaw that followed the unexpected collapse of the Soviet empire opened half of Europe to vast new possibilities. For many nations and peoples, this meant a leap, with mixed success so far, toward democracy and capitalism. For others, the new freedom opened a Pandora's box of age-old attitudes, aspirations, and animosities. Both responses demonstrate the extent to which communism failed to fulfill its promise of developing "new men." Instead, it did little more than lock in place ancient habits of mind. And while the risk of global destruction is surely diminished, we have scarcely entered an era of peace.

In the diplomatic and scholarly scramble to understand and explain the altered architecture of international affairs after the Cold War, much of the speculation has focused on alternative potential futures for Russia, the continuing unification of Western Europe, and the singularity of the role of the United States. Events, however, have tended to force attention toward other issues, especially the dangers of renewed ethnic conflict in Europe. In one sense, the salience of this subject should not be surprising. The map of the continent today, after all, is no more congruous with nationalities than it was after previous conflicts.

Indeed, since the fall of the Berlin Wall, scores of conflicts have broken out around the globe. For American leaders, virtually all these hot spots, such as the Persian Gulf and Somalia, presented novel challenges to policy. But it is in the former Soviet states, the region that in many ways continues to pose the greatest risks, that stability seems the hardest to imagine. Quite simply, as of early 1996, the future of Russia and the other formerly communist nations remains unknowable.

As a result, the Twentieth Century Fund has been continuing a program that started with this last decade of the twentieth century: support for a series of books and monographs that explore the uncharted terrain of the post-Soviet world. Our authors have completed numerous projects, beginning with Elizabeth Pond's *After the Wall*, that bravely attempt to inform policy. I say "bravely" because writing about these matters as kaleidoscopic changes occur around the globe requires a certain willingness to take risks. But events will not wait for our understanding to jell—or for a democratic consensus to form about foreign policy in these nations. Today, statesmen continue to feel their way in a gingerly fashion regarding the most fundamental question about future security arrangements: just what will the various publics of these democracies support in terms of expense, risk, and action? So each of these works has an importance that transcends the normal scholarly tests; they provide significant background, commentary, and advice for those who do not have the luxury of waiting for more settled times. During this difficult period of change, the Fund has published James Chace's *The Consequences of the Peace*, Rosemary Righter's *Utopia Lost*, Gil Loescher's *Beyond Charity*, Thomas Baylis's *The West and Eastern Europe*, Tony Smith's *America's Mission*, Richard Ullman's *Securing Europe*, Patrick Low's *Trading Free*, Janet Heininger's *Peacekeeping in Transition*, and Jonathan Dean's *Ending Europe's Wars*. In addition, a number of books on similar issues will soon be published: Michael Mandelbaum's analysis of the future of NATO, John Ruggie's study of multilateralism, and Monteagle Stearns's look at the American diplomatic effort.

This volume represents a significant addition to that list. Steven Burg, professor of politics at Brandeis University, is one of a handful of scholars qualified to explain the developments in Eastern Europe and the resurgence of ethnic conflicts in these former communist states. Author of *Conflict and Cohesion in Socialist Yugoslavia*, Burg is providing critical materials for the work of the Center for Preventive Action, a relatively new organization housed at the Council on Foreign Relations and supported by both the Carnegie Corporation and the Twentieth Century Fund.

In this book, Burg traces the development of the newly noncommunist states of Central and Eastern Europe. He stresses the "need for a stable framework for international peace," including the creation of an institutionalized capacity to deal with challenges in both domestic and international affairs. He offers practical advice about how to support democratization within these new states and appropriate outside response mechanisms for multilateral crises. Even though Burg completed his writing before the decision to dispatch American forces to Bosnia as part of the NATO peacekeeping force, his observations about the former Yugoslavia remain powerfully apt. The deployment of U.S. troops, of course, opens a new chapter in our relations with this part of world and in the history of the Atlantic Alliance. Moreover, this initiative represents the most ambitious American involvement in any effort to end ethnic violence. Readers of the pages that follow will find that Burg helps unravel the complex policy issues that surround the upsurge of nationalism throughout the region. He places U.S. policy in a valuable historical context, showing how the United States and its allies have tried to deal with rising ethnic conflict in a host of formerly communist states. Finally, Burg's contention that the use of force does not represent a long-term solution to ethnic conflict is sure to be borne out in Bosnia.

Ultimately, the test today of a book about these issues is whether it helps policymakers on both sides of the Atlantic. By that standard, Steven Burg's work is an unqualified success. On behalf of the Trustees of the Twentieth Century Fund, I congratulate and thank him.

Richard C. Leone
PRESIDENT
THE TWENTIETH CENTURY FUND
JANUARY 1996

INTRODUCTION

FOR MORE THAN FORTY YEARS, Western policymakers defined the revolutionary, expansionist ideology and activities of world communism as the central threat to international peace and stability. They met that threat by confronting it with a counterbalancing threat of force and pursuing a strategy of containment. With the collapse of communism, the nature of the threat to peace and stability in the Euro-Atlantic community has changed. The external threat of Soviet expansionism has been supplanted by a powerful, internal threat arising out of the clash of competing ethnic nationalisms. This challenge cannot be met by the threat of force alone or neutralized through a strategy of containment. It requires Western states to act decisively to influence the internal political development of the post-communist states themselves.

Mounting scholarly research and the evidence of day-to-day developments in the post-communist states support the view that democratic development offers the best prospect for the peaceful settlement of disputes and the most reliable guarantee of long-term international peace. In this book, therefore, I argue that the United States and its allies share a strategic interest in the consolidation of democracy in post-communist Europe. The emergence of nationalist regimes and movements in these states represents a powerful challenge to the development of internal democracy and, therefore, to the stability of international peace. The strategic interest of the United States thus demands efforts to meet and defeat that challenge, not by opposing or eliminating ethnic identities, but by fostering the development of multiethnic democracies.

Because political boundaries rarely match ethnographic ones, clashes between nationalist regimes and their ethnic minorities are inevitable when political authority is linked to ethnic identity rather than to democratic processes of selection and decisionmaking. The repression of internal ethnic minorities, legitimated by the claims of a majority to ethnic self-determination, contradicts the fundamental principles of democracy and often engenders a violent response. Such conflicts are easily escalated by individual acts of brutality and can result in enormous human destruction. Ethnic conflicts are difficult to prevent from spilling over into neighboring states, and thus they often assume international dimensions.

Competing nationalisms blocked democratization of the former Yugoslavia. With the onset of the crisis, a national army was transformed into a nationalist one, and its conventional firepower was dispersed and redirected from defense against external aggression to offensive internal war against both armed opponents and defenseless civilian populations. The internal conflict rapidly became internationalized, involving a widening circle of actors.

In the former Soviet Union, where control over a much larger and more destructive inventory of conventional and tactical nuclear weapons has also become dispersed, and where concern over their security against diversion to guerrilla organizations is well justified, the danger of escalation is especially ominous. It imperils more than the security of local actors. The threats by South Ossetian separatists and Azerbaijanis to use nuclear weapons,[1] the threats by Serb nationalists to conduct a terror campaign against the West in response to any military intervention in Bosnia-Herzegovina, and the threat by the Bosnian Muslim vice president to conduct such a campaign if the West does *not* intervene,[2] should serve as forewarnings of the potentially catastrophic consequences of failing to address ethnic grievances in the region before they turn violent.

Policymakers thus confront a difficult problem: how to oppose the emergence or consolidation of nationalist regimes that block democratic development and threaten international peace without becoming unduly involved in the domestic politics of other states or being drawn into interminable local wars. Unfortunately, policymakers and scholars alike have found it difficult to define the policies and practices that most effectively support the development of democracy or prevent the rise of nationalist authoritarianism. Moreover, ethnic and other social and political tensions are compounded by the difficulties inherent in the transformation of state-dominated and centrally planned economies into market-based systems. As recent elections demonstrate, the social costs of progress toward private ownership and marketization undermine popular support for democratic leaders who sponsor such reforms. Democratization itself may empower precisely those sectors of society most resistant to meaningful economic reform. The consolidation of democracy may therefore require—at least in the short run—social policies that sacrifice the speed of economic transformation for the sake of political stability. However, such a strategy may result in the preservation of a statist rather than fully democratic system.

Western policymakers, as well as their East European counterparts, must therefore decide how to reconcile two seemingly contradictory goals: progress toward privatization and marketization of the economy, and democratization of the political order. I argue here that democratization of the East European and post-Soviet political systems should be seen as a higher-order priority for Western policymakers than the realization of radical plans for economic transformation. Such "shock therapy" may in fact make democratization more difficult. Democratization, on the other hand, may serve to ameliorate the statist threat to reform inherent in a gradual approach to economic transformation.

Although the collapse of communism ended the strategic threat to American and West European security, policymakers cannot become indifferent to developments in the former communist states. Failure to contain the conflicts that have already broken out, forestall future ones, secure the democratization of the successor states, and sustain the prospect of economic well-being for their populations would have negative effects on the economic, political, and security interests of the West. The most immediate impact would be felt in Western Europe. But the larger political forces unleashed by such developments would certainly affect the global economic, political, and security interests of the United States as well.

The destructive combination of ethnic fighting in the former Yugoslavia, the fear of such fighting elsewhere, and simple economic hardship throughout the region has already produced an increasing flow of refugees westward. By July 1993, over 800,000 people from the former Yugoslavia were seeking asylum elsewhere in Europe.[3] These refugees are relatively few compared to the number that might well be produced by ethnic upheaval in Ukraine, Russia, or Russian-populated territories of the other former Soviet republics. Yet they have already produced disputes between West European states over their respective immigration policies, as well as a sharp increase in domestic social and political tensions. These tensions are reflected not only in incidents of violent assault on immigrants and "guest workers" by German neo-Nazi groups, but also in the growth of electoral support for nationalist and other parties of the extreme right in Western Europe.

It is in the interests of both the West and the post-communist states themselves to mitigate the flow of East Europeans to the West. Emigration threatens to siphon off significant intellectual resources and entrepreneurial energies from the post-communist states at a time when these energies are crucial to social, economic, and political reconstruction. Within Eastern Europe, the flight of refugees from ethnically mixed areas of conflict to neighboring states dominated by their own ethnic groups reinforces reactionary, nationalist, and often extremist elements in these states and contributes to the destabilization of domestic and regional politics.

Economic hardship compounded by the threat of violence weakens the popular appeal of democracy itself. In the absence of substantial external support, and especially in the aftermath of prolonged violence, it will be extremely difficult for most democratic governments in post-communist Europe to deliver tangible short-term benefits to broad segments of their populations. Weak democratic governments that fail to improve popular well-being are vulnerable to displacement by opponents less committed even to gradual transformation of the state-dominated economy and the social and political relations that grow out of it. The electoral victories of reformed communist parties in Lithuania, Poland, and Hungary and the appeal of nationalist parties in Slovakia and Romania, for example, can be attributed in part to the hardships of transition. Elsewhere, more authoritarian opponents of change may adopt the strategy of Slobodan Milosevic in Serbia and attempt to legitimize themselves by pursuing extreme nationalistic agendas. The substantial electoral support garnered by the extreme nationalist party of Vladimir Zhirinovsky in the December 1993 Russian elections reflects the strength of this threat.

Left unattended, the rise of nationalist regimes in Eastern Europe, the flow of refugees and émigrés westward, and the consequent increasing political appeal of nationalism in Western Europe would stimulate further violence by neo-Nazi and other ethnocentric groups in the West. This in turn would elicit strong reactions from responsible governments. If sustained for long periods, however, such reactions might themselves become real threats to civil liberty. Thus, the long-term security of liberal democracy in the West (especially in Germany, a state with a relatively short history of democratic development) may depend on the strength of democracy in the East.

The military issues raised by continuing conflicts in the East have already complicated the deeper political integration of the European Community and undermined the cohesiveness of the Atlantic Alliance. In the face of a reduced Russian military threat to Western Europe, NATO itself must be redefined so as to address the new security challenges arising out of the internal instabilities of the post-communist states. The vast changes that are occurring in the post-communist states heighten the urgency of establishing a new international security framework among the North American, West European, and post-communist states to replace the obsolete architecture of the Cold War, but they also make this more difficult to achieve.

The security arrangements of the Cold War era succeeded in preventing East-West conflict in Europe and global nuclear war, but they are ill suited to meeting the challenges of the post-Cold War era. The Yugoslav crisis has revealed the weaknesses in NATO, the European Community, the Conference on Security and Cooperation in Europe (CSCE), and the UN Security Council system. There is a clear need to develop a new framework for the prevention of such conflicts and for the peaceful resolution of those that cannot be prevented.

Although it is often argued that the instabilities within and among the post-communist states could be resolved if NATO membership were extended to them immediately, I argue here that NATO membership by itself is insufficient for reestablishing Euro-Atlantic security in the post-Cold War environment. Western experience suggests that it was the *simultaneous* presence of democratic political regimes, economic integration through the European Community and other international organizations and agreements, and military-security cooperation through NATO that produced international stability and security in the postwar Euro-Atlantic community. In the post-communist era, American policy must once again be directed toward achieving such multidimensional integration. Premature expansion of NATO—that is, expansion in the absence of the democratization and economic integration of the post-communist states—would introduce political instabilities and perhaps even conflicts that the alliance is ill prepared to handle and would contribute to a new division of Europe.

The failure of the United States and its allies to deal with the issues raised by the nationalist conflicts in the former Yugoslavia increases the incentives for other competing groups within Europe and elsewhere to turn to violence to solve their own problems. Russian nationalists point to the Serbs' use of force in the former Yugoslavia as a model for Russian action in the Baltic republics where, they claim, the rights of the Russian populations are endangered. The conflict in Chechnya and other areas of the Caucasus, not to mention the many active nationalist-separatist movements in the Third World, Western Europe, and North America, raise many of the same issues as those in the former Yugoslavia.

The appeals of nationalist-separatist groups to the principle of national self-determination, which at least appears to have been legitimated by Western actions in Yugoslavia, challenge the principles of state sovereignty, territorial integrity, inviolability of borders, and noninterference in the internal affairs of other states that were central to the postwar international system. This challenge must be addressed if peaceful mechanisms for the resolution of ethnic conflict are to be established and the stability of the international system in the post-Cold War era is to be preserved. Extremist politicians in both Western and Eastern Europe have already raised territorial claims against neighboring states based on ethnohistorical identity. And ethnic group leaders have raised demands for secession in several otherwise well established states. To prevent the proliferation of such claims across the Euro-Atlantic community, policymakers must carefully redefine the principles of self-determination and sovereignty, as well as the obligations that arise out of them.

In this book I argue that the right of self-determination must be defined in terms of basic human rights. Competing claims to the rights of self-determination, sovereignty, and territorial integrity, such as have been central to violent ethnic conflicts in the post-communist states, must be assessed in terms of the democratic credentials of the claimants rather than in ethnic terms alone. By demanding that claimants meet internationally recognized standards of human rights and democratic government before the international community will sanction the exercise of such rights, the United States and other democratic states can reduce the appeal of secessionism or irredentism and increase the incentives for emerging leaderships to commit themselves to democratic formulas for governance and intergroup accommodation.

The successful democratization of the post-communist states and the establishment of peaceful international relations in the region will also require greater direct involvement on the part of the United States. But Washington will have to coordinate its policies with its European allies, whose own interests in the region may, in some cases, differ from or even conflict with those of the United States. As the Yugoslav crisis has demonstrated, in the absence of coordinated action, instability and conflict in the post-communist states can undermine Western cohesion. However, instability and conflict can be met in ways that further the integration of the Euro-Atlantic community through the institutionalization of multilateral mechanisms for the prevention and peaceful resolution of conflict.

American efforts must be multidimensional, addressing the social and political aspects of democratic development, as well as providing direct economic assistance. In October 1991, Vaclav Havel, then still president of a united Czechoslovakia, appealed for direct American involvement. He asked "American scholars [to] come to our country as often as possible and teach us about civic society, about the kind of legislation and institutions it requires and about what relationships should exist between these institutions and the citizens, and among the citizens themselves."[4] Any such efforts, however, must avoid patronizing local leaders. And they must be tailored to the specific nature of the threat to democracy in each state.

Where democracy is threatened by ethnic conflict, special efforts must be devoted to establishing counterweights to the appeals of nationalism based on a close understanding of local circumstances. Clearly, any external power—European or American—that attempts to impose solutions on such conflicts will find it very difficult to succeed. The challenge to the United States and its allies, therefore, is to find ways to help structure social, economic, and political conditions so that the contending parties themselves are motivated to resolve their disputes and initiate and sustain efforts to defuse ethnic tensions.

While the crisis in Yugoslavia may seem at first glance to suggest the impossibility of achieving such a goal, closer examination offers important lessons on how it might be pursued more effectively. The Yugoslav crisis demonstrates the importance of concerted international action to prevent and resolve conflicts before they turn violent. In this book I use lessons drawn from the Yugoslav crisis to suggest a variety of peaceful means by which the community of democratic states, working through multilateral institutions, can prevent the outbreak of similar crises elsewhere. I call the pursuit of such activities a strategy of "preventive engagement." While difficult, this strategy can be coordinated with, and reinforce, efforts to promote the democratic development of new governments.

The difficulty of moving toward a more activist policy focused on peaceful, preventive measures designed to influence the internal development of other states can be attributed, in part, to the persistence, among theorists and practitioners alike, of the so-called realist theory of international relations. Realist theory focuses narrowly on relative military capacities, to the exclusion of internal social and political processes. With the fall of communism, however, the importance of internal structural and political conditions, including the emotional power of nationalism to elicit extraordinary sacrifice, can no longer be ignored in the formulation of American policies to preserve the peace.

The strategy of preventive engagement put forward here differs radically from the realist approach to conflict resolution and international security. Realist theory holds that the behavior of states is constrained by the deterrent or coercive force of external power. Realists argue, therefore, that conflict is best prevented and violence is most effectively ended when each party to a conflict is equally well armed. Realists argue that between competing ethnic groups, as in relations between states, it is a balance of military power that ensures peace.

In the post–Cold War world, realism supports a fundamentally neo-isolationist view of international relations. In this view, security is achievable through the unilateral acquisition of military power. There is no need for collective action. Hence, realists suggest the delivery of arms to secessionist groups in Yugoslavia, rather than efforts to address the fundamental sources of the conflict in the region, both as the means by which conflict could have been prevented and the means by which violent conflict can be brought to an end.[5] But the behavior of Serb, Croat, and Muslim nationalist extremists suggests that prudent policymakers ought not to place much confidence in a strategy that relies on arming all sides in such conflicts.

The realist approach to international security is a prescription for an unending arms race in the former Yugoslavia and everywhere else competing nationalisms engender conflict. As the wars in the

Balkans and the Caucasus as well as in Northern Ireland, the Middle East, Afghanistan, and Vietnam have demonstrated, there is no such thing as a stable balance of power or a simple military deterrent to ethnic mobilization for war. Military force alone cannot resolve ethnic conflict short of the destruction of one group by another.

The dramatic events of recent years heighten the temptation to resort to political hyperbole. But the fact remains that the West does confront a historic opportunity to encourage the democratic development of states that have not been democratic for most of the twentieth century. The democratization of the post-communist states would provide the most effective basis for avoiding the kind of crises that in the past have led to international war.

The collapse of communism does not in itself guarantee these positive outcomes, however. The strength of nationalisms throughout the region provides a powerful instrument for the construction of new authoritarian regimes. A nationalist authoritarian government in Russia would present dangers many orders of magnitude greater than those that have resulted from the establishment of an authoritarian regime in Serbia. Amelioration of the nationalist threat to democracy in the post-communist states must therefore be recognized and treated as a strategic interest of American foreign policy. American policymakers must resist the neo-isolationist temptation to substitute arms exports for foreign policy and instead make a sustained effort to influence the course of political development in the post-communist states.

CHAPTER 1

Nationalism, Democracy, and International Peace in Post-Communist Europe

THE DEMOCRATIZATION of the post-communist states presents policymakers with a vexing dilemma: The collapse of authoritarianism has unleashed forces that make the establishment of liberal democracies difficult. The suppression of these forces, however, would entail actions that might make the establishment of liberal democracies impossible. Some accommodation of the national aspirations of local populations is essential if violent conflict is to be avoided and the legitimacy of new democratic institutions is to be strengthened. It will also be necessary if these populations are to endure the material sacrifices associated with the transition to democracy. There is, moreover, a moral virtue in creating opportunities for the expression of national cultures. Thus, institutional and procedural formulas must be found so that ethnic minorities are not relegated to the status of permanent political minorities. At the same time, however, democracy cannot be held hostage by an intransigent minority. The central challenge to policymakers therefore involves the creation of incentives to cooperation between competing groups.

If the United States is to assist the post-communist states of Eastern Europe in meeting this challenge, American foreign policy must undergo a radical shift—from a strategy of containment to one of active engagement. By nurturing and stabilizing the new democracies, the United States will not only contribute to the collective interests of the international community of states—establishing a stable and enduring international peace—but it will also provide for the national interest by securing American access and influence in a region of future economic and political significance.

NATIONALISM AND INTERNATIONAL CONFLICT

The Conference on Security and Cooperation in Europe (CSCE), or Helsinki process, was the product of the Soviet-American détente of the 1970s. The United States and its Western allies used the process to reaffirm the principles of human rights and individual freedom, as well as to establish principles of transnational freedom of contact and cooperation, in the hope of weakening the grip of communist governments over their peoples. The Soviet Union and its allies, in contrast, sought affirmation of the territorial and political status quo in Eastern Europe. While the Helsinki Agreement adopted in 1975 did ratify the international status quo, it also established an important basis on which both the West and, more important, domestic groups in the communist states themselves could legitimately pursue political change. The Helsinki Accords promoted the formation by dissidents in the communist countries of small but active grassroots political organizations. The increased cultural contacts between East and West that followed the signing of the accords reinforced a process already under way among the broader, nondissident social elites in Eastern Europe: the development of both increasingly liberal political values and increasing national consciousness.

The liberalization of values and the increasing salience of national identity among critical internal elites were the products of communism's postwar success at social modernization relative to the prewar past.[1] Mikhail Gorbachev's attempt to reform the Soviet system introduced new opportunities for grassroots political activity, and intellectuals in the economically more developed non-Russian republics of the Soviet Union—among whom these values had been more widespread—rapidly organized popular movements in pursuit of independent national states. At the same time, a parallel increase in what might be considered liberalizing nationalism was unfolding among the subordinate nations in the multinational states of Eastern Europe in the 1980s.

The apparent marriage of liberalism and nationalism in the communist states in the 1970s and 1980s echoed a similar marriage between these forces in Central Europe in the mid-nineteenth century. The earlier alliance resulted in the devolution of power to nationalist leaderships, but it did not produce democracy.[2] Nationalism constituted a liberalizing force only in opposition to ethnically alien, authoritarian rule; once in power, nationalism became itself an ideology of repression.

The implosion of the Soviet domestic political order, the emergence of independent states in the former territories of the Soviet Union, and the emergence of new regimes in Eastern Europe have resulted in an analogous devolution of power to national states. As a result, nationalism has again become a powerful legitimating force for new governments with uncertain bases of popular support. It also threatens to become once again an ideology of repression.

Although some have argued that the collapse of communism leaves no alternative to liberal democracy as an ideological foundation on which to legitimate new governments,[3] it remains to be seen whether the post-communist regimes will be able to transform the bases of their legitimacy from nationalist to democratic principles. The work of political scientist David Easton—perhaps the most influential theorist on this issue—suggests that newly democratic and democratizing regimes must demonstrate their effectiveness in the short term in order to garner the instrumental, or pragmatic, support of their populations. And benefits must be delivered to the population over a long period in order for pragmatic support for particular incumbent governments and their policies to develop into deeper, affective support for the political system in general and for democracy as a way of life.[4]

Ethnic diversity by itself represents a major obstacle to the development of this affective support, which has been defined by Easton as "a sense of we-feeling, common consciousness, or group identification."[5] But it is not an insurmountable obstacle. In the absence of pragmatic bases of support for existing arrangements, however, diversity presents a powerful basis for the delegitimation of a transitional democracy and the mobilization of support for a nationalist alternative. In several of the post-communist states the instability of incumbent governments, the fragmentation of ruling coalitions, and the social costs of economic transformation make it difficult for democratic regimes to deliver benefits to the population and thus raise the prospect of democratic breakdown.

The increased salience of nationality in post-communist Europe has rekindled many of the ethnic and territorial issues of the late nineteenth and early twentieth centuries. The powerful combination of internal discontent and external ambition may again lead some of these states toward more authoritarian arrangements, as nationalisms are transformed from mobilizing ideologies of opposition into exclusionary, alienating ideologies of internal oppression and external aggression. Indeed, in some of these states governments still face significant disloyal opposition from unreformed communists, extreme nationalists, neofascists, and other authoritarian forces ready to exploit such discontents and ambitions. The specter of Weimar haunts the region.

Throughout the Soviet Union and Eastern Europe, national self-assertion has been characterized by the equation of ethnic identity with a right to political independence. Sovereignty has been defined in the popular mind as freedom from rule by an ethnically alien group. This popular attachment to the right of ethnic collectives to sovereignty represents a powerful obstacle to the creation of economic and political institutions that cut across ethnic differences and create the foundations of a shared political community.

Yet Eastern Europe is an ethnically diverse region in which political borders do not correspond with precision to either the territorial distribution of ethnic groups or their self-defined historical homelands. Boundaries were established as the result of treaties negotiated after World War I, representing imperfect attempts to apply the principle of national self-determination to the region. Further changes followed World War II and the Soviet occupation of the region. Within the multinational Soviet and Yugoslav states, borders and even the status of entire territories were subject to change by the central leadership with little opportunity for expression of the popular will.

Some ethnic groups in postwar Eastern Europe ended up largely within the confines of a single state. These included those that formed "homogeneous" national states of their own, those that found themselves part of multinational states, and those that became national minorities. Other ethnic groups were divided by state borders or by internal borders within multinational states. The presence of an overarching political authority, however, moderated the impact of these divisions. The Serbs, while divided by internal borders, remained part of a single Yugoslav state, and the Russians remained part of a highly centralized Soviet Union. Similarly, Soviet hegemony suppressed cross-border issues in relations between states in Eastern Europe.

The collapse of communist power was followed by international recognition of entities that had attained republic status in the multinational Soviet and Yugoslav federations. Units of lesser status under the old regimes were not recognized. Whereas the former were conceded a right to self-determination, the latter were not. Nor were national groups divided by internal borders conceded this right. Along with the rapid accession of the newly recognized states to membership in such international organizations as the United Nations and the CSCE came the formal legal protections afforded by the international principles of state sovereignty and the right of states to defend their territorial integrity.

The Helsinki Accords had ratified "the equal rights of peoples and their right to self-determination," which was defined as "the right, in full freedom, to determine when and as they wish, their internal and external political status." Despite the reference to "peoples" in the Helsinki Accords and the follow-up documents of the CSCE (as in the UN Charter), the United States had supported the right of self-determination in the Helsinki context because it had understood it to mean the right of the states under Soviet domination to a free and autonomous existence. As communism collapsed, however, and the international community recognized successor states on the basis of formerly internal borders, some ethnic groups sought to reconfigure those borders based on their claims as peoples to a right of self-determination. The efforts of nationalist regional leaderships to achieve independence raised important questions about conflicts between the right of secession and recognition based on the principle of self-determination, and the right of states to defend their territorial integrity.

Serbs, Croats, Bosnian Muslims, Romanians, Moldovans, Armenians, Azerbaijanis, Georgians, Ossetians, Abkhazians, Chechen, Ingush, and Russians have all been drawn into conflicts fueled by conflicting claims legitimated by these principles. Albanians, Macedonians, Hungarians, and Slovaks may soon be added to this list. In the absence of effective democratic frameworks for the resolution of conflict deriving from the competing claims of groups within previously recognized states, such conflicts too easily escalate into violence and threaten to draw neighboring states into direct involvement.

The boundaries of the Hungarian national state that had been part of the Austro-Hungarian Empire before World War I, for example, were severely truncated as the result of the postwar settlement. Approximately two-thirds of its territory and more than a quarter of its ethnically Hungarian population were assigned to neighboring states by the Treaty of Trianon, concluded in 1920. From the perspective of the Czechoslovak, Romanian, and Yugoslav states that exercised sovereignty over them, the formerly Hungarian territories represented potential foci of Hungarian irredentism. During World War II the Hungarian government, in alliance with Nazi Germany, reclaimed parts of these former territories. These seizures were reversed after the war but left a renewed suspicion of Hungarian ambitions on the part of neighboring states. It is these very states that have now all become highly unstable with the collapse of communism, and in which the status of Hungarian minority populations has been threatened by the rise of Slovak, Serb, and Romanian nationalisms.

The first democratically elected Hungarian prime minister, József Antall, escalated these suspicions when, shortly after assuming power in May 1990, he declared that he considered himself the prime minister of fifteen million Hungarians (only ten million Hungarians reside within the borders of the Hungarian state). Antall later claimed that he was "talking about this not in the legal sense but in the spiritual, emotional context." But at the same time he noted that as the result of the Treaty of Trianon, "one-third of Hungarians, without having left their homeland or country, became citizens of a foreign country."[6] That he harbored ambitions to reclaim these territories was clear. Such statements were also consistent with popular sentiment in the country. In a public opinion survey conducted in May 1991, 68 percent of all Hungarians expressed the view that territories in neighboring countries actually belonged to Hungary.[7] Concern over the fate of Hungarians in Romania was particularly pronounced: some 42 percent of Hungarians surveyed identified Romania as their "main enemy."[8]

The expansionist ambitions of Hungary's leaders apart, these expressions of concern for Hungarians abroad reflect the threats posed to these populations by the erosion of conditions in the neighboring states and the rise of Slovak, Serb, and Romanian nationalisms. Hungarians from Vojvodina have been fleeing across the border in increasing numbers to escape persecution by Serbs. They, as well as Hungarians from Slovakia, actively seek the physical and political protection of the Hungarian state.

According to the 1992 Romanian census, there were 1.6 million ethnic Hungarians in Romania.[9] Others estimate the number to be much larger. Hungarians constituted almost 24 percent of the population in the province of Transylvania, and over 21 percent in Crisana-Maramureş. Within these regions, Hungarians constituted large majorities in two counties and large minorities in others. The clash between Hungarian and Romanian nationalisms in Transylvania led to the outbreak of violence in the region in 1990 and has been a source of continuing conflict since. Even modest attempts to express Hungarian identity have met with repressive responses. The nationalist Romanian mayor of the Transylvanian city of Cluj, for example, has been particularly active in attempting to suppress Hungarian identity in his city.[10] Such conflicts contributed to expanding electoral support for Romanian nationalist parties in parliamentary elections held in September 1992.[11]

Since 1992, the governing party in Romania, the Party of Social

Democracy in Romania (the direct descendant of the National Salvation Front, later Democratic National Salvation Front, which was composed predominantly of former communists and which assumed power after the overthrow of Ceauşescu in December 1989) has become increasingly dependent on the support of nationalist parties to retain power. Early in 1994, it entered into a formal coalition that included two extreme nationalist parties: the Party of Romanian National Unity (PRNU) and the Greater Romania Party (GRP). In mid-1994, the PRNU entered the cabinet, followed by the GRP in early 1995.[12] The growing reliance of the former communists on the extreme nationalists for political survival has contributed to growing tensions between the government and the Hungarian population in Transylvania.

Romanian nationalist forces in Transylvania are led by Gheorghe Funar, the mayor of Cluj, and the PRNU. They draw their support from ethnically Romanian communist-era elites of the region, whose power would be threatened by the full civic incorporation of the large Hungarian minority, and from the local ethnic Romanian population who fear that increased government attention to the interests of Hungarians will necessarily result in decreased attention to their own interests, and who ultimately fear any takeover of the region by Hungary.[13] These fears are reinforced by demands on the part of the Hungarian Democratic Federation of Romania, the main political organization of the Hungarian minority in Romania, for greater local cultural and even territorial autonomy. Such demands engender hostile responses not only from the radical Romanian nationalist parties, but from liberal opposition leaders and the independent media as well.[14]

Romanian nationalist extremists benefit from popular fears with respect to the demands of the Hungarian minority. These are sustained, in part, by intemperate statements on the part of politicians in Hungary. At the May 1995 meeting of the HDFR in Cluj, for example, the most stridently nationalist statement came not from the ethnically Hungarian politicians from Romania, but from the leader of the Independent Smallholders Party of Hungary, József Torgyan, who opposed the conclusion of a treaty between the two states that might incorporate a negotiated compromise, and called for the unification of all Hungarians in a single state. His statement was repudiated by a representative of Hungary's ruling Socialist Party. But Romanian nationalists were once again provided the opportunity to link HDFR demands for autonomy to the aspirations of nationalist politicians in Hungary.[15]

A similar linkage between domestic ethnic relations and interstate relations exists in Slovakia. Since 1989, the Hungarian population of Slovakia has become increasingly well organized. New Hungarian cultural and political organizations formed almost immediately after the collapse of communism, and already existing organizations became more active in the defense of Hungarian interests. The concern of ethnic Hungarians to secure their fundamental rights has been heightened by the rise of distinctly anti-Hungarian sentiments among Slovaks, as manifest in nationalist demonstrations in several ethnically mixed areas of the republic in early 1990, in calls for the expulsion of Hungarians and the creation of a "pure Slovak state," and in the attempt by the Matica Slovenska, the Slovak national cultural society, to outlaw the use of the Hungarian language.[16] In a survey conducted in May 1991, 65 percent of respondents in Slovakia expressed hostility toward the Hungarian minority.[17]

Concern on the part of the Hungarian government for the status of ethnic Hungarians in Slovakia has contributed to the tension in relations between these two countries since the collapse of communism. Slovak politics has been dominated since 1992 by Vladimir Meciar and his party, Movement for a Democratic Slovakia (MDS). The MDS won over 37 percent of the vote in elections to the republic parliament in 1992 and established a coalition government with the Slovak National Party (SNP).[18] While the MDS was nationalist in its orientation toward relations with the Czechs and intolerant of the Hungarian minority, the SNP represented the extreme right-wing nationalist tendency in Slovak politics. Thus, the Meciar-led government contributed to the escalation of tensions between the state and its Hungarian minority, and thereby worsened relations with Hungary.

With the fall of the Meciar government in March 1994, a left-right coalition took control in Slovakia, led by Jozef Moravcik. The Moravcik coalition brought together those parties seeking to distance the state from both its communist and its fascist past, and thus was more liberal than its predecessor in its ideological orientation toward the Hungarian minority. It was also dependent on the support of the two Hungarian parties to maintain its parliamentary majority. Thus it moved to ease relations with the Hungarian minority while pursuing domestic economic reform and an international rapprochement with Hungary. Despite gains registered under the Moravcik government, however, Meciar's MDS scored a surprising electoral victory in the September 1994 elections, securing 35 percent of the popular vote. The MDS entered into an alliance with the SNP and the leftist Association of Slovak Workers to take control of the government once again in December 1994. The Meciar government moved immediately to strengthen state control of the media, slow down the privatization effort renewed by the Moravcik government, and increase cultural pressure on the Hungarian minority.[19]

Hungary refused, until 1995, to conclude a treaty affirming the inviolability of the Slovak-Hungarian border, citing the treatment of Slovakia's Hungarian minority as one of "many unresolved problems" in bilateral relations.[20] Only under pressure from the European Union was a treaty finally concluded. But the March 1995 treaty has been the subject of divergent interpretations between the two governments and has been the cause of renewed conflict in Slovakia between the Hungarian parties and the SNP.[21]

Parallels can be drawn between the Hungarian government's concern for the status of ethnic Hungarians in neighboring states and the concerns in Albania over the status of ethnic Albanians in Kosovo, southern Montenegro, and western Macedonia. Indeed, these situations may be even more volatile because of the conflict in Bosnia, the extremely high tensions between Serbs and Albanians in Kosovo, the uncertain international status of Macedonia, and the potential territorial ambitions of other states in the region. Albania is a weak state unlikely to pursue aggressive action against its neighbors on its own. But it could easily be drawn into a conflict with

Serbia over Kosovo, as could several other Balkan states. Such conflict might be sparked by an escalation of Serbian repression in Kosovo or the resort to force by Kosovar Albanians either to establish their independence or to unite with Albania.

Disturbing parallels to conditions in Eastern Europe can be found in the former Soviet republics. The most intense and long-lasting interethnic violence in the former Soviet Union has occurred in the Caucasus, a region that is both larger and more populous than the combined republics of Croatia and Bosnia-Herzegovina. The levels of interethnic hostility and violence surrounding the competition for control over disputed territory here parallel those found in the former Yugoslavia. The potential for powerful surrounding countries to be drawn into local conflicts is at least as great here as in the Balkans. And the international consequences of such involvement would be no less important.

In the Nagorno-Karabakh region of Azerbaijan, a violent conflict between the local majority population of ethnic Armenians, who are seeking autonomy and union with the Armenian national state, and the Azerbaijani state, which exercises sovereignty over the region, has continued for more than eight years.[22] Nagorno-Karabakh, like the Caucasus as a whole, is located at the historical intersection of three competing, culturally distinct imperial powers: Turkish, Iranian, and Russian. Despite attempts by the predominantly Armenian population of Nagorno-Karabakh (about 89 percent of the population, according to the 1926 Soviet census) to unite with Armenia, the region was placed under Azerbaijani sovereignty in the Soviet period. From 1921 on, Nargorno-Karabakh remained a part of the predominantly Muslim, Turkic republic of Azerbaijan. The local population in Nagorno-Karabakh, however, remained predominantly Armenian—84.4 percent in 1959, and 76.9 percent in 1989.[23]

With the onset of glasnost, the aspirations of Armenians in Nagorno-Karabakh for union with Armenia, which had been suppressed by Moscow, found renewed public expression. They were reinforced by a sharp decline in economic conditions in the region. By February 1988, Armenian activists were calling openly for transfer of the region to the Armenian republic, with the support of mass demonstrations in Yerevan and in Nagorno-Karabakh. The Azerbaijani population responded to rising Armenian national assertiveness with a bloody attack on Armenians living in the Azerbaijani city of Sumgait. The February 1988 Sumgait riots began the progressive escalation of interethnic violence. By January 1990 the violence had become open warfare. Not even the deployment of large numbers of Soviet troops could suppress it.

The continuing fighting in and around Nagorno-Karabakh contributed to the growing instability of the entire Caucasus. Following the collapse of the Soviet Union in August 1991, Russian president Boris Yeltsin attempted to broker a peaceful settlement of the conflict in September. An apparent agreement between the Armenians and Azerbaijanis soon collapsed, however. This pattern of outside attempts to broker a settlement, the conclusion of an apparent agreement, and its subsequent collapse has been repeated several times since.[24] Regional actors concerned about local security issues, including Russia, Iran, and Turkey, have all attempted to facilitate a settlement. But each has been suspected by one side of excessive sympathy for the other, and the effort has failed. In the case of Russia, there is good reason to doubt the sincerity of its efforts to broker a peace settlement: there is strong evidence that Russian troops acting as mercenaries, as well as elements of the Russian army in Nagorno-Karabakh and Armenia, have been fighting on behalf of the Armenians.[25]

International organizations, including the CSCE and the United Nations, have also failed in their efforts to facilitate a settlement. The CSCE undertook a series of missions to the region in 1992 to explore the establishment of a cease-fire. A conference on Nagorno-Karabakh was created in March 1992 to undertake negotiations, but this failed to produce results. A cease-fire finally was arranged under Russian sponsorship in May 1994. But no third party mediator has been able to resolve the contradiction between the competing principles of legitimation that are at stake in this conflict: Azerbaijani representatives have grounded their claims to Nagorno-Karabakh on the principle that boundaries of the former Soviet republics have achieved international recognition and that Azerbaijan therefore has the right to protect its sovereignty and territorial integrity. Azerbaijan thus has refused to accept representatives of Nagorno-Karabakh as negotiating partners. Armenians in Nagorno-Karabakh, on the other hand, claim the right of national self-determination.[26] Thus, in many respects, the conflict in Nagorno-Karabakh represented a foretaste of the conflicts that would erupt in Yugoslavia and that still threaten other East European states.

Violent conflict has also occurred in the Georgian republic, between Georgians and two regional ethnic minorities: the Abkhazians and the Ossetians. The Abkhaz, an ethnically Turkic, Muslim people, had been agitating for increased autonomy under Soviet rule and continued to do so as Georgia achieved its own independence.[27] In April 1991, Abkhaz and Georgian leaders in Abkhazia formulated a power-sharing agreement that essentially ratified the status quo by giving the Abkhaz disproportionate representation in the local parliament. But this agreement was nullified by the Georgian nationalist president, Zviad Gamsakhurdia, who responded to Abkhaz demands with exclusionary and repressive actions. The result was a rapid disintegration of relations between Abkhazia and Georgia. By August 1992, fighting between Georgian military units on one side and an alliance of Abkhazians and other Caucasian mountain peoples on the other had turned into civil war.[28]

The Georgian leadership found it particularly difficult to offer concessions to the Abkhazians because this was not the only secessionist movement or potential movement it confronted. The ethnic Azerbaijani population was agitating for the establishment of an autonomous region of their own within the republic, and the Ossetians of the South Ossetian autonomous oblast in north central Georgia had been seeking to expand their autonomy since 1989. Ossetian aspirations to unite with the North Ossetian Autonomous Republic, from which they are separated only by the Georgian-Russian border, clashed with the growing support among Georgians for independence from the Soviet Union and gave rise to violent conflict between Ossetians and Georgians. Repressive measures by the Gamsakhurdia government led to the escalation of interethnic violence.[29] Fighting between the South Ossetians and Georgians was ended by a cease-fire in July 1992, enforced by Russian, Georgian, and Ossetian peacekeeping troops. This arrangement effectively removed the region from Georgian control and threatened to lead to its eventual separation from the republic.

More recently, the secessionist aspirations of a small nation and the determination of the Russian state to defend its territorial integrity have led to violence in Chechnya, a North Caucasian region of the Russian republic. Chechen resistance to Russian rule reflects centuries-long efforts by the Chechen people to free themselves from foreign domination and more recent grievances arising out of mistreatment during the Soviet period.[30] Like many other regional leaderships in the former Soviet Union, local Chechen leaders seized the opportunity to declare local sovereignty in 1990. The failed coup in Moscow in 1991 set off an internal political struggle for control of Chechnya, won by radical nationalist-separatist forces led by Dzhokhar Dudaev, a former Soviet air force general.

After winning election as president in an apparently rigged election in October 1991, Dudaev blocked an attempt by Russian president Boris Yeltsin to restore central control, and a prolonged political stalemate set in. During this period, Dudaev exercised increasingly authoritarian rule, and ethnic tensions intensified between the Chechen and the large Russian minority—almost 25 percent of the total population of Chechnya in 1989 and over 50 percent of the population of Grozny, the capital. The Russian decision finally to use force against Chechnya in December 1994 involved consideration of a number of domestic and international economic and security issues. Perhaps the dominant consideration, however, was the Russian geostrategic interest (following the conclusion of a major agreement providing for Western investment in the exploitation of Azerbaijan's substantial oil reserves) in ensuring the security of the existing oil pipeline between Baku and the Russian Black Sea port of Novorossiisk, which crosses Chechnya.[31]

From an ethnopolitical perspective, Chechen insistence on independence from Moscow represented only one of the several possible challenges that might arise from growing unrest among the peoples of the North Caucasus. The Russian leadership successfully negotiated a compromise solution to similar conflicts with other regional leaders—most notably with Tatarstan in February 1994—but chose not to pursue this strategy in Chechnya.[32] But the use of force against Chechnya has proven ineffective as a means to end Chechen resistance.

The demands of the Chechen, Abkhaz, and Ossetian minorities, like those of the Armenians in Nagorno-Karabakh and the warring groups in the ethnically mixed territories of the former Yugoslavia, throw into sharp relief the urgent necessity to resolve the apparent contradiction between the principles of self-determination, sovereignty, and territorial integrity, which are central to the international political order. They also reinforce the view that ethnic conflicts cannot easily be resolved by the use of force—at least not without enormous human cost.

The breakup of the Soviet Union left large Russian minority populations in the non-Russian successor states. Altogether, more than twenty-five million ethnic Russians, or over 17 percent of the 1989 ethnic Russian population of the Soviet Union, were left outside the Russian republic. The policies and practices of some of the successor state governments are politicizing the Russian minority populations and creating conditions for their mobilization in much the same way that Serbian identity was mobilized in Croatia and Bosnia-Herzegovina.

Concerns about the status and treatment of Russians outside Russia also reinforce an emerging tendency toward what one analyst has called "Russian imperial nationalism."[33] For example, Russian defense minister Pavel Grachev stated in June 1992 that he would respond to any violation of "the honor and dignity of the Russian population" in any part of the Commonwealth of Independent States with "most resolute measures."[34] This perspective is reflected in the revised Russian military doctrine made public in November

1993, in which suppression of the rights of Russians abroad is identified as a threat to Russian security.[35]

Even if the Russian state leadership chooses not to pursue irredentist policies, ethnic Russians in the successor states may raise such claims on their own. And as events in the former Yugoslavia demonstrate, nationalist unrest among dispersed members of the once-dominant nation of a former multinational state can lead to military intervention by "their" national state on behalf of its conationals on the peripheries. The continuing presence of large contingents of the former Soviet, and now Russian, army in the successor states raises the prospect of intervention by predominantly ethnic Russian military units to defend Russian minority populations against perceived threats from the local ethnic majority.

The Serbs' use of force in precisely this way against the neighboring states of the former Yugoslavia provides a ready model for the Russian imperial nationalists. Russians in Moldova adopted such an approach as early as August 1990, when they declared a "Dniester Soviet Socialist Republic." The strength of their resistance, their ability to engage in violent conflict against the Moldovan government, and especially their ability to secure control over the territory east of the Dniester are attributable entirely to the weapons, other logistical support, and manpower provided by the Russian Fourteenth Army, which is based in the region.

The conflict in Moldova is an example of the kind of conflict that is most likely to occur between Russia and the other successor states. Although it has an ethnic component, it is primarily an ideological and political conflict. Part of the local Russian population seeks to oppose the consolidation of an ethnically alien political order. Loyal to an imperial concept of Russian identity, these diaspora Russians are allied with conservative forces in Moscow intent on restoring Moscow's power over the former Soviet peripheries. The outbreak of conflict between diaspora Russians and local elites sets the stage for the use of force by Moscow—either indirectly in support of an uprising by the Russian minority, or through direct intervention under the pretext of protecting the rights of local Russians or even of "restoring order." Such a scenario may yet unfold in Estonia, over the Russian enclave surrounding Narva, or in Ukraine, over the Crimea. If political discontent in the heavily Russian eastern regions of Ukraine leads to open rebellion against Kiev, the conflict that might ensue between Ukraine and Russia would be of far greater consequence than those in Croatia or Bosnia-Herzegovina.

The wars in the former Yugoslavia are a tragic example of such escalation and the unpreparedness of the international community to prevent such conflicts or bring them to a peaceful conclusion once they have started. The costs and controversy over Western involvement in such conflicts place a premium on their prevention and especially their resolution before they turn violent.

DEMOCRACY AND INTERNATIONAL PEACE

In sharp contrast to the wars in the former Yugoslavia and the Caucasus and the violent conflict in Moldova, negotiations among the democratically elected governments of East Central Europe and their active engagement in the CSCE and other international organizations have contributed to the maintenance of generally peaceful relations. Their behavior reflects, in part, the powerful norms of negotiation, compromise, and peaceful behavior that prevail among democratic governments. It also reflects the power of economic interest. Just as peaceful cooperation in postwar Western Europe was reinforced by economic interdependence, so the anticipation of economic gain acted as an incentive to cooperation between Poland, Hungary, and Czechoslovakia (now the Czech Republic and Slovakia) and between these states and the European Community.

In a recent empirical study of international conflict, political scientist Bruce Russett has found that the more democratic any pair of states are, the less likely a militarized dispute will break out between them or that any dispute between them will escalate.[36] Although there is no single, agreed definition of "democracy," Diamond, Linz, and Lipset have enumerated three "essential conditions" that usefully summarize the characteristics that distinguish democratic regimes. They are

> [1.] meaningful and extensive *competition* among individuals and organized groups (especially political parties) for all effective positions of government power, at regular intervals and excluding the use of force; [2.] a highly inclusive level of *political participation* in the selection of leaders and policies, at least through regular and fair elections, such that no major (adult) social group is excluded; and [3.] a level of *civil and political liberties*—freedom of expression, freedom of the press, freedom to form and join organizations—sufficient to ensure the integrity of political competition and participation.[37]

The establishment, operation, and consolidation of these essential features of a liberal democratic regime require a sufficiently widespread commitment to peaceful participation and competition so as to preclude the use of force against citizens exercising their constitutionally guaranteed rights or against legitimately constituted authorities exercising their constitutional powers. These conditions produce the institutionalization of political accountability on the part of decisionmakers. Under conditions of social diversity, the demands on decisionmakers, as well as the policies they adopt, are moderated and constrained by the interactions of competing interests. This principle of free interaction among diverse, organized interests lies at the heart of the concept of pluralist democracy.[38]

Numerous studies affirm the close relationship between democracy and international peace. Russett, however, finds that the pacific effect of democracy operates independently of other factors often assumed to account for peaceful relations between states. These include wealth and, significantly for the realist theories of international relations, the military balance between states. Russett found that the strength of the democratic effect was most closely related to the strength of democratic norms, or democratic culture, in these states. Not surprisingly, he found that democratic peace was also explained by the institutional constraints on the ability of democratic governments to go to war.

The importance of the development of domestic democratic norms and institutions in the post-communist states to the security interests of the Western democracies blurs the traditional distinction between internal and international issues. Developments within the CSCE reflect this. Since 1989, member states, including the Soviet Union and, later, the post-communist states, have placed an increasing emphasis on the resolution of ethnic conflict and the protection of human rights and fundamental freedoms as the most effective means of securing international peace.[39] Furthermore, in Vienna in 1989, in Copenhagen in the spring of 1990, and at the Geneva meeting of experts on national minorities in July 1991, the member states purposely did not reaffirm the principle of nonintervention in the internal affairs of other states adopted at Helsinki in 1975. Instead, at Copenhagen, they affirmed that "pluralistic democracy and the rule of law are essential for ensuring respect for all human rights and fundamental freedoms."[40]

The Geneva meeting of experts on national minorities, which convened just as war broke out in Slovenia, concluded that issues concerning the rights of national minorities "are matters of legitimate international concern and consequently do not constitute exclusively an internal affair of the respective state."[41] This view was reiterated at the conference on the human dimension held in Moscow in the fall of 1991, in the wake of the failed August coup attempt.[42]

The political limits on Western involvement in the internal development of the East European political systems have thus radically contracted as both the West and the successor states themselves have sought to construct a new framework for security in the post-Cold War world. The expanded opportunities for influencing internal developments in the post-communist states must therefore be exploited to ensure the democratization of these states. However, in order to do so, the West must formulate effective responses to the most immediate challenge to democracy among the post-communist states: nationalism.

NATIONALISM AND THE TRANSITION TO DEMOCRACY

Nationalism can be, and has been, a positive force for democratizing change. Historian Boyd Shafer, for example, has chronicled the historical connection in Europe and America between popular nationalism and republicanism. "Popular nationalism was," he argues, "part of the general movement toward republicanism and democracy, of the revolt against monarchical, aristocratic, and clerical domination."[43] The nation-states constructed after 1815 were instruments for securing material advantage and physical security for national elites. They also strengthened and consolidated cultural identity and fostered the growth of expanded political communities defined on the basis of ethnic identity. In the multinational Austro-Hungarian Empire, nationalism and liberalism were allied against autocracy. The liberalism of nationalist legitimation was severely limited, however. While it produced a devolution of power to the nationalist regime in Hungary, for example, that regime was characterized by a growing intolerance of its own ethnic minorities.[44]

Nationalisms played a similar role in the modern multinational states of Yugoslavia and the Soviet Union. In an effort to strengthen the legitimacy of communist rule, these regimes attempted to accommodate popular identities through the creation of federal structures. These were intended to serve as an alternative to, and weaken support for, the creation of independent nation-states. The ethnic structures of these states grew increasingly important under the impact of social modernization, which altered popular consciousness, increased political awareness, and spread the inclination to participate more broadly through the educated sectors of the ethnically indigenous populations. Both the Soviet and the Yugoslav regimes gradually expanded the political authority of the ethnically defined federal republics and increased the opportunities for participation in these states by ethnic elites.

Concessions to individual political rights and opportunities for political activity were substantially greater in Yugoslavia than in the Soviet Union, at least until the onset of glasnost under Gorbachev.

But none of the other essential conditions characteristic of democratic regimes were established in either state under communist rule. Ultimately, however, sufficient civil and political freedom was created in each of these regimes to allow the ethnic political structures they established and the national political identities they supported to be transformed by ethnic elites into bases for nationalist movements.

"Nationalism" is used here to refer to mass political movements that arise among groups that conceive of themselves as potentially sovereign political communities.[45] This consciousness of community often derives from a shared cultural framework based primarily on a common language and common historical experiences. Intragroup communication across time and territory is central to the growth of this consciousness and to the mobilization and organization of mass political action. A common language and a linguistic elite that preserves and extends the common culture, as well as the spread of literacy and the expansion of popular participation, are therefore central to the emergence of group consciousness and the formation of a mass political movement based on it. Hence, it is not surprising that one consequence of modernization processes among socially, economically, or politically aggrieved groups may be the rise of nationalism.[46]

The specific elements defining such identities may vary from group to group or over time within a single group. The existence of aggrieved groups alone, however, does not account for the rise of nationalist movements. For such movements to take root, individuals and, ultimately, mass populations must perceive an opportunity to redress their grievances through organized action.[47] Thus, political entrepreneurs—whether ethnic elites of the old regime seeking to maximize their own power or new counterelites seeking to overthrow the old order—play an important role in defining such movements. Depending on the resources of such a movement relative to the regime, simple repression may prevent it from threatening the regime. For a nondemocratic regime, the cost of such repression may be calculated in terms of its effects on social and economic development. But the consequences of such repression for a newly established democracy may be very grave, indeed: the repression of free expression strikes at the heart of democratic principles. In either circumstance, repression may prove counterproductive by strengthening the appeal of a nationalist movement among its ethnic constituency.

Nationalism is distinguished from social movements that arise among other aggrieved groups by the powerful affect, or emotion, associated with it. In extreme cases, nationalist movements evoke a willingness to fight and die on behalf of the cause. This derives from the notion that what is at issue is group survival. Nationalist demands for official protection and support for languages and cultures reflect this concern for group survival.

Nationalist movements cannot, however, be understood as solely "primordial" in nature. They are most often also organizational vehicles for the articulation of arguments over rights, goods, status, power, and other material and political issues. Hence, the conflicts between Serbs and other groups in the former Yugoslavia and between Armenians and Azerbaijanis in Nagorno-Karabakh may be exceptional cases by virtue of the disproportionately powerful role of primordial hatred and the extreme violence that has taken place. But their ultimate solution must involve the redress of grievances pertaining to rights, status, and power that also motivate and mobilize the populations—and especially their leaders—in these conflicts.[48] In this sense, use of the term "ethnic conflict" tends to overemphasize a single—albeit extremely important—dimension of intergroup conflict.

The strength of nationalist political movements, the popular appeal of avenging long-held ethnic grievances, and the resultant escalation of ethnic conflict impede the transition from authoritarianism to democracy. As political scientist Daniel Levine points out, "When regimes change, rules of the game are in flux, new leadership groups emerge, and different kinds of issues, demands, and interests clamor for a place in the political sun."[49] The essence of a transition to democracy under such conditions consists in the fact that, while the eventual *outcomes* of the interplay among these new political forces may remain in doubt over an extended period, a lasting and legitimate agreement is reached on the common *rules* by which outcomes are to be obtained. The political challenge inherent in the process of democratization, therefore, is to create stable political institutions and processes "that make conflict, change, and conciliation possible without institutional collapse."[50]

Nationalist conflict, however, suppresses the salience and, in some cases, even the emergence of multiple issues, demands, and interests. Nationalist leaderships attempt to subordinate all issues to the effort to attain a particular outcome. Unless institutional and procedural safeguards are established, the rise of nationalism among a numerically dominant group relegates all others to the status of a permanent minority, unable to defend their interests even under conditions of competition, participation, and individual liberty. Nationalism in a dominant group, however, makes it unlikely that such safeguards can be established or that minorities will continue to enjoy genuine individual liberties. Under these circumstances, nationalist movements among the minority most often demand autonomy and pursue separatist goals. They seek a separate existence for their nation, denying the existence or salience of commonalities, shared interests, or even mutual dependence. In extreme circumstances, nationalist conflicts turn violent, destroying the fabric of society. Nationalist movements thus strike at the very heart of the process of democratization: they represent collectivist bases for regime legitimation that compete with the individual rights-based legitimation of a liberal democratic order.

The political organizations characteristic of nationalist movements and state institutions and processes legitimated primarily through the fulfillment of nationalist aspirations are therefore ill suited to the conciliation of competing demands characteristic of democratic regimes. Nationalist organizations and governments may compromise the aspirations of their ethnic constituencies only at the risk of losing their popular support to more radical elements. They tend, therefore, to adopt exclusivist rather than inclusivist policies; they tend toward extremism rather than moderation. In this way, the politics of nationalism is contrary to the very essence of the liberal democratic process.

The deeply dislocating effects of simultaneous economic and political transformation contribute to the powerful attraction of nationalism for both political elites and the mass population. The material hardships imposed on the population by the transition make it difficult, if not impossible, for governments to win popular support on the basis of the benefits they can deliver to the population. This heightens the effectiveness of appeals to national sentiments, which can be satisfied through actions more easily under the control of the state. The declaration of sovereignty, the establishment of cultural supremacy, or even the threat of military action are all promises more easily fulfilled than an improvement in the standard of living. Moreover, such acts strengthen state power and secure the positions of political incumbents far more effectively than efforts to institutionalize the civil liberties of the population. The latter, in fact, facilitate criticism of the government and the activities of an opposition, making them less attractive to incumbent politicians.

The nationalist legitimation of new states is thus likely to impede the development of political competition, prevent the adoption of inclusive principles of participation, and delay the institutionalization of individual liberties that are essential to democratic systems. Several of the post-communist governments, for example, have attempted to redress ethnic grievances of the majority or the eponymous population through policies and practices that effectively discriminate against minorities. New laws with respect to citizenship, language rights, and voting rights, and other issues have heightened tensions between dominant and minority groups.

In both Estonia and Latvia, radical nationalist-populist movements sought to disenfranchise individuals who entered the republics during the period of Soviet rule. The Congress of Estonia and the Latvian Citizens' Committee are extreme examples of attempts to establish a nationalist, exclusivist basis of legitimation for emerging regimes.[51] Such efforts often engender nationalist-separatist reactions among compact minority settlements. The city of Narva on the Estonian-Russian border, for example, is 97 percent Russian and a potential locus of separatist activity if the Estonian regime were not to moderate its exclusionary policies, especially if economic discontent in the area becomes politicized.[52] Such discontent was apparent in the referendum of July 1993, which produced an overwhelming vote of support among local Russians for territorial autonomy.[53]

The parliamentary strength of nationalist and right-wing parties in Latvia increased between the June 1993 and September 1995 elections. In 1993, the nationalist For Fatherland and Freedom Party secured just over 5 percent of the vote, and six seats in the hundred-seat parliament.[54] In 1995, this party won fourteen seats, as the Latvian electorate shifted its overall support to parties of the right, abandoning its support for the moderate center represented by Latvia's Way. The latter lost more than half its parliamentary strength, declining from thirty-six to seventeen seats.[55]

The popular support exclusionary measures evoke among majority populations suggests the great difficulty of establishing a broad social and political commitment to the pluralistic concept of civil society that underlies Western liberal democracy. The cold reception President Clinton received in Latvia in July 1994 when he urged a crowd of tens of thousands to grant equal status to non-Latvians is one indication of the depth of popular feeling on such issues.[56] The prospect of successfully establishing the political culture of tolerance for differences that underlies American democracy would seem to be impossible, therefore, in the absence of concerted efforts by local political leaderships to construct legal and political structures to defend the rights of minorities.[57]

The policy response of independent Ukraine to its ethnic minorities stands in sharp contrast to that of the Baltic states: it has been inclusionary and has aimed at affirming political equality. The much greater size, socioeconomic complexity, and ethnic and political diversity of Ukraine in comparison to the Baltic states multiplied the number of interests and groups that emerged in Ukraine under glasnost. This moderated the appeal of narrowly nationalist politics in Ukraine and increased the importance of compromise and coalition building for mobilizing support in Ukrainian politics. Thus, both national-cultural and civil-political concerns came to be reflected in the opposition movement that emerged in 1989.

Ukraine is a heterogeneous society, characterized by distinct cultural and historical variations even among ethnic Ukrainians. There are strong cultural distinctions between the seven oblasts of western Ukraine, incorporated in the republic after World War II and making up 18.9 percent of the total population, and the rest of the republic. The proportion of Russians in the population of this region is relatively low. Smaller proportions of Ukrainians declared Russian as their mother tongue in the 1989 Soviet census in this region. Western Ukrainians are also more "national" in their orientation. Electoral support for independence and for the more nationally oriented candidate for president in the December 1991 elections was stronger here than in more Russified regions of the country.

At the same time, western Ukraine includes the largest non-Russian minority populations. Hungarians make up 12.5 percent of the population in the Transcarpathian region (Zakarpattia) that borders Hungary. Here, the local Hungarian population has voted its support for both Ukrainian independence and local autonomy, including administrative recognition for the Hungarian minority.[58] Romanians (including both those who declared Moldovan and those who declared Romanian identity in 1989) account for some 19.7 percent of the population in the Chernivtsi region, bordering both Moldova and Romania. These border territories might represent fertile grounds for secessionist or irredentist activity were it not for the policies of the new Ukrainian government. The citizenship law adopted in October 1991 granted citizenship to all individuals resident in Ukraine at the time, making no distinctions based on ethnicity. The declaration on national minorities adopted by Ukraine in November 1991 and the law adopted in June 1992 guarantee the full equality of citizens, including their linguistic and cultural freedom. The response of independent Ukraine to demands for local autonomy has also been concessionary and inclusive instead of repressive and exclusionary.

The proportion of ethnic Russians, as well as the proportion of culturally Russified Ukrainians, is highest in the eastern regions of the republic, especially in the Donbas. However, the high proportion of Ukrainians who declare Russian as a mother tongue in these areas is not due solely to the Russifying impact of large numbers of Russians in the local population. It also reflects the centuries-long history of ethnic Russian settlement here and the adoption of Ukrainian identity by populations whose historical or ancestral language always was Russian. Thus, the very meaning of Ukrainian identity differs between the western and eastern regions of the country. It is not surprising, therefore, that Ukraine has opted for a more liberal definition of rights and has so far avoided a narrowly nationalist definition for legitimation of the state.

Concentration of the Russian population in the eastern regions of Ukraine nonetheless raises the question whether Russians in eastern Ukraine might not lay claim to local autonomy of their own or perhaps even secede in favor of union with Russia. Economic unrest in the heavily industrialized provinces of Donetsk and Luhansk in eastern Ukraine creates the potential for a political alliance between leftist forces, including the former communists, opposed to economic reform and seeking continued state support for the social welfare of the population, and Russian nationalist forces seeking to exploit fears of Ukrainianization among the largely Russian and Russian-speaking local population.[59] Such an alliance might give rise to a powerful separatist movement in eastern Ukraine akin to that which emerged in Slovakia after 1990. Even in these regions, however, from 75 percent to over 90 percent of the electorate voted for independence in the December 1991 referendum. Only the Crimean electorate was closely divided on this issue; just over 54 percent supported independence.

Under Soviet rule, the Crimea remained part of the Russian republic until 1954, when it was transferred by administrative decision to Ukraine. The population of the peninsula is predominantly

Russian, and the proportion of Russians has grown steadily as the result of colonization, the expansion of Soviet military facilities on the peninsula, and the deportation of the indigenous population of Crimean Tatars, carried out in 1944. By 1989, the population was 67 percent Russian and 25 percent Ukrainian. Moreover, almost half the Ukrainian population was linguistically Russified. It is not surprising, given these conditions, that resistance to Ukrainian independence was strongest among this population.

The status of the Crimea represents a potentially explosive issue in Ukrainian politics. The strong desire for autonomy among the local majority Russian population has been met by resistance on the part of the Ukrainian government. The latter has encouraged resettlement of the native Crimean Tatar population, exiled by Stalin after World War II, as a means of increasing the population opposed to autonomy, or at least opposed to union with Russia. Interest among Russian nationalists in securing Crimean autonomy and union with Russia raises the possibility that a local secessionist movement might receive support from Russia.

Russian interest in the Crimea is reinforced by the basing of the Black Sea fleet on the peninsula. The status of the fleet represents a potential flashpoint in relations between Ukraine and Russia and has been the object of intense political dispute between the two states since the breakup of the Soviet Union. Despite periods of heightened rhetoric, this conflict has been negotiated peacefully. Neither leadership can risk the potential escalation of conflict that might result. While the leadership of Ukraine must be wary of inciting a Russian separatist movement in eastern Ukraine and alienating the millions of Russians who play important roles in the economy of Ukraine, the leadership of Russia must be wary of engendering unrest among the millions of ethnic Ukrainians who populate key areas in Siberia and the Far East and perform critical economic, political, and administrative functions in Russia. Moreover, any escalation of nationalisms represents a potential threat to the political survival of both the Ukrainian and the Russian governments, each of which faces political challenges from forces that might exploit nationalist conflict to their domestic political advantage. The economic and political incentives for maintaining peaceful relations and the potential costs of conflict appear so great as to compel the Russian and Ukrainian leaderships to negotiate the peaceful resolution of their differences. By doing so, they are likely to avoid adding an interethnic dimension to conflicts between their states.

Even where common economic and other interests might provide a pragmatic basis for interethnic cooperation and the preservation or establishment of common economic or political institutions, the power of nationalist-separatist sentiments among mobilized ethnic groups in the post-communist states makes it difficult for local leaders to act on them. Indeed, even the distribution of economic interests and resources itself may be in dispute as illegitimate legacies of the old regime for which contemporary compensation is due. Moreover, if postwar German experience is any guide, the transformation of political culture may require that democratic institutions be accompanied by significant improvements in the material well-being of the population.[60]

With the onset of competitive elections, politicians may gather substantially greater support—and therefore greater political power—by exploiting the coincidence of regional economic differences and inclinations toward ethnic self-assertion than by advocating economic compromise and political unity. The perception of material conflicts in ethnic terms by the mass populace, the acceptance or exploitation of such ethnic definitions by elites, and especially the frequency with which conflicts defined in this way produce violence make the resolution of differences over the distribution of governmental functions and over economic and other issues much more difficult. If liberal democracy depends on mastery by political leaders of the art of compromise, then successful transition to democracy is made more difficult by the fact that East European leaders, facing populations whose nationalist aspirations are unconstrained by other competing interests and aspirations, enjoy little leeway in which to develop this art.

Among the post-Soviet states, in the former Yugoslav states, and in Czechoslovakia, the transition from authoritarianism was turned into a simultaneous "end-of-empire" process. Once it was perceived in these terms, intellectual, economic, and other groups who might otherwise have been inclined to support such a transition were drawn toward more nationalistically determined positions. The Slovenian and Croatian challenges to rule from Belgrade, for example, stimulated a conservative and even reactionary response from some Serbs whose earlier support for the democratization of Yugoslavia ultimately proved less powerful than their attraction to Serbian nationalist agendas. Similarly, the opportunity to establish an independent national state proved more appealing to democratic activists in Slovenia than the task of democratizing a common Yugoslav state. In Czechoslovakia, the alliance of Czechs and Slovaks opposed to communism soon disintegrated, and electoral support in both Slovakia and the Czech Republic shifted to leaders and parties intent on pursuing regional interests at the expense of the federation.

The rush to affirm the political authority of national identities and the legitimacy of national states has also led in some cases to the partial legitimation or relegitimation of antidemocratic aspects of national political history. The fascist and Nazi collaborationist regimes established in Hungary under Miklos Horthy, in Slovakia under Josef Tiso, and in Croatia under Ante Pavelic have each been the object of public and in some instances de facto official reevaluation. New governments in Lithuania and Slovenia have pardoned Nazi collaborators, and the Croatian government has appointed former officials of the collaborationist regime to new positions of authority. Such actions are one dimension of the reaffirmation of collective identity in the region and a reflection of the powerful urge to reject any negative judgments of them. They also reflect, however, the weakness of concerns for individual and human rights in the contemporary politics of the region and insensitivity or even hostility toward ethnic minorities. The institutionalization of individual and human rights is, however, essential to the success of any transition from nationalist to democratic bases of regime legitimation.

Democratically inclined leaderships in the region are thus confronted with the task of establishing an enforceable boundary between legitimate national identification and cultural self-affirmation on the part of the majority and nationalist oppression of the minority, between democratically acceptable and unacceptable political behavior. This is an immensely difficult and ever-changing political challenge. Debate over this issue continues in the United States even after two hundred years of institutionalized democratic experience. It should not be surprising, therefore, that this is so difficult to achieve in the post-communist states, for it is clear that most of these states cannot yet depend on either a mass civic culture or their own accumulated legitimacy to insulate them from popular discontent. Nor do they have the resources to deliver sufficient material benefits to their people to counterbalance the social, economic, and political hardships that confront them.

The electoral victories of post-communist parties in Lithuania, Poland, and Hungary demonstrate that support for parties and governments remains highly volatile throughout the region and that popular discontent over material conditions is easily translated into political power. Where intergroup relations or the frustration of group ambitions create ethnic tensions or conflict, these may be joined to material dissatisfactions to create powerful bases for nationalist, antidemocratic movements. Historical experience as well as the contemporary examples of Yugoslavia, Hungary, Romania, Slovakia, and Moldova make it clear that widespread reversion to nationalist authoritarianism in Eastern Europe can easily lead to international conflict. Local conflicts inevitably threaten to escalate, spread, and draw in outside powers, including the United States. This has already happened in the former Yugoslavia. The West, therefore, has a clear security interest in the consolidation of democracy in the post-communist states; the establishment of democratic structural constraints on the ability of leaders to resort to violence to solve the many outstanding ethnoterritorial and ethnopolitical issues within and between the states of the region; and the longer-term establishment of democratic political cultures that will reduce their inclinations to do so.

The construction of a stable framework for international peace in the Euro-Atlantic community cannot wait for the effects of a transformation from centrally planned economies to market-based systems to produce the social, economic, and cultural foundations of democracy. Indeed, there is no agreement among analysts as to the specific social and economic "preconditions" of a democratic political order. Moreover, as political scientist Terry Lynn Karl has suggested, what appear to be the social *preconditions* for democracy may, in fact, represent the *outcomes* of democratic processes. Socioeconomic development, greater equality, and even the emergence of a civic culture, she argues, "may be better treated as the products of stable democratic processes, rather than as the prerequisites for their existence."[61] In view of this uncertainty, American policy must focus on strengthening democratic political institutions and processes in the post-communist states against the threat of authoritarian nationalisms.

CHAPTER 2

Ethnic Conflict and the Euro-Atlantic Community: The Yugoslav Crisis

THE REEMERGENCE OF national conflicts in Eastern Europe and the successor states of the former Soviet Union presents the United States and its allies with strong challenges to international peace. The immediate consequences and longer-term implications of such conflicts require European, Euro-Atlantic, and international organizations to adapt to the more difficult demands of maintaining peace under conditions of economic and political transformation and mobilized ethnic identities.[1] Nationalist demands to redefine political relationships within existing states, establish new states, or redefine boundaries between existing states defy the traditional distinction between internal and external conflicts. They involve many dimensions of human interaction and are subject to conflicting interpretation by outside actors attempting to deal with their consequences. The solution of any one such conflict must be seen as a potential precedent for others, not only among the successor states of post-communist Europe, but in the Third World and among the Western states as well.

Several Western states face or have faced internal challenges to their political unity based on regional ethnic identities. These experiences are inevitably reflected in differing views with respect to ethnic conflicts within states, especially conflicts that cut across the borders of states. The reemergence of political diversity among the post-communist states also contributes to policy differences among Western states as they pursue opportunities to advance divergent national interests. It is not surprising, therefore, that progress toward the establishment of a consistent, agreed set of principles for dealing with such conflicts has been slow and that even agreement on ad hoc responses to severe crisis has been extremely difficult to achieve.

International responses to the crisis in Yugoslavia were dominated by the great powers. Britain, France, and Germany, as well as the United States and the Soviet Union—later, Russia—played critical roles in shaping collective responses to the crisis. Throughout, each of these actors pursued its own, often conflicting, national interests. But they also acted in concert. Among them, Britain, France, Germany, the United States, and the Soviet Union/Russia dominated the activities of the CSCE, the European Community/European Union, the United Nations Security Council, and NATO; and through these organizations, they influenced the actions of others. Some Islamic states, for example, became increasingly involved in the crisis. But their options and opportunities were severely limited by the constraints imposed by decisions of the Security Council and the actions of the great powers.

Thus, the legitimate authority to address the crisis in Yugoslavia through multilateral institutions and organizations was dispersed, while the influence and resources to do so were concentrated in the hands of a few key states. This is an inherently weak and politically ineffective arrangement for crisis management. But the international community and particularly the Western powers were further hampered by several factors: the rapid obsolescence of key principles of international order characteristic of the postwar system and the organizations developed to uphold them; the as yet incomplete process of articulating and establishing consensus around new principles for resolving conflict in the post-Cold War system; and growing differences among the perceived national interests of the major powers. These contributed to the inability to resolve the conflicts in Yugoslavia before they threatened international peace, to prevent these conflicts from turning violent, and to end them once they did.

The Yugoslav crisis represents an extreme example of the destructive power of ethnic conflict. But the conditions that gave rise to that crisis are by no means unique. Some of the same social, economic, and political conflicts that contributed to the mobilization of ethnic identities in Yugoslavia are already present elsewhere in Eastern Europe and the former Soviet Union. Only a few of these have turned violent, and many still remain subject to resolution through negotiation. In attempting to develop tactics and strategies for the peaceful resolution of ethnic conflicts elsewhere, we must therefore ask why conditions in Yugoslavia gave rise to violence and examine whether domestic and international actors might have acted differently to achieve a peaceful settlement.

PRINCIPLES AND INSTITUTIONS IN FLUX

By the time the Yugoslav crisis exploded, in 1991, principles of international order in the Euro-Atlantic community were undergoing rapid change. The Helsinki Final Act, adopted by the CSCE in 1975, included ten such basic principles.[2] These included some that ratified the postwar configuration of states in the region by establishing their sovereignty and territorial integrity, affirming the inviolability of their borders, and establishing the principle of nonintervention in the internal affairs of other states. Other principles committed the signatories to peaceful relations by disavowing the threat or use of force and calling for the peaceful settlement of disputes. Others committed them to respect for "human rights and fundamental freedoms" and "the equal rights of peoples and their right to self-determination." The Final Act established the freedom of individuals, including members of national minorities, to exercise equal civil, political, economic, social, and cultural rights. It also established the right of peoples to determine their own political status. In effect, the Helsinki principles established Western concepts of individual liberty and collective democracy as the Euro-Atlantic political standard and applied that standard to all the signatory states, from North America to the USSR. However, more than a decade of additional negotiations and revolutionary changes in the domestic and foreign policies of the Soviet Union was required before the CSCE could begin to play an important role in the Euro-Atlantic security framework.[3] The third CSCE follow-up meeting, which lasted three years and concluded in Vienna in January 1989, reflected the increasing interest of the Soviet leadership under Gorbachev in East-West cooperation and the determination of the West to use that interest as leverage to obtain further progress on human rights, the peaceful settlement of disputes, and other issues. After 1989, modest progress was achieved through the CSCE framework toward the construction of mechanisms for the peaceful resolution of conflict. The Yugoslav crisis made clear, however, that these still required substantial improvement.

The concluding document adopted at Vienna reiterated and deepened the Helsinki Accords by adding more detailed statements and definitions by which adherence to each of the ten principles established in Helsinki might be judged. With regard to the peaceful settlement of disputes, the Vienna Document included the acceptance, in principle, of "mandatory involvement of a third party when a dispute cannot be settled by other peaceful means." It also initiated efforts to create a mechanism by which participating states might enforce implementation of commitments in the area of "human rights and fundamental freedoms, human contacts and other issues of a related humanitarian character." This human dimension mechanism required participating states to respond to requests and representations by other participating states on questions related to the human dimension of the CSCE, and to hold bilateral meetings to examine such questions when requested to do so. It also permitted participating states to bring such issues to the attention of other participants and raise them at meetings of the conference on the human dimension to be held each year, as well as at the main CSCE follow-up meetings.[4]

In this way, the CSCE legitimated inquiry and involvement by participating states in the internal affairs of other participating states and weakened the principle of noninterference in internal affairs as a defense for activities that violated human rights principles embodied in the CSCE agreements. The Vienna Document therefore did not reiterate the sixth principle adopted at Helsinki in 1975, which prohibited direct or indirect intervention in the internal affairs of other states. Indeed, the Geneva meeting of experts on national minorities held in July 1991, which convened just as war broke out in Slovenia, acknowledged the political realities of ethnic conflict in Europe by specifically concluding that issues concerning the rights of national minorities "are matters of legitimate international concern and consequently do not constitute exclusively an internal affair of the respective state."[5] This view was reiterated at the conference on the human dimension held in Moscow in the fall of 1991 in the wake of the failed August coup attempt.[6]

The dramatic changes in Eastern Europe in 1989 and the continuing changes in the USSR permitted the United States and other Western states to engage in more direct advocacy of democratic change through the CSCE. The document produced by the conference on the human dimension in Copenhagen in the spring of 1990 reflected these efforts. It contained extensive statements defining the general institutional and legal elements of pluralistic democratic systems and asserted that "pluralistic democracy and the rule of law are essential for ensuring respect for all human rights and fundamental freedoms." It also established minority rights as an essential element of democracy. But there was continuing disagreement among member states over such issues as "how to curb intolerance while preserving the integrity of the principle of freedom of expression," the definition of what constituted a "minority," and, most contentious of all, "the extent to which states should take an active role in protecting and promoting minority identities, rather than refraining from blocking or inhibiting minorities' efforts to protect and promote themselves." Because of these differences, the Copenhagen Document imposed few specific obligations on member states.[7]

The great sensitivity of issues surrounding minority rights and the corresponding difficulty of achieving consensus among the states of the CSCE were also evident at the Geneva meeting of experts on national minorities, in July 1991.[8] The rights of national minorities, especially the right to self-determination, were in dispute throughout Eastern Europe and the Soviet Union, and by this time had become the focus of violent conflict in Yugoslavia. It is not surprising, therefore, that the Yugoslav delegation fought unsuccessfully to include a statement explicitly denying the right of self-determination to national minorities. However, unlike previous CSCE documents, the Geneva Document does not contain an explicit affirmation of the right to self-determination.[9]

Limited progress in the definition of minority rights was paralleled by limited progress toward the establishment of institutions and organizations empowered to implement the Helsinki principles. The Charter of Paris for a New Europe, adopted at the November 1990 CSCE summit meeting in Paris, established a Council of the CSCE Ministers of Foreign Affairs, which would meet regularly, at least once a year. It also established a Committee of Senior Officials (CSO) to prepare meetings of the council, carry out its decisions, review current issues, and take appropriate decisions, including recommendations to the council. The Paris Charter mandated the development of provisions for convening emergency meetings of the CSO, which it did at its meeting in Berlin in June 1991. The emergency meeting mechanism was activated in response to the outbreak of armed conflict in Yugoslavia. The first emergency meeting, held in early July, was followed by four additional such meetings on Yugoslavia in 1991 alone.

The Paris Charter also established a permanent Secretariat of the CSCE in Prague, an Office of Free Elections in Warsaw (later renamed the Office of Democratic Institutions and Human Rights [ODIHR] and given an expanded mandate by the council in January 1992), and a Conflict Prevention Center in Vienna. The Office of Democratic Institutions became the institutional locus of the human dimension mechanism; the Conflict Prevention Center was created to reduce the risk of conflict through CSCE confidence- and security-building measures, including consultations and cooperation with respect to "unusual military activities." Both the human dimension mechanism and "unusual military activities" procedures were called into operation by CSCE states as part of their effort to deal with the Yugoslav crisis.

Three major stumbling blocks continued, however, to prevent successful management within the CSCE framework of international crises arising out of ethnic conflicts. The first obstacle was the continuing contradiction inherent in the simultaneous commitment to the principles of self-determination and territorial integrity of existing states. There was little prospect that agreement could be reached on how to determine what groups are entitled to exercise the right of self-determination, or even what such a right entailed. Sovereignty of states remains the cornerstone of the international political order and the basis of membership in the CSCE. Few states are secure against such claims. Moreover, the principle of self-determination offers few guidelines for the resolution of conflicts between groups that make competing claims to sovereignty over the same territory.[10]

In actual practice, the principle of territorial integrity enjoyed clear priority in the international system. This was reflected, for example, in the results of the January 1991 Valletta meeting of the CSCE on peaceful settlement of disputes. The modest procedure adopted there could neither be invoked nor continued if a party to the dispute declared that its territorial integrity or sovereignty was at issue.[11] This effectively rendered the procedure useless in cases such as the Yugoslav crisis or the Soviet use of force against Lithuania, which took place as the Valletta meeting opened.

The second obstacle to successful management of crises lay in the CSCE's continuing reliance on consensual decisionmaking. This rendered it vulnerable to the effective veto of any single member. The Soviet use of force against Lithuania, for example, constituted a flagrant violation of the CSCE principles, but the solitary opposition of the Soviet delegation prevented the convening of an emergency CSCE meeting to consider the situation in the Baltic states. Similarly, Yugoslav resistance to CSCE involvement in the resolution of its own crisis was the source of continuing frustration to other participating states.

The lack of any enforcement mechanism constituted a third and perhaps most serious obstacle. The Soviet leadership could use force against the Baltic states, Yugoslavia could use force against Slovenia, and other CSCE member states might elect to use force against their own populations with relative impunity. There was no possibility of a response in kind from the CSCE.

The Western states did have the capacity to conduct multilateral military operations that could support political efforts to achieve the negotiated, peaceful resolution of such conflicts, or to enforce peace against the will of conflicting parties. But that capacity was located in NATO, which was organized against what these states perceived as the main threat to international peace in the postwar period: Soviet military attack. In addition to joint military capabilities, the North Atlantic states developed an extensive network of political and economic consultative relationships under the NATO umbrella. The development of close consultative and cooperative behavior among the NATO countries was facilitated both by the perception of a common external threat and by the evolution of a shared democratic political culture among almost all the member states. The latter made it largely unnecessary to develop formal mechanisms for carrying out conflict resolution or peacekeeping functions between the member states.

The military-security integration achieved through NATO was an important element securing international peace in Europe. But it is difficult to imagine that peace in Western Europe or democratic political systems in the less stable postwar states could have been secured as quickly or as effectively in the absence of rapid economic recovery and deliberate economic integration. Both developments were encouraged and supported by the United States through the Marshall Plan. Economic integration, however, was primarily the product of deliberate efforts on the part of European leaders determined to prevent renewed conflict.

The economic and political integration of Western Europe in the European Union (EU) (formerly the European Community [EC]) produced a gradual transfer of partial sovereignty from individual member states to common institutions in many areas of economic and social policy. The latter have thus become important arenas for political consultation and the negotiation of policy differences among member states.[12] But the member states of the EU are unlikely to cede sovereignty over the definition of either their national territories or their domestic political institutions and processes to the EU. Indeed, the very process of ratifying the 1991 Maastricht Treaty establishing the European Union affirmed the sovereign power of domestic authority.

The tension between national sovereignty and transnational authority is reflected in the European approach to human rights issues as well.[13] The Council of Europe has established a European Commission on Human Rights to hear complaints against member states of the council for failing to secure the rights and freedoms specified in the European Convention on Human Rights, to which states now must accede as a condition of membership. However, the Commission on Human Rights may act only after all domestic remedies have been exhausted, and it may accept petitions from individuals only if the government concerned agrees. Thus, the convergence of European states around a set of human rights norms must be attributed more to the consolidation of democratic regimes and cultures in the states than to any institutional arrangements for adjudicating disputes over these rights, including the rights of ethnic minorities. With the important exception of the conflict in Northern Ireland, the strong democratic institutions in each member state provide sufficient capacity for the peaceful resolution of domestic intergroup conflicts. In the case of Northern Ireland, bilateral negotiations between the two well-institutionalized democratic states directly involved appear likely to lead to eventual multilateral negotiations over a peaceful solution among all involved parties.

The conflict between Greece and Turkey over Cyprus suggests the importance for international peace and conflict prevention in the Euro-Atlantic community of *simultaneous* economic and military-political integration on the one hand, and the evolution of common democratic political values on the other. Unlike in Western Europe since World War II, economic and political convergence between Greece and Turkey did not proceed simultaneously with military-security integration into NATO. Until relatively recently, neither country enjoyed stable democratic government. The absence of stable democracy ruled out membership in the European Community and its network of integrative economic relationships. Greece was therefore not admitted until democracy was reestablished. Turkey has not yet been admitted. NATO relationships by themselves proved inadequate as instruments for dispute resolution between member states. Even in Northern Ireland, British military-political dominance alone was insufficient to overcome the accumulated legacy of intercommunal violence and economic inequality that underlies the conflict there. Thus, it would appear that in the absence of a widespread network of common material and other social interests associated with economic integration, and in the absence of the deeper values associated with stable democratic systems, military-political integration alone appears to provide insufficient bases for the peaceful resolution of disputes.

In the case of Cyprus, it is the peacekeeping capability of the United Nations that made the peaceful management of the Cyprus conflict—but not its solution—possible. UN peacekeeping operations are primarily political and diplomatic missions, carried out by military contingents.[14] They are intended to maintain, or keep, a peace or cease-fire agreed to by warring parties, and facilitate further negotiation aimed at a peaceful settlement of the conflict. They do not by themselves represent solutions. Nor do they represent attempts by the United Nations to impose or enforce its own solutions. Consistent with the political nature of peacekeeping operations and the United Nations Charter principle of noninterference in domestic affairs, the success of such operations requires the consent and cooperation of the conflicting parties, usually a host country or countries. Conditions of internal war make it difficult, if not impossible, to secure consent from all parties involved and are therefore ill suited to such operations.

Where peacekeeping forces are interposed between conflicting parties who cannot agree on anything other than a cease-fire, it is likely that their deployment will at best mark the beginning of protracted negotiations and effectively "freeze" the status quo. It is also likely that fighting will be resumed in the future, since peacekeeping contingents do not present a powerful military deterrent. Any party to the conflict may therefore choose to take up arms at any time. The deployment of UN peacekeepers to Cyprus, for example, was not followed by further agreement between the Greek and Turkish communities. It did not prevent further violent episodes or, in July 1974, a coup d'état followed by a Turkish military invasion and full-scale fighting. Since the cease-fire established in August 1974, the island has been partitioned de facto. The UN force in Cyprus has controlled a buffer zone between the Greek- and Turkish-controlled regions of the island, and negotiations between the communities have made little progress. In a worst case, peacekeeping forces may themselves become the target of attack by parties who view a cease-fire as contrary to their interests.

The weaker the political support of the conflicting parties for a peaceful settlement, therefore, the stronger the military capability required of any peacekeeping operation. However, the use of force must remain a last resort for United Nations peacekeepers if the diplomatic and political mission of such operations is to be achieved. The use of force for purposes other than the self-defense of peacekeeping troops would alter the character of such operations, converting them into enforcement operations, whether de jure or de facto. The line between peacekeeping and enforcement operations may therefore be determined by the local political and military conditions under which such operations are undertaken, as well as by the intent of the Security Council.

United Nations enforcement operations under the provisions of Chapter VII of the UN Charter provide a basis for more extensive military operations to enforce international peace, even in the absence of local consent. Enforcement missions cannot be neutral operations. They require identification of a threat to international peace against which force is to be directed. The political effect of using military force is to support, displace, or overthrow the existing authority, or to establish a new one, in the area of operations. Such operations can easily bring the Security Council into direct confrontation with the principle of state sovereignty. All members of the Security Council necessarily share an interest in protecting their own sovereign authority against encroachment. This interest plays an important role when they consider whether to invoke the authority of Chapter VII and mandate coercive action against the wishes of another state. Nonpermanent members, especially, have been concerned not to legitimate intervention by the great powers in the internal affairs of less powerful states. But great powers, too, have been concerned not to allow the authority of the United Nations to constrain their freedom of action. UN peacekeeping operations remain subject to the political influences of the great powers, who exercise veto power over the decisions of the Security Council.

Thus, when the wars in the former Yugoslavia broke out, the capacity of the Euro-Atlantic political community to respond to interethnic conflicts that threatened international peace remained dispersed and uncoordinated. The articulation and international ratification of the principles of democratic government and the rule of law, as well as progress toward the institutionalization of mechanisms for the peaceful resolution of conflicts surrounding the exercise and protection of the rights embedded in these principles, had proceeded furthest within the CSCE framework. But serious internal contradictions between some of the most basic of these principles remained unresolved. Legitimate international authority to enforce agreed solutions or impose solutions externally was lodged in an entirely separate institutional arena, with overlapping but not identical membership: the United Nations Security Council. The Security Council, in turn, required a consensus among its permanent members in order to provide such authority. Even when authorized, United Nations peacekeeping efforts operated under severe political restraints. The primary military organization of the Western democracies, NATO, was still organized to meet the receding threat of Soviet military attack and was as yet unprepared to confront the threat to Western security posed by ethnic conflicts within and among the post-communist states.

The great powers, acting in concert and led by the United States, still commanded sufficient military and political resources to galvanize international institutions and mount a credible threat of peace enforcement when their vital national interests were at stake. Their decisive reaction to the Iraqi invasion of Kuwait stands in sharp contrast to their inaction in Yugoslavia. But in the case of Yugoslavia, the challenge to Western interests and to international peace was less obvious and thus commanded less attention from policymakers. Even as the Yugoslav crisis intensified, however, divisions among the great powers and the dispersion of relevant authorities, responsibilities, and resources among differing institutions, organizations, and individual states further weakened the ability of Western states to respond.

PRELUDE TO WAR

The collapse of Yugoslavia must be explained in terms of several factors. Structural factors, in the form of mutually reinforcing ethnic, regional, economic, and political cleavages, contributed to the intensification of the conflict and its definition in ethnic terms. Political factors, manifest in the inability or unwillingness of regional leaders to compromise, contributed to a political stalemate. Institutional factors, in the form of constitutional arrangements that granted each ethnoregional leadership a veto over decisionmaking, transformed interregional stalemate into governmental paralysis and, finally, breakdown.

By the mid-1970s, Yugoslavia had become a highly decentralized federation, in which the constituent republics dominated the federal center. Political leaderships in the regions jealously protected their interests and consistently sought to expand their prerogatives at the expense of federal authorities. The potential for interregional conflict to become ethnic conflict was constrained by the overwhelming common interest of the regional communist leaderships in the preservation of the political order that shielded them from responsibility and accountability.[15] Like the other regimes of Eastern Europe, the multinational regime in Yugoslavia was legitimated by the benefits it delivered to the population. It provided rapid economic development, social modernization, and improved living standards. It delivered physical security from the internal turmoil of the prewar regime and the fratricidal conflict of the wartime state, as well as the satisfactions of belonging to a community that enjoyed a disproportionately high level of international prestige, derived from the international prominence of President Tito.[16]

Legitimation of the multinational political community was reflected in the spread of a "Yugoslav" civic identity in the 1970s. The growth of this identity remained modest, however. The proportion of the population that declared "Yugoslav" identity in the national census increased from 1.3 percent in 1971 to 5.4 percent in 1981. This suggested that processes of ethnic and political integration were taking hold, but the distinct ethnic, or national, identities of the regional populations continued to command their affective loyalties and provide the most powerful bases for political mobilization.[17]

The ethnically defined territorial structures of the Yugoslav system reinforced the political strength of these identities and the political divisions in the leadership. Federal political bodies in both the government and the party, including the collective state presidency and the party's presidium, were composed of representatives of the republics and provinces selected by the regional leaderships. Individual leadership positions in these bodies, including the country's prime ministership and presidency, rotated according to an explicit agreement between the regions. Only the military remained a unified, all-Yugoslav organization, although it was dominated by ethnic Serbs.

By the mid-1980s, the collective leadership bodies of the country were divided between those who supported an even looser association between the regions and those who continued to support a strengthened federal government. This division was reinforced by differences over the scope and pace of further economic and political reform and by the coincidence of these differences with ethnic cleavages.[18] By the late 1980s, political differences among the regional leaderships had become even more volatile as the result of the increasingly violent conflict between Serbs and Albanians in Kosovo.

Devolution and power sharing, two strategies often cited as possible solutions to ethnic conflict,[19] thus intensified nationalist conflict in Yugoslavia. First, they increased the autonomous power of leaderships whose regional constituencies were defined largely by the identities of their dominant ethnic groups, and second, they contributed to both the redefinition of interregional conflict in ethnic terms and the politicization of ethnic identities.[20] However, the populations of the units to which power was devolved were not homogeneous. With the exception of Slovenia, the leaderships could not seek to fulfill the nationalist aspirations of their ethnic majorities without alienating substantial minority populations.

Only the population of the Slovenian republic approached homogeneity. Equally important, over 98 percent of all Slovenes in Yugoslavia resided in Slovenia. Thus, efforts by ethnically Slovene regional leaders to advance Slovene national-cultural interests and strengthen Slovenian autonomy effectively encompassed all Slovenes. They neither threatened the status of a large minority within Slovenia nor challenged the power of any other group over its own republic by encouraging large Slovene minority populations elsewhere to demand autonomy.

The case of the Croats and Croatia differed sharply from that of the Slovenes and Slovenia. Eighty percent of the Croats in Yugoslavia in 1991 resided in the Croatian republic, where they constituted 77.9 percent of the population. Serbs accounted for 12.2 percent of Croatia's population. Thus, Croat leaders could not pursue exclusionary nationalist policies within the context of the Croatian state defined by the borders inherited from the communists without the risk of alienating a large ethnic minority with strong links to conationals beyond Croatia's borders.

Croats were themselves divided by the internal borders of the

Table 2.1

REGIONAL DISTRIBUTION OF MAJOR ETHNIC GROUPS
IN FORMER YUGOSLAVIA, 1991

Regions	Slovenes	Croats	Hungarians	Serbs	Muslims	Albanians	Montenegrins	Macedonians	"Yugoslavs"	Total Population
Slovenia	1,718,318	53,688	8,499	47,097	26,725	3,558	4,233	4,412	12,237	1,962,606
Croatia	23,802	3,708,308	23,802	580,762	47,603	14,281	9,521	4,760	104,728	4,760,344
Vojvodina	2,563	74,226	340,946	1,151,353	6,079	2,959	44,721	16,641	168,859	2,012,517
Serbia*	5,777	26,827	4,430	5,081,766	173,871	76,012	75,258	30,936	145,810	5,824,211
Bosnia-Herzegovina	—	755,895	—	1,369,258	1,905,829	—	—	—	239,845	4,364,574
Kosovo**	—	8,161	—	195,301	57,408	1,607,690	20,045	—	3,070	1,954,747
Montenegro	407	6,249	—	57,176	89,932	40,880	380,484	860	25,854	615,267
Macedonia***	—	—	—	44,159	—	427,313	—	1,314,283	—	2,033,964
GROUP TOTALS	1,750,867	4,633,354	377,677	8,526,872	2,307,447	2,172,693	534,262	1,371,892	700,403	23,528,230

*Excludes Vojvodina and Kosovo.

**Data for ethnic Albanian population, which boycotted the census, is an estimate generated by the Kosovo Provincial Statistical Institute.

***Data for certain areas of the republic were extrapolated from a limited census.

Source: Savezni Zavod Za Statistiku (SZS), "Nacionalni sastav stanovnistva po opstinama," Statisticki Bilten broj 1934 (Beograd: SZS, 1992).

Table 2.2

COMPOSITION OF REGIONS BY MAJOR GROUPS (HORIZONTAL) \ REGIONAL DISTRIBUTION OF MAJOR GROUPS (VERTICAL)

GROUPS

(In each group, the first value is the horizontal figure, printed lower left in the cell, and the second is the vertical figure, printed upper right.)

REGIONS	Slovenes		Croats		Hungarians		Serbs		Muslims		Albanians		Montene-grins		Macedon-ians		Yugoslavs		Region Total
Slovenia	87.6	98.1	2.7	1.2	0.4	2.4	2.4	0.6	1.4	1.2	0.2	0.2	0.2	0.8	0.2	0.3	0.6	1.7	100.0
Croatia	0.5	1.4	77.9	80.0	0.5	6.3	12.2	6.8	1.0	2.1	0.3	0.7	0.2	1.8	0.1	0.3	2.2	15.0	100.0
Vojvodina	0.1	0.1	3.7	1.6	16.9	90.3	57.2	13.4	0.3	0.3	0.1	0.1	2.2	8.4	0.8	1.2	8.4	24.1	100.0
Serbia	0.1	0.3	0.5	0.6	0.1	1.2	87.3	59.3	3.0	7.5	1.3	3.5	1.3	14.1	0.5	2.3	2.5	20.8	100.0
Bosnia-Hercegovina	—	—	17.3	16.3	—	—	31.4	16.0	43.7	82.6	—	—	—	—	—	—	5.5	34.2	100.0
Kosovo	—	—	0.4	0.2	—	—	10.0	2.3	2.9	2.5	82.2	74.0	1.0	3.8	—	—	0.2	0.4	100.0
Montenegro	0.1	0.0	1.0	0.1	—	—	9.3	0.7	14.6	3.9	6.6	1.9	61.8	71.2	0.1	0.1	4.2	3.7	100.0
Macedonia	—	—	—	—	—	—	2.2	0.5	—	—	21.0	19.7	—	—	64.6	95.8	—	—	100.0
Group Total		100.0		100.0		100.0		100.0		100.0		100.0		100.0		100.0		100.0	

Source: Table 2.1.

former Yugoslavia. Over 16 percent of Croats resided in the neighboring republic of Bosnia-Herzegovina, where they constituted 17.3 percent of the population. The Croats in Bosnia-Herzegovina were clustered in regions bordering on Croatia itself, where they constituted the overwhelming majority of the local population and formed a Croatian ethnic irredenta. Serbs constituted an even larger proportion of the population in Bosnia-Herzegovina—31.4 percent in 1991—and comprised the majority in some counties of the republic. Bosnia's Muslims constituted 43.7 percent of the population and represented the majority in other counties. Thus, no group could claim the overall majority in the republic. In many counties there was no single ethnic majority. Within a single county, rural areas might be ethnically homogeneous or dominated by a single group, while urban areas were ethnically mixed.

The emergent multiethnic civil society characteristic of urban Bosnia-Herzegovina was reflected in the fact that, in 1981, almost 8 percent of the republic's population declared "Yugoslav" identity, and over 75 percent of these individuals were resident in urban areas. In the larger cities, "Yugoslavs" constituted from one-fifth to one-quarter of the population. Given this complex pattern of ethnic settlement in Bosnia-Herzegovina, no ethnic leadership in the republic could advance exclusionary nationalist ambitions on behalf of its ethnic constituency without alienating vast portions of the population—including members of its own group who had become part of the urban civic culture.[21]

The population of the republic of Serbia also contained geographically concentrated ethnic minority populations. In the province of Vojvodina, the concentration of ethnic Hungarians in the northern counties near the border with Hungary meant they were viewed from both Budapest and Belgrade as a potential Hungarian irredenta. In the province of Kosovo, the overwhelming majority of the population consisted of ethnic Albanians. Serb resentment over the increasing power of the ethnic Albanians in Kosovo reinforced long-standing concerns among Serbian nationalists over the division of the Serb nation among the several republics of Yugoslavia. The

Serbs of Croatia comprised 6.8 percent of all Serbs in Yugoslavia in 1991, and those in Bosnia-Herzegovina, 16 percent. The increasing autonomy of the republics from one another and the growing interregional conflict of the 1980s stimulated fears among Serb nationalists that large portions of the nation might be "cut off" from Serbia. Such fears were easily manipulated by Slobodan Milosevic to defeat his political opponents in the Serbian Communist Party leadership, mobilize the Serbian masses around nationalist slogans, reverse the devolution of power to the provinces, reassert Belgrade's control over Kosovo and Vojvodina, and consolidate a new authoritarian regime in Belgrade.

Milosevic represented a powerful synthesis of Serb nationalism, political conservatism, support for centralism, and resistance to meaningful economic reform. Developments in Serbia under his leadership stood in stark contrast to those in Slovenia, where the growth of popular nationalism took the form of demands for political democracy and rapid economic reform, the pluralization of group activity in the republic, and support for further confederalization of the Yugoslav regime. In Serbia, the republic remained under the continuing control of the unreformed Communist Party, which renamed itself and co-opted some prominent noncommunist figures into its leadership, but remained under Milosevic's control. The Slovenian communist leadership, in contrast, cooperated with emergent social and political forces to move rapidly toward a more pluralistic order.[22] Rather than seeing organized popular pressure only as a threat, the Slovenian leadership under Milan Kucan viewed it as an important and necessary asset in its struggle for economic and political reform of the federation. The increasing divergence of Slovenian and Serbian economic interests and political tendencies in the mid-1980s was reflected in increasingly antagonistic relations between both the political and the cultural elites of these two republics, Slovenia having embarked on a secessionist strategy and Serbia having embarked on an effort to recentralize power and authority in Belgrade.

In the past, the most explosive conflict in Yugoslavia had been

Yugoslavia: Ethnic Majorities

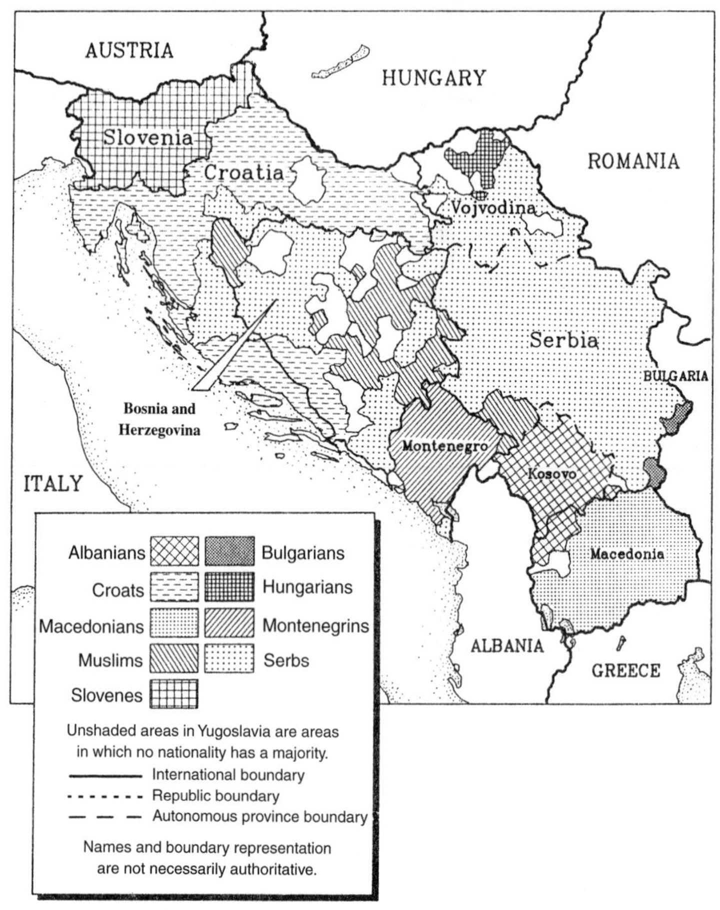

Ethnic Majorities in Bosnia-Herzegovina

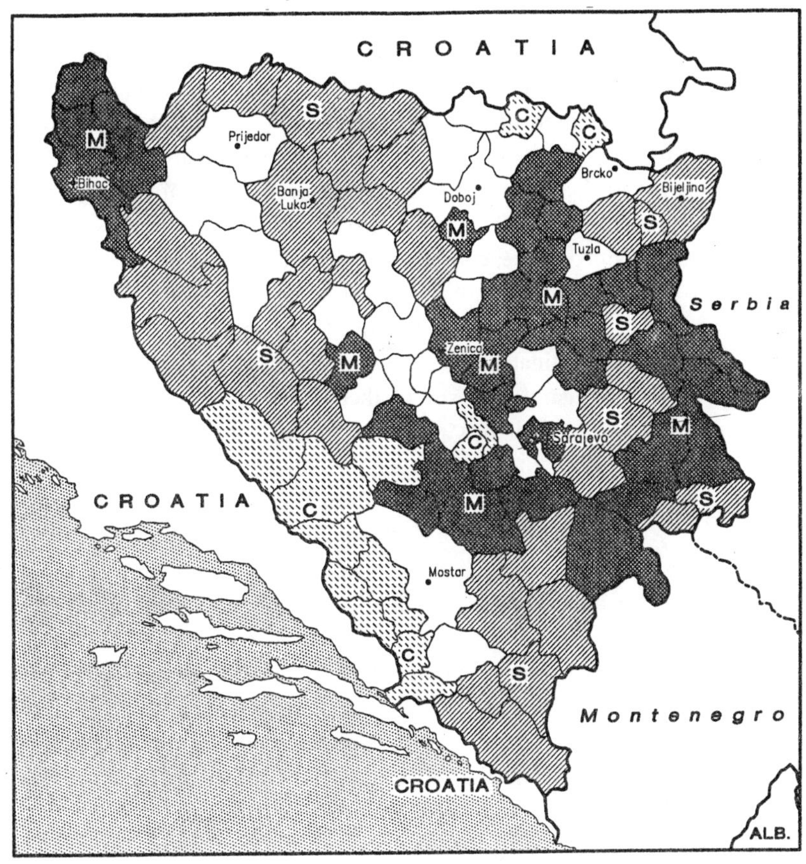

ETHNIC MAJORITY AREAS

- M — Muslim
- S — Serb
- C — Croat
- No majority in Bosnia and Herzegovina

Serbia and Montenegro have asserted the formation of a joint independent state, but this entity has not been formally recognized by the United States.

Names and boundary representation are not necessarily authoritative.

between the political aspirations of Croats and those of Serbs; the historical and imagined national homelands and claims to sovereignty of these two groups overlapped. This was the conflict that destabilized the interwar regime and threatened to destabilize the communist regime in 1971. In December 1971, Tito used military force to suppress the mass nationalist movement that had arisen in Croatia and then went on to purge the leaderships of Croatia and the other republics.[23] As a result, Croatian communist leaders in the 1980s remained more conservative than their Slovenian counterparts, although they also supported a confederationalist view of Yugoslavia. More important, because Croatian leaders traced their origins to the antinationalist purges of the early 1970s, they did not enjoy the popular legitimacy of their Slovenian counterparts and remained vulnerable to a political challenge from the nationalist opposition. With the breakup of the Yugoslav Communist Party (formally, the League of Communists of Yugoslavia) in January 1990 and the onset of competitive elections in the republics, the Croatian leadership was decisively defeated. The electoral victory in May 1990 of the Croatian Democratic Union, a nationalist coalition led by Franjo Tudjman, polarized relations between Croats and Serbs in that republic and set the stage for a renewed confrontation between Croatian and Serbian nationalisms.

By early 1990, definition of the emerging post-communist order in Yugoslavia became the object of open conflict between several competing and even mutually contradictory nationalist visions. The Serbian vision allowed for two fundamentally different outcomes: either the federation would be sufficiently strengthened to assure the protection of Serb populations everywhere in the country, or the dissolution of the federation would be accompanied by the redrawing of boundaries to incorporate Serb-populated territories in a single, independent Serbian state. This did not preclude the accommodation of the Slovene vision of an entirely independent Slovenian state. But it did deny Croatian aspirations for an independent state defined by the borders inherited from the old regime, and it contradicted extreme Croatian nationalists' pretensions to an expanded

Croatian state encompassing Croat-populated territories in Bosnia-Herzegovina.

Serb and Croat nationalist aspirations might still have been accommodated through the creation of independent states that exercised sovereignty over their respective ethnic territories. But such a solution would have required a substantial redrawing of existing borders and would thereby have called into question the continued existence of Bosnia-Herzegovina as a multinational state of Muslims, Serbs, and Croats. Moreover, any agreement openly negotiated by the Serbian leadership that legitimated claims to self-determination based on the current ethnic composition of local populations would have strengthened the ethnic Albanian case for an independent Kosovo and raised the prospect of Serbia either giving up that province peacefully or escalating the level of repression there.

Kosovar Albanians declared their independence and adopted their own constitution in the summer and fall of 1990. Were borders to be changed on the basis of ethnicity alone, Kosovar Albanian leaders might lay claim to a large swath of western Macedonia where, according to the 1991 census, ethnic Albanians constituted the majority or plurality of the local population. They might also lay claim to the bordering Serbian county of Presevo, where ethnic Albanians constituted the majority. While the largest ethnic Albanian party in Kosovo, the Democratic Alliance, has pursued a moderate course, the more radical nationalist Albanian General Party has called for the unification of all ethnically Albanian territories.[24] Similarly, Muslim nationalists in Bosnia might lay claim to the several counties of the Sandzak region of southern Serbia in which Muslims constitute the majority.

In August 1990, Serbs of the central Dalmatian region of Croatia—Croatian Krajina—began an open insurrection against the authority of the Zagreb government. Already fearful of the nationalist campaign themes of the governing Croatian Democratic Union and mindful of the violently anti-Serb character of the most recent episodes of extreme Croatian nationalism, the Serbs of Dalmatia viewed the Tudjman government's effort to disarm ethnically Serb local police forces and replace them with special Croatian police units as a portent of further repression to come.[25] They declared their intention to remain part of a common Yugoslav state or, alternatively, to become an independent Serb republic. Their uprising should have been a clear warning to all concerned: the republic borders established by the communist regime in the postwar period were extremely vulnerable to challenges from ethnic communities that did not share the identity on which new, nationalist post-communist governments sought to legitimate themselves. Such communities were alienated or even threatened by the nationalistic legitimation of these new governments. If existing borders were to be preserved, substantial political guarantees would have to be provided for the ethnic minority enclaves in the republics.

In Slovenia, the overwhelming declaration of support for a sovereign and independent state by 88 percent of the electorate in a referendum held December 23, 1990, made the secession of that republic all but inevitable. The decision by Yugoslav leaders in February 1991 to begin determining how to divide the country's assets among the regions suggested still more clearly that the breakup of Yugoslavia was at hand. But the threat by the Yugoslav minister of defense in December to use force to prevent Slovenia or Croatia from seceding signaled the likelihood that the breakup would not be peaceful.

The ensuing wars in Croatia and Bosnia-Herzegovina demonstrate the violent consequences of pursuing secessionist or irredentist strategies by force in disputed territories. These wars have been driven by a Serb effort to carry out the consolidation of a Serb nation-state encompassing all ethnic Serbs—even to the extent of seizing multiethnic territories—and the disregard by Croat and Muslim leaders of Serb interests. The brutality of the Serbs and the brutality of the responses to their actions reflect the extremism that follows from attempts to establish exclusive ethnic control over disputed territories. The wars in the former Yugoslavia thus illustrate the extreme consequences that may result when the principle of national self-determination is defined in exclusivist ethnic terms and applied by any one group to ethnically mixed territories. They also illustrate the inherent contradiction between the principle of national self-determination and the principles of monolithic state sovereignty and unitary territorial integrity.

PRESERVING THE STATUS QUO

A narrow window of opportunity for negotiating a peaceful solution of the growing dispute between the republics and addressing the demands raised by the different ethnic communities appeared to remain open until March 1991. Western inaction in late 1990 and early 1991 can be attributed in part to the preoccupation of West European leaders with the negotiations over European integration. Collective action through the EC was further stymied by the clear differences in perspective among Britain, France, and Germany. U.S. policymakers, on the other hand, consciously chose to distance themselves from the issue.

The Bush administration was well equipped to deal with the crisis. Deputy secretary of state Lawrence Eagleburger, national security advisor Brent Scowcroft, and other high officials in the foreign policymaking establishment knew Yugoslavia exceptionally well. By late 1990, press leaks suggested that the American intelligence community had concluded that Yugoslavia was on the verge of disintegrating.[26] However, the White House failed to accept the warnings of intelligence analysts and did not attempt to lead a coordinated Western response to the gathering crisis.

The attention of Western policymakers generally, and American policymakers in particular, was diverted by two other problems: the continuing political crisis in the Soviet Union and the preparations for the military effort to reverse the Iraqi invasion of Kuwait. The latter commanded the attention of military planners. Political leaders were occupied by the efforts to shore up the shaky Soviet regime under Mikhail Gorbachev. Any effort to facilitate a peaceful breakup of Yugoslavia appears to have been precluded by the fear that it might create an undesirable precedent for the Soviet Union. To the extent that policymakers paid any attention to the crisis in Yugoslavia, they devoted their energies almost entirely to supporting the status quo.

No better example of the futility of American policies in this period can be found than in the diplomatic effort invested in getting the Yugoslavs to adhere to their own rules for rotation of the chairmanship of their collective presidency in May 1991, instead of addressing the underlying disagreements. The West's failure to act once the inevitability of dissolution (as suggested in its own intelligence estimate) became apparent or to develop principles on which such dissolution might be achieved peacefully reduced Western influence over the secessionist regional leaderships and encouraged the use of force by those seeking to hold the country together.

Intensive negotiations among the regional leaders during April and May 1991 failed to produce a formula for accommodating the demands of some regions for greater independence and the needs of others to maintain a common relationship. These talks took place against the background of escalating interethnic violence. In early May, the Yugoslav minister of defense allowed that a civil war was already under way and made it clear that the army was prepared to intervene if the political leadership could not settle the ethnic conflicts pulling the country apart.

A referendum in Croatia in May 1991, boycotted by most of the Serb population of the republic, produced a 92 percent vote in support of Croatian sovereignty and independence. The Serbs of Dalmatia organized their own referendum. They voted to secede from Croatia and either remain part of Yugoslavia or join an expanded Serbian state. This pattern was to be repeated elsewhere as ethnic minority communities, understanding their status as a permanent numerical minority on political issues infused with ethnic meaning, refused to participate in voting on such issues. This represented an effort—poorly articulated as such—to delegitimate the claim of the ethnic majority to victory based on simple majoritarian principles.

Western concern over the use of force in Yugoslavia was expressed in a series of diplomatic warnings and the application of mild economic and political pressures. But Western states remained firmly committed to the status quo in Yugoslavia. They failed to address the growing probability that the Serbian leadership in Belgrade and their Serb allies in the military would resort to force either to prevent the secession of Slovenia and Croatia or to detach Serb-populated territories of Croatia and Bosnia-Herzegovina and annex them to Serbia. No effort was made to encourage Yugoslav leaders to hold the federation together by addressing the special concerns of the territorially compact communities of ethnic minorities rather than by using force. Statements issued by the European Community and the United States stressed instead support for the continued territorial unity of Yugoslavia.

EC leaders visiting Belgrade in May reminded Yugoslav leaders of "the Community's attachment to certain principles such as adherence to the existing institutional framework and respect for territorial integrity, [and] the need for dialogue to seek a peaceful settlement to the issue of the country's new structures *within current internal and external borders.*"[27] This represented an ill-advised extension of the Helsinki principles from internationally recognized borders to internal borders that had been established, whether by negotiation or diktat, as part of an effort to institutionalize a particular political regime. But it simply sustained a position adopted in March by the European Parliament.[28] Washington expressed support for "democracy, dialogue, human rights, market reform, and unity" in Yugoslavia, defining unity as "*the territorial integrity of Yugoslavia within its present borders.*" The U.S. statement went on to suggest that dismemberment would worsen ethnic tensions and that unity must be democratic and based on mutual agreement. "The United States will not encourage or reward secession," and if borders were to be changed, they would have to be changed by "peaceful consensual means."[29] This appeared to leave open the possibility of redrawing internal borders as part of a dissolution process. But the United States offered no support for such border changes, even as a means of avoiding violence. By failing to do so, it lost an opportunity to influence the character of the new regimes that were already emerging in the republics.

In an apparent effort to stimulate a peaceful resolution of the conflict, U.S. secretary of state James Baker visited Belgrade in June. In remarks following his meeting with Yugoslav leaders, he stressed the "importance of . . . continuing a dialogue to create a new basis for unity" and "the need to avoid unilateral acts that could preempt the negotiating process." He remarked a few days later in Washington, following the declarations of independence by Slovenia and Croatia and the onset of fighting in Slovenia, that he "found an air of unreality [in Belgrade], an inability on the part of several republic leaders to understand the dangerous consequences of their actions." He reiterated that

> we will not reward unilateral actions that preempt dialogue or the possibility of negotiated solutions, and we will strongly oppose intimidation or the use of force. The United States continues to recognize and support the territorial integrity of Yugoslavia, including the borders of its member republics. At the same time, we can support greater autonomy and sovereignty for the republics—in other words a new basis for unity in Yugoslavia—but only through peaceful means.[30]

European governments and the EC similarly disapproved of the Slovenian and Croatian actions.

Thus, the United States and its European partners remained firmly committed to the territorial integrity of the former Yugoslavia. They rightfully insisted on the peaceful redefinition of relationships among the federal units of the old federation. But they made no provisions for recognition of the single most powerful factor driving the federation toward disintegration: the growing nationalisms of the various peoples of Yugoslavia. Those nationalisms not only called into question the survival of the federation but also raised doubts about the viability of some of the republics. The same principle of self-determination that might justify the claim of

Slovenes and Croats to independent statehood could also be used to justify the Dalmatian Serbs' demands for separation from Croatia. Similarly, the principles of sovereignty and territorial integrity employed by Croats to justify their claims to Croatia could be used just as easily by Serbs in Belgrade to justify defending the integrity of the former Yugoslavia. Neither the United States nor the Europeans made any attempt to confront these issues. Indeed, by extending premature recognition to internal borders, they contributed to the intransigence of all parties to the growing conflict.

FROM WAR TO DISSOLUTION

The outbreak of fighting in Slovenia prompted the West European states—especially those sharing borders with Slovenia—to activate CSCE conflict management mechanisms, and a Conflict Prevention Center (CPC) consultative committee was convened in early July at the behest of Austria and Italy. Yugoslav representatives used the occasion to argue for their government's right to use force against an illegal declaration of independence. The committee appealed for an immediate cease-fire, without effect. The first emergency meeting of the Committee of Senior Officials of the CSCE was convened shortly thereafter. It issued an urgent appeal for a cease-fire, offered a "good-offices" mission to facilitate dialogue, and supported an EC initiative to send a mediation team of senior officials to Yugoslavia. The chair-in-office (Germany) was empowered to hold additional meetings as necessary to deal with the crisis, and four additional meetings were held during 1991.[31] The CSCE remained severely constrained in its ability to respond to events, however, because Yugoslavia exploited the principle of consensual decisionmaking to veto CSCE action.

The prominence of the EC and, to a lesser extent, the CSCE in early efforts to end the conflict in Yugoslavia, as well as the lack of involvement of NATO military/political resources, reflected a number of factors. First, up to the outbreak of war in Croatia, it seemed possible to resolve the conflict by political rather than military means, and the Europeans appeared intent on pursuing a political settlement. NATO involvement would necessarily have shifted the emphasis to the military dimension of the conflict. Second, NATO involvement and the preponderant role of the United States in NATO might have worked against the efforts of some European leaders to keep the crisis a European affair. The resistance of some European leaderships to U.S. involvement reinforced the reluctance of the American administration to be drawn into the crisis. The absence of American and NATO involvement, however, denied Western mediators an important asset for compelling the parties to reach an agreement and enforcing any agreement that might be reached.

Joint Western action was also constrained by genuine disagreement over the probable consequences of particular actions and by the divergent interests and concerns of individual states. American and European policymakers differed, for example, in their estimates of the probable effects of diplomatic recognition of Slovenia and Croatia. The United States and France opposed recognition. French foreign minister Roland Dumas warned, for example, that recognition would "throw oil on the flames." German, Austrian, and Danish officials, in contrast, urged the EC to recognize the breakaway republics as a means of exerting pressure on the Serbs to abandon the use of force.[32]

The responses of individual states were also affected by concerns about the precedent they might be setting for parallel problems elsewhere, especially in their own countries. The activity of Corsican nationalists in France, Britain's experience with nationalist movements in Scotland and Wales and the continuing conflict in Northern Ireland, and Italy and Spain's experience with regional autonomy movements made these countries reluctant to extend immediate recognition to Slovenia and Croatia. "Tomorrow what we have done for Yugoslavia would be applied to other cases," warned Foreign Minister Dumas.[33]

Germany, in contrast, perhaps because of the recent experience of national unification, was more eager to support the claims of the

Slovenes and Croats to self-determination. Conservative opinion in Germany, as reflected in the *Frankfurter Allgemeine Zeitung,* was openly supportive of Croatian and Slovenian aspirations from at least the beginning of 1991.[34] Some voices warned that recognition would not contribute to a resolution of the conflict. Others questioned the logic of recognizing Slovenian claims to independence by asking what such action might imply "if the Bavarian parliament and senate recommended in unanimity, solemnly, and emphatically the dissolution of the federal republic?"[35] Even those in Germany who initially criticized calls for recognition, however, came to agree with them in the wake of the fighting in Slovenia.[36] By August, it was clear that the German government was committed to recognition.

However, Germany remained unwilling to act alone. Decisive action through the CSCE remained blocked by Yugoslav and Soviet opposition. The Soviet Union had a vested interest in denying the CSCE any precedent for intervention in support of the Baltic states, which had already declared independence, or other Soviet republics that might do so in the future. Action through the United Nations was similarly precluded because of the threat of a Soviet veto in the Security Council. The Bush administration appeared to have "disengaged" from the issue, having defined it as a European matter, thus precluding unilateral intervention by the United States or an American-led NATO response. Member states were as yet unprepared to expand NATO's collective defense mission to encompass peacemaking or peacekeeping, or to extend its range of operations to the Balkans. This left the EC as the only venue through which Germany might act.

The European Community appears to have been led to act by four factors. First, Yugoslavia was clearly perceived as part of Europe. The conflict thus presented an opportunity to demonstrate the coordination of national policies for which the European political cooperation mechanism had been created. Success would contribute to deepening such cooperation, a process that lay at the core of negotiations then taking place over the eventual Maastricht Treaty on European union. Second, the Yugoslav crisis presented the EC with an opportunity to demonstrate international leadership akin to that shown by the United States in Kuwait, and to do so independently of the United States. Third, all EC member states shared a common interest in opposing the use of force to settle disputes in Europe. Fourth, and perhaps most important, Germany's manifestly strong support for Slovenia and Croatia raised the threat of German unilateral action, which might derail European integration. Forestalling such action required the Community to develop a more active, common approach to the conflict.

The EC approach, supported and assisted by the CSCE, combined assistance in negotiating and monitoring a cease-fire, the facilitation of peace talks, the imposition of sanctions, and, when the fighting spread to Croatia, the threat of force. The EC initially dispatched a mission to Yugoslavia to promote negotiations, while adopting an embargo on arms shipments and suspending financial assistance to Yugoslavia.[37] Strenuous and tense negotiations involving Yugoslav leaders and the EC mediation team produced an agreement among the representatives of all six republics, which was concluded on the island of Brioni on July 7.[38] This agreement called for a cease-fire in Slovenia, the withdrawal of Yugoslav People's Army (Jugoslovenska narodna armija, or JNA) troops from Slovenia and their return to barracks in Croatia, a three-month delay in implementation of the Slovenian declaration of independence, and the initiation of new talks on the future structure of the federation. The Slovenian parliament ratified this agreement but emphasized that Slovenia was not giving up its sovereignty by doing so.[39] In fact, the agreement itself represented de facto European—that is, international—recognition of republic borders.

The ability of European negotiators to broker this agreement reflected the apparent convergence of interests between Slovenia and Serbia. Slovenian and Serbian actors had been attempting to negotiate a political agreement for several years. Slovenian and Serbian dissidents had been engaged in discussions aimed at finding some common ground for the development of a Yugoslav political order since 1985.[40] Janez Drnovsek, the communist youth organization candidate who had been elected Slovenian representative to the Yugoslav presidency by direct, competitive elections in April 1988, was engaged in intensive negotiations with Milosevic and the Yugoslav military throughout the spring of 1991. According to another member of the Slovenian political leadership of that period, interviewed in 1994, Drnovsek may even have discussed the conditions under which Slovenia might be allowed to secede peacefully. Indeed, Drnovsek is reported by several Slovenian sources to have claimed that he could have achieved this.

Slovenian president Milan Kucan had held his own direct talks with Milosevic. In January 1991, he and Milosevic appeared to have worked out an agreement permitting the secession of Slovenia within its existing borders in exchange for Slovenian acquiescence to Serb efforts to redraw other borders. In a joint statement, the two leaders noted that "Serbia acknowledged Slovenia's interests to secure unhampered realization of the right of the Slovenian people and the Republic of Slovenia to its own path and its own commitments concerning the form of ties with other Yugoslav nations" and that "Slovenia, on the other hand, acknowledged the interest of the Serbian nation to live in one state and that the future Yugoslav accord should respect this interest."[41] In keeping with this understanding, Milosevic declared at Brioni that those who wished to leave Yugoslavia should be permitted to do so but that the JNA should be allowed to continue to defend those who wished to remain part of a common state. The latter, he made clear, included the Serbs outside Serbia. He justified their right to remain part of a newly configured state by reference to "their right to self-determination."[42]

This statement signaled a clear willingness to allow Slovenian independence, coupled with a determination to hold on to those ethnically Serb territories of other republics that had declared their desire to remain part of a Yugoslav federation. EC mediators thus did not have to deal in this instance with the most vexing issue in the breakup of the country: the status of Serb communities outside Serbia. The Brioni Agreement also served important Serbian interests by permitting the withdrawal of JNA troops and equipment from Slovenia and their redeployment to Croatia, where they later were engaged in the war against Croatian secession.

The European Community faced far greater difficulties in attempting to end the growing violence in Croatia, where Serb communities had already become mobilized against the Zagreb government and Serb irregular forces were already waging war against ethnically Croat populations. The G-7 leaders, meeting in mid-July, concluded that war could not be prevented in Croatia and called for the establishment of a UN peacekeeping mission to that republic. But such action was clearly premature, as no agreement of any kind had yet been reached between the conflicting parties. Action was, in any event, blocked by the opposition of the Soviet Union, which was determined to avoid establishing a precedent for UN intervention in its own internal conflicts.

In response to the outbreak of fighting in June, the Soviet Foreign Ministry had reaffirmed Soviet support for "the existence of a single, independent Yugoslavia." It argued that international efforts to restore peace should be carried out in cooperation with the Yugoslav government and aimed at the "preservation of Yugoslavia's integrity and independence."[43] In August, the Soviet government cautioned against interference in Yugoslav internal affairs and warned that "to take the side of one of the parties to the conflict . . . would mean to automatically put oneself in conflict with others, both inside and outside Yugoslavia." Moscow specifically warned against recognition of Croatia and Slovenia.[44]

The Serbian refusal to agree to a cease-fire in Croatia in late July marked the failure of the European Community's effort to mediate a Croatian-Serbian settlement and led the EC foreign ministers to call for UN intervention. The EC considered mounting an intervention effort of its own but was unable to reach agreement. Germany, France, and Luxembourg supported such an effort, but policymakers were deterred by an analysis prepared by British military specialists on the scope of the effort that would be required. The European states turned instead to threats of economic sanctions and diplomatic recognition of the breakaway republics in an effort to compel the Serbian leadership to abandon its use of force against Croatia.

European efforts had no effect, however, until the August coup attempt in Moscow radically altered the international parameters of the conflict. The collapse of the Soviet Union eliminated the major political deterrent to Western support for the dissolution of Yugoslavia, as well as the threat of a Soviet veto in the UN Security Council. The EC's Declaration on Yugoslavia of August 27, 1991, reflected these changes. It referred to the Serb and JNA military actions in Croatia as an attempt to change borders by force and characterized the results of these actions as "territorial conquests." The EC leadership thus clearly adopted the view that Yugoslavia would be divided along existing republic borders. Yet there is no evidence that this approach ever was subjected to critical analysis or policy debate among European or American leaders. The principle of the inviolability of borders enshrined in UN and CSCE documents, heretofore applied to international borders, was now applied to previously internal borders.

Altered international circumstances led to quick acceptance of the EC's call on August 27 for the convocation of a peace conference on Yugoslavia. The EC approach involved negotiations between representatives of the federal and regional leaderships and the leaders of the European Community, based on the principles of "no unilateral change of borders by force, protection for the rights of all in Yugoslavia and full account to be taken of all legitimate concerns and legitimate aspirations." It also called for the establishment of an arbitration procedure to decide issues submitted to a five-judge panel by the conflicting parties, who were to nominate two of the judges.[45] By again referring to borders and by inviting representatives of the regions to participate on an equal basis with representatives of the Yugoslav state, the EC again signaled its de facto recognition that Yugoslavia was disintegrating and that it would recognize the existing federal units as its successors.

Harsh debates at the EC peace conference, which opened in the Hague on September 7 under the chairmanship of Lord Carrington, made it clear that only the Serbian and Montenegrin leaderships favored continuing the federation. Slovenian, Croatian, and Macedonian leaders favored independence. The Muslim-dominated leadership of Bosnia-Herzegovina favored federation only if both Croatia and Serbia participated. The Serbian delegation refused even to discuss most of the Community's proposals, arguing that the drafts assumed that Yugoslavia did not exist anymore, a proposition it was unwilling to accept. None of the delegations were prepared to consider giving up territory.[46] Such intransigence was reinforced by the European approach. By extending recognition to existing borders, the EC encouraged the expectations and demands of each local leadership for sovereign control over its territory and immunity from external interference in domestic affairs, and eliminated a potentially important incentive to accommodate their respective minorities or explore alternative political formulas for establishing peaceful relations with their neighbors.

The scope and intensity of the conflict in Yugoslavia accelerated while the Europeans debated their next steps. In an effort to limit the conflict, the CSCE Committee of Senior Officials agreed on an arms embargo covering all combatants in early September. The UN Security Council voted unanimously on September 25, 1991, to impose a total arms embargo on Yugoslavia. This and later efforts would have little effect on the ability of Serb and JNA forces to wage war, however. They controlled considerable stockpiles of material established as part of the defensive strategy of the old regime. Both the Croats and the Bosnian Muslims would receive supplies from international arms merchants.[47] Each would also establish domestic capacities to produce arms.[48] The Bosnian government forces, however, surrounded on all sides by either Croat or Serb opponents and in control of substantially less territory and fewer former JNA military production facilities, would feel the effects of the arms embargo more acutely than their opponents.

The United States used the occasion of the September 1991 Security Council debate to criticize all the parties to the conflict. Secretary of State Baker repeated his earlier assertion that "unilateral acts, including by republics, have foreclosed options for peaceful negotiations and have made the resolution . . . more, not less, difficult and complicated." He accused the Serbian leadership of "actively supporting and encouraging the use of force in Croatia by Serbian militants and the Yugoslav military" and the JNA of "outright military intervention against Croatia." Despite Baker's warning that "the United States cannot and will not accept repression and the use of force," there was little reason to believe that the conflicting parties would heed his call for a peaceful settlement or be much persuaded by a vague threat of further action.[49]

Early in October, the leadership of the Conference on Yugoslavia viewed dissolution as irreversible and focused its efforts instead on developing alternative arrangements for political and economic relations among the existing republics. The republics were expected, according to one high official of the conference, to choose from among the various alternatives "on an à la carte basis." The draft convention finally proposed by the EC mediators amounted to little more than a common economic market, with fewer common institutions and less central authority than the EC itself.

The ineffectiveness of these negotiations led the EC foreign ministers to ask the UN secretary-general in October to use the coercive powers granted him under Chapter VII of the UN Charter to bring peace to the region.[50] Following the adoption of the arms embargo by the Security Council in September, the secretary-general's special envoy, former secretary of state Cyrus Vance, traveled to Yugoslavia three times, and on November 23 in Geneva, he secured agreement to a Croatian-Serbian cease-fire. He later negotiated an agreement on the deployment of a UN peacekeeping mission to Croatia.[51] Serbia's willingness to accept the UN role, in contrast to its resistance to EC involvement, can be explained in terms of the constraints inherent in the deployment of UN peacekeeping troops: as primarily political and diplomatic instruments, such troops could only "freeze," not reverse, the situation in Croatia. Moreover, the agreement included the specific provision that it "would not prejudge" the final outcome of the dispute, thus implying that the status of the territories to be protected by the United Nations was in doubt. This was precisely why Germany opposed the UN-sponsored cease-fire.[52]

Acceptance of the Vance-mediated UN peace plan did not represent a commitment by either Serbia or Croatia to the peaceful resolution of their conflict. Each continued its military actions following the Geneva agreement and sought to exploit the opportunities for gain inherent in the UN presence. Thus, the fundamental political conditions on which successful UN peacekeeping operations depend were, in fact, absent in Croatia.

By the time Secretary Vance had negotiated the deployment of peacekeeping troops to Croatia, Yugoslavia was in obvious dissolution. The arbitration commission under French jurist Robert Badinter established as part of the EC Conference on Yugoslavia rendered a decision to this effect in December 1991. The resignation of Yugoslav prime minister Ante Markovic later in the same month, marking the end of the old federation, passed with hardly any notice.

The United States and its European allies remained divided, however, over the timing and consequences of diplomatic recognition of the breakaway republics. German insistence on early recognition led the EC to act in mid-December. Britain and other member states opposed to early recognition are alleged to have acquiesced in exchange for German concessions on the European monetary union then being negotiated as part of the Maastricht Treaty. Underlying this concession was an apparent consensus that a decision that was bad for Yugoslavia but maintained European unity was better than a decision that was good for Yugoslavia but divided the Europeans and derailed the Maastricht process.[53]

The December 1991 EC decision stipulated that in order to be recognized, the former Yugoslav republics would have to meet a broad range of political criteria. These included internal democracy; a good-faith commitment to the peaceful negotiation of their disputes; respect for the UN Charter, the Helsinki Final Act, the rule of law, human rights, and the rights of ethnic and national minorities as called for by the draft treaty convention prepared by the EC Conference on Yugoslavia; respect for the inviolability of borders and the principle that they may be changed only by peaceful means and common agreement. No mention was made of a right to self-determination. The EC also stipulated that states applying for recognition would have to accept the peace process embedded in the EC Conference on Yugoslavia.[54]

Bosnia-Herzegovina, Croatia, Slovenia, and Macedonia all submitted applications for recognition by the European Community. The Serbs of Croatian Krajina and the Albanians of Kosovo also submitted applications, but the EC refused to accept them. The EC continued to support the preexisting borders of the republics and to deny ethnic communities not granted republic status under the old regime the right to self-determination that had been accorded the Croats and Slovenes by virtue of their having been granted such status. Serbia and Montenegro, claiming they were the successor to Yugoslavia, did not submit applications.

In a series of decisions handed down in January 1992, the Badinter Commission provided belated legal justification for recognizing republic borders as international borders. It ruled that Macedonia and Slovenia satisfied the criteria for recognition. But it also ruled that Croatia should not be recognized until it had fully complied with provisions of the draft treaty convention granting "special status" to minority territories. Despite these decisions, the European Community states succumbed to increasing political pressure from Germany and agreed in December 1991 to recognize Slovenia and Croatia, but not Macedonia. In the case of Bosnia-Herzegovina, the Badinter Commission noted that the government's efforts to declare an independent unitary state within the existing republic borders were contradicted by the declarations of Bosnian Serbs in favor of continued membership in a Yugoslav state. It therefore ruled that "the will of the peoples of Bosnia-Hercegovina to constitute the SRBH [Socialist Republic of Bosnia-Hercegovina] as a sovereign and independent state cannot be held to have been fully established." It suggested "a referendum of all the citizens of the SRBH without distinction" as a possible means by which the popular will might be determined.[55]

The suggestion of a referendum as a means of establishing legitimacy in Bosnia-Herzegovina was based on a widely accepted principle of democracy: majority rule. But it failed to take into account that the accommodation of ethnic identity was crucial to the establishment of authority and legitimacy in Bosnia-Herzegovina. The communist regime had been based on a form of consensual decisionmaking by representatives of the three major ethnic groups. This pattern was continued in 1990, when the tri-ethnic coalition government adopted its own principle of consensus. But this principle had already broken down in practice when the Badinter Commission called for a referendum. By permitting international—if not internal—legitimacy to be won on the basis of a simple majority, the commission encouraged the Bosnian Muslims and Croats to forge an alliance of expediency through which they could establish an electoral majority to overthrow the old principle once and for all and negate Bosnian Serb opposition to separating the republic from Yugoslavia.

THE BOSNIAN DEBACLE

The commitment of Bosnian Muslim leaders to establishing the independence of Bosnia-Herzegovina was already apparent by late 1991. In October, an alliance of the Muslim and Croat government parties, together with other smaller parties in Bosnia-Herzegovina's parliament, had declared the sovereignty of the republic and its neutrality in the conflict between Croatia and Serbia. With this act, they appeared to embark on the same path toward secession followed by Slovenia and Croatia. They did so over the objections of the Serbian Democratic Party, the third member of the government coalition, which argued that this action violated the coalition agreement to rule by consensus. Serb members of parliament then formed their own parliamentary body, the Bosnian Serb Assembly, and conducted a referendum in November 1991 that recorded the preference of Bosnia's Serbs for union with Serbia in a Yugoslav state. In response to the Badinter Commission's call, the parliament of Bosnia-Herzegovina scheduled a referendum on the issue of independence for February 29–March 1, 1992, again over the objections of the Serbs. Bosnian Serbs boycotted the referendum, but the Bosnian Muslims and Croats voted overwhelmingly in favor of independence. On the basis of this result, President Alija Izetbegovic declared independence on March 3. Sporadic fighting broke out in the republic during the days that followed.

The United States delayed diplomatic recognition of Croatia, Slovenia, and Bosnia-Herzegovina, and the Europeans delayed recognition of Bosnia-Herzegovina, in the hope of encouraging peaceful solutions to the conflicts that divided Serbs, Croats, and Muslims. It had been clear to all Western leaderships, at least from the beginning of the fighting in Slovenia, that the fate of Bosnia-Herzegovina represented the most difficult and dangerous of all the problems deriving from the disintegration of Yugoslavia. Both Lord Carrington and Secretary Vance had attempted, unsuccessfully, to address the Bosnian question in the course of their respective negotiations and had advised German foreign minister Hans-Dietrich Genscher against recognition. UN secretary-general Javier Pérez de Cuellar did the same in letters sent in December 1991. Professional analysts within the German foreign policymaking apparatus warned that recognition of Croatia and Slovenia in itself, let alone recognition of Bosnia-Herzegovina, could lead to war.[56]

Nonetheless, the United States and its European partners agreed in March 1992 to a coordinated approach that led to the recognition of Bosnia-Herzegovina in April. Neither the threat nor the reality of diplomatic recognition was enough to lead the Serbs in Croatia and Bosnia or the Serbian leadership in Belgrade to negotiate peaceful resolutions of the conflicts in Croatia and Bosnia-Herzegovina. Indeed, the notion that recognition would bring an end to the conflict over Bosnia, or at least put an end to Serbian ambitions with respect to Bosnia, appeared to be based on a fundamental misreading of events in Croatia. It was not the threat and, later, reality of international recognition that brought an end to the fighting in Croatia. It was the implicit recognition on the part of UN mediators of the disputed status of Serb-held territories and the implicit acknowledgment that the definition of Croatian sovereignty and, perhaps, borders was subject to further negotiation. The prospect that the de facto recognition extended to existing republic borders by the EC-mediated Brioni Agreement of July 1992 might be reversed may have contributed to the haste with which Germany imposed its preferences on its European partners. Formal recognition effectively ended the possibility that solutions to these conflicts could be found by negotiations on borders, or by negotiations within the framework of the EC-mediated Conference on Yugoslavia or the subsidiary negotiations devoted exclusively to Bosnia.[57]

The EC had attempted to bring about the peaceful "cantonization" of Bosnia-Herzegovina into autonomous ethnic territories through negotiations chaired by Portuguese ambassador José Cutiliero in February and March. These talks produced an agreement between the three ethnic parties on a statement of principles for new constitutional arrangements in mid-March. Bosnia was to be divided into three "constitutive units" defined primarily in ethnic terms. Although details were never worked out, the general principles agreed to in March granted an effective veto to each of the three major groups. Thus, the EC plan for Bosnia-Herzegovina amounted to the "Yugoslavization" of the republic and its de facto partition along ethnic lines. Moreover, each "constitutive unit" was to be "allowed to establish and maintain links with other republics and their organizations providing their relations and links are in accordance with the independence and integrity of Bosnia-Hercegovina."[58]

Both the Bosnian Serbs and the Bosnian Croats supported the plan, the latter having abandoned the tactical alliance established with the Muslims as a means of separating Bosnia-Herzegovina from Yugoslavia, in favor of aligning themselves with the Serbs as a means to secure the de facto union of Croat-populated territories with Croatia. But the plan failed to satisfy the Muslim-led government. After eight rounds of talks over a period of three months, during which time armed conflict in the republic intensified, the EC effort to mediate a solution was suspended.

In light of the failure of negotiated cease-fires to take hold and the rapidly increasing level of force being used by the Bosnian Serbs and Yugoslav army to seize control over much of the republic, international actors began to view the conflict in Bosnia in narrowly military terms, and none was prepared to intervene. Lord Carrington, for example, averred that "there is only one way of stopping them, and that is by intervening with military force and separating them, and I don't see any way in which anybody is going to do that. I don't see NATO doing it, I don't see the UN doing it, I don't see the Community doing it, I don't see the WEU doing it."[59] The clear absence of any immediate threat to intervene encouraged the continued use of force on the part of the Serbs.

The Muslims were encouraged in their pursuit of independence for the republic by the informal advice of the American ambassador to hold out for a better deal.[60] Such advice reinforced the conviction of some Muslim leaders that they could win a military victory by drawing the West, particularly the United States, into the conflict on their side. The Bosnian Serbs, meanwhile, acted unilaterally to create their own Bosnian Serb state. Moreover, the EC-sponsored negotiations failed to take into account the ambitions of leaders in Croatia and Serbia, whose aspirations to divide Bosnia between their respective states and concomitant support for separatist Serb and Croat forces inside Bosnia contributed greatly to the violence there.

By taking a more comprehensive approach, the international community might have been able to mediate between the contradictory values and goals of local actors. Extreme demands for the right to self-determination on the part of the Serbs in Croatia and Bosnia might have received less support from a Serbian leadership in Belgrade faced with the prospect that adoption of such a principle might lead to the loss of Kosovo. Croatian ambitions with respect to western Herzegovina might have been similarly moderated by their desire to hold on to the Krajina. Under such circumstances, it might have been possible to achieve an overall settlement based on tradeoffs and moderated application of the concepts of sovereignty and self-determination. But such an approach would have required the international community to place the peaceful settlement of conflicting demands for self-determination through negotiation above the principle of territorial integrity of states. At the very least, it would have required the United States and the European Community to abandon their support for the preexisting borders of the republics of the former Yugoslavia as the basis for establishing new states. The rush to recognize Croatia in November and December 1991 effectively shut the door on this approach. Moreover, such an approach stood the best chance of success before the cycle of ethnic violence set in. Once it had begun, even mutual concessions were made more difficult.

Formal recognition of Bosnia-Herzegovina in early April 1992 provided the spark that ignited the political tinderbox there and brought the UN peacekeeping mission in Croatia to the verge of collapse. Understandably, the Croats now sought to avert a Cyprus-like de facto partition that would give control over Croatia's territory to local Serbs. And neither Serbia nor Croatia gave up its pursuit of territories in Bosnia-Herzegovina.

The Serbian and Montenegrin leaderships proclaimed a new, truncated Yugoslav state on April 27 and formally disavowed both territorial claims on neighboring states and the use of force to settle disputes. Shortly thereafter, the new Yugoslav regime renounced control over JNA forces in Bosnia-Herzegovina. It formally released soldiers of Bosnian origin from service and pledged to return troops of Serbian origin to Serbia. This effectively converted large numbers of ethnically Bosnian Serb JNA troops into the military arm of the Bosnian Serb political leadership.[61] However, the Serb military leadership in Bosnia-Herzegovina remained in close contact with the Serbian command of the new "Yugoslav" army in Belgrade.[62] Moreover, departing JNA troops transferred large supplies of weapons and other material to the Bosnian Serbs, and heavy weapons and air units of the Serbian (Yugoslav) military continued to cross from Serbia into Bosnia in support of actions by Bosnian Serb forces.

Even as UN troops began their deployment in Croatia in April, heavy fighting broke out in Bosnia-Herzegovina. Serb forces undertook the "ethnic cleansing" of territories that fell under their control, engaging in widespread terror against non-Serb civilian populations and subjecting predominantly Muslim or ethnically mixed cities and towns in the territories they claimed to fierce artillery and heavy weapons attack. Local Croatian forces, with the direct support of military forces of the Croatian republic, established control over the largely ethnically Croatian territories in western Herzegovina and effectively annexed them to Croatia. Throughout the republic, large numbers of civilians were killed, many were taken prisoner and subjected to cruel tortures, and hundreds of thousands fled the fighting to become refugees in neighboring former Yugoslav republics and other European countries.

The international community reacted to the escalation of the conflict in Bosnia-Herzegovina by adopting severe economic sanctions against the new Yugoslav state (Serbia and Montenegro) and increasing its political and diplomatic isolation. In May 1992, the CSCE's Committee of Senior Officials invoked a consensus-minus-one principle of decisionmaking on issues relating to Yugoslavia, citing a "pattern of clear, gross and uncorrected violations of CSCE commitments" to justify this change. Russian opposition to a U.S.-EC effort to expel the new Yugoslav state from the CSCE led instead to its suspension in July.[63] Croatia and Slovenia were admitted to the CSCE in March, and Bosnia-Herzegovina in April. In May, all three states were admitted to the United Nations. The new Yugoslav state's claim to a seat in the United Nations as the legal successor of the former Yugoslavia was denied. Despite Russia's initial objection, the UN Security Council required the new Yugoslav state to reapply for admission.[64] Thus, within a few months of the start of open warfare in Bosnia-Herzegovina, the international community had ratified the dissolution of Yugoslavia, refused to permit the Serbian-Montenegrin federation to succeed it, and granted recognition to all the former republics except Macedonia as independent states.

This "internationalization" of the ongoing conflict failed to bring the fighting to an end. The war in Bosnia-Herzegovina was viewed by some as a war of aggression by one state (Serbia-Montenegro) against another (Bosnia-Herzegovina), and by others as a civil war among Serbs, Croats, and Muslims. The latter view undermined the political appeal of claims by the Bosnian government to sovereignty and the rights to territorial integrity and self-defense. Although the conflict took on greater political urgency in the United States in the summer and fall of 1992 with the approach of a presidential election, neither Washington nor its European allies were ready to come to the military defense of, or provide overt military assistance to, the Bosnian government. The United Nations also appeared to be reluctant to be drawn into more extensive involvement.

The scale of the tragedy in Bosnia-Herzegovina, the failure of the EC to find any basis for a negotiated solution, the growing flow of refugees,[65] and the scope of Western media attention devoted to the attack on Sarajevo had led some European and other states to seek direct UN intervention. However, the UN undersecretary-general for peacekeeping operations recommended against such an undertaking in the absence of a political agreement between the warring factions, and the secretary-general concluded that a UN peacekeeping operation of the scale that would be required to keep the peace in Bosnia-Herzegovina was "not at present feasible." The secretary-general suggested in mid-May 1992 that a European effort might be more appropriate.[66]

Secretary of State James Baker had earlier been reported to be "disappointed with the lack of success of earlier United States efforts to influence events in Yugoslavia" and to have "decided to disengage from the issue" because "there [was] no solution."[67] On May 12, Baker's official spokesperson justified such disengagement by declaring that no U.S. security interests were at stake in the Yugoslav crisis.[68] Ten days later, however, American policy underwent a significant shift. Baker declared the situation in Bosnia-Herzegovina "unconscionable" and a "humanitarian nightmare."[69]

With the support of the EC, which had already adopted an embargo of its own, the United States called on the United Nations to impose a total embargo on Serbia, and in response the Security Council adopted Resolution 757 on May 30. In addition to instituting an economic embargo against the Serbian and Montenegrin federation, the resolution affirmed that borders could not be changed by force, and it renewed the Security Council's demands for an immediate cease-fire as well as an end to outside interference, the withdrawal or disarming of JNA and Croatian military units in Bosnia-Herzegovina, and the disarming and disbanding of all irregular units. The Security Council also called for an end to forced expulsions of local populations and for the establishment of a "security zone" around Sarajevo airport to facilitate a humanitarian airlift effort. The enforcement authority of Chapter VII was invoked to impose these sanctions almost one year after the onset of violence.

Secretary Baker's call for the delivery of humanitarian aid appears to have been an attempt by the Bush administration to forestall demands for more decisive action. The siege of Sarajevo differed little from the siege of Vukovar in October and November 1991, when Serb forces had subjected that Croatian city to an artillery assault that effectively destroyed it. The major difference for American policymakers was the growing public concern over events in Bosnia and the proximity of presidential elections.

The international responses to the mounting crisis continued to ignore local political realities. Serb-Croat negotiations over the fate of Bosnia—which ignored Muslim interests—were resumed; they culminated in an agreement, signed in Graz, Austria, in May for the partition of the republic.[70] This was followed by discussions between the Croats and Muslims in Split, Croatia, over the establishment of a confederation between Croatia and Bosnia-Herzegovina.[71] Thus, the Muslims, Serbs, and Croats all seemed to be moving toward a solution involving partition, some form of union between the Croats and Bosnian Muslims, and the creation of a separate Bosnian Serb entity. At the same time, however, international actors remained focused on affirming the integrity of Bosnia-Herzegovina as it had existed within the former Yugoslavia. Yet they remained unwilling to undertake the military action that would have been required to achieve such an end.

When Secretary Baker met with European leaders in Lisbon in

late June 1992 he argued that military intervention should be viewed as a last resort, to be used only after all diplomatic, political, and economic measures were exhausted. The American administration was internally divided over the use of force,[72] as were the Europeans. French and Italian leaders were reported to have pushed for the use of force to reopen Sarajevo airport. But the British continued to oppose any effort to impose peace by force.[73]

The use of force was also opposed by Russia. Moscow had supported sanctions only reluctantly, allegedly under pressure from the EC.[74] That support engendered considerable domestic opposition. The Yeltsin government, particularly Russian foreign minister Andrei Kozyrev, was exposed to intense criticism at home in the communist, nationalist, and moderate press.[75] Kozyrev defended Russian policy by arguing that it was intended "to support reasonable forces in the Yugoslav leadership and society" against "national-Communists in Belgrade and the Yugoslav Army" and "Serbian national-Bolsheviks." Opposition to such forces was in Russia's own interest. "After all," he argued, "in Moscow today essentially the same forces are consolidating as are doing so in Belgrade. They are trying to push us into the same abyss. With Bolshevik straightforwardness, they are replacing the communist mythology with pseudopatriotic mythology, placing the same reliance on arguments of force instead of the force of arguments."[76]

By framing the issue in this way, Kozyrev helped make the issue of Russian policy toward the former Yugoslavia a point of growing conflict between the Yeltsin government and its opponents. Opposition was particularly vigorous in the parliament.[77] Positions with respect to Yugoslavia became a point of difference between those advocating cooperation with the West and those inclined toward a more nationalist, even anti-Western, foreign policy. The intensity of domestic opposition to Russian cooperation with the West led Kozyrev to warn his CSCE colleagues in December 1992 of the potential for a nationalist, militaristic backlash in Russia.[78]

The reopening of Sarajevo airport under UN control in June 1992 was achieved after a dramatic surprise visit to Sarajevo by French president François Mitterrand and without the use of force. But the ensuing airlift of humanitarian supplies did not contribute to lowering the level of hostilities. As Bosnian government officials complained at the time, the UN-negotiated agreement to reopen the airport did not require a cease-fire; it required only that local forces not fire on the airport. This allowed even those Serb forces under direct UN supervision to continue to shell the city. Moreover, by establishing control over the airport, the United Nations inadvertently helped complete the encirclement of Sarajevo by dividing the city from government-held territory on the far side of the airport.

The decision by Western leaders to go ahead with the humanitarian relief effort in Bosnia-Herzegovina in the absence of a broader political settlement made it clear that Western leaders did not expect such a settlement to come quickly. The decision not to use force to deliver such relief reflected both Russian opposition and the unwillingness of some European and American policymakers to become more deeply involved in the conflict. U.S. defense officials believed that the use of force would inevitably lead to ground combat.[79]

Those in Washington who viewed the crisis in the former Yugoslavia as a civil war, as did the secretary of defense, argued that it did not threaten international peace or require Western intervention. Those who saw the conflict as a case of international aggression against a sovereign state, as did the secretary of state, argued for greater and more direct Western intervention. Secretary Baker, for example, was reported to have suggested that "the only way to solve [the situation in Bosnia-Herzegovina] is selective bombing of Serbian targets, including Belgrade."[80] However, President Bush made it clear that the United States would act only as part of a UN-sanctioned multinational effort aimed at humanitarian relief and would not attempt to solve the political conflict by force.

By July 1992, a political settlement appeared to have slipped out of reach. Representatives of the Bosnian Serbs, Bosnian Croats, and the Bosnian government had met in London in the middle of the month for indirect talks under the sponsorship of Lord Carrington.

Communicating with each other through an EC mediator, because each refused to meet directly with the others, the parties apparently agreed to a truce and to place their heavy weapons under UN supervision. They further agreed to begin indirect talks on future constitutional arrangements for the republic and to allow refugees to return to their homes. But, as was the case with so many previous agreements, no cease-fire was actually established. Serb shelling of Sarajevo did not let up even during the visit a few days thereafter of British foreign minister Douglas Hurd, who was led to remark that "where there is no will for peace we cannot supply it."[81]

Bosnian government officials revealed what little interest they had in seeking a negotiated solution when they admitted that "the only reason the Government signed the accord in London was that failure to do so would have allowed the Serbian leaders to present the Government as the party obstructing peace, and because Western nations, including the United States, had placed 'intense pressure' on Bosnian officials to go along."[82] Thus, the EC-mediated negotiations had ceased to function as a means of achieving a political settlement and an end to the fighting. They had deteriorated into a means by which each warring party sought to gain political advantage over the others and to strengthen the position of its fighting forces on the ground. In some circumstances, local leaders had to be coerced into participating.

The July talks in London had opened to public scrutiny a major weakness of the international effort to date: the lack of coordination among the major actors. Secretary-General Boutros Boutros-Ghali objected to the proposal to place heavy weapons under UN supervision, which he alleged had been put forward by EC mediators without UN authorization. Officials responsible for UN peacekeeping and enforcement operations, and EC authorities engaged in peacemaking mediation processes attempted to bring their efforts into closer coordination by convening a conference of the concerned parties in London in August under joint sponsorship. The International Conference on the Former Yugoslavia (ICFY) was established with the aim of bringing all parties to the conflicts in the former Yugoslavia under the umbrella of a coordinated negotiating authority. The organizers hoped that as a result of intensified pressure on those at war, hostilities would cease and a settlement could be reached. They also wished to encourage the settlement of those disputes in the former Yugoslavia that had not yet led to open warfare.

The mediation effort that began at the London Conference was also motivated by the desire on the part of Western governments to demonstrate to their publics that they were responding to the issues and concerns raised by the collapse of the Carrington-led talks. The public outcry generated by media coverage of the Sarajevo bread-line massacre in May and the revelations in August of atrocities committed on inmates at Serb-run detention camps elsewhere in Bosnia-Herzegovina had given rise to increased pressure for Western military action to stop the fighting and, in the United States, to accusations by the Democratic candidate for president that the Bush administration had failed to act forcefully enough.[83] President Bush and American foreign policymakers therefore briefly assumed more active roles in attempting to strengthen Western responses to the mounting tragedy in Bosnia-Herzegovina.

President Bush was reported to be seeking allied support for the use of force to deliver humanitarian supplies to Sarajevo, by deploying European ground troops in a more aggressive role than UN peacekeepers, and by using NATO airpower to protect them. But Secretary-General Boutros-Ghali cautioned that the threat of force might make UN troops already in Sarajevo the direct targets of attack. The British reminded the Americans publicly that "the only objective that would justify the massive use of force would be the achievement of a peace settlement."[84]

The Security Council adopted Resolution 770 in August 1992, carefully limiting its authorization for the use of "all measures necessary" to the delivery of humanitarian assistance, not to the imposition of an overall settlement. Meanwhile, American enthusiasm for the use of force was quickly dampened in light of estimates of the scale of the commitment that would be required. A senior aide to the chairman of the Joint Chiefs of Staff told Congress in August that 60,000 to 120,000 troops would be necessary to secure a land route from the coastal city of Split to Sarajevo and to establish a twenty-mile secure zone around the Sarajevo airport for the protection of relief flights. As many as 400,000 troops would be needed to impose a cease-fire throughout Bosnia-Herzegovina.[85] In the absence of a political settlement between the warring parties, however, even intervention on this scale held out little promise of settling the conflict. Moreover, under such conditions it would be difficult to define the specific mission of an intervention force and therefore impossible to determine when its mission had been completed and it could be withdrawn. The recent experience of UNPROFOR/Croatia suggested that a traditional peacekeeping mission would lead only to an unstable, de facto partition of the republic and the continuation of ethnic violence both within and across partition lines. The prospect of intervention becoming an open-ended commitment ensured that it would not take place.

The absence of a credible threat of the use of force clearly reduced the incentive of the Bosnian Serbs, who enjoyed military dominance, to make concessions in the interest of achieving a settlement with the Muslims and the Croats. At the same time, the continued hope on the part of the Muslim-led government of outright Western military intervention, kept alive by incremental increases in Western involvement such as that represented by the August Security Council resolution and by discussions of intervention within the American administration, reduced the willingness of the government to concede military victory to the Serbs and negotiate a political settlement. Despite these difficulties, the Americans and Europeans nonetheless launched a renewed effort to encourage a negotiated agreement between the warring parties.

THE VANCE-OWEN PLAN AND U.S. POLICY

The International Conference on the Former Yugoslavia convened in London at the end of August 1992 under the cosponsorship of the United Nations and the European Community.[86] It brought together all interested parties to discuss the conflicts in the former Yugoslavia. These discussions reflected the great differences in positions among the participants. Although some advocated direct military intervention by an international force, none sought to circumvent the recognized authority of the UN Security Council to legitimate any such action. At the same time, it was clear that none of the permanent members of the Security Council were as yet ready to support such action. The conference thus reduced the prospect that force might be used in the short term to bring the fighting to an end.

The conference adopted a statement of general principles for the negotiation of a settlement that included calls for the cessation of fighting, an end to the use of force, nonrecognition of gains won by force, recognition of the sovereignty and territorial integrity of states, and the inviolability of recognized borders. Significantly, the principle of national self-determination was not reiterated. Instead, the conference stressed respect for individual rights as embodied in existing international conventions, implementation of constitutional guarantees of the rights of minorities, and the promotion of tolerance. Thus, the international community appeared to be moving toward the substitution of human rights and the protection of civil liberties for ethnic-based claims to national self-determination as a means of strengthening support for existing borders, although it did not dispense with the potentially problematic concept of "minority rights." The conference explicitly condemned forced expulsions and called for the closing of detention camps, the safe return of refugees, adherence to the Geneva Conventions, and the settlement of questions of state succession by consensus or arbitration.

No consideration was given to redrawing borders as a means of encouraging a political settlement. Russian foreign minister Kozyrev, who drew a distinction between external borders, which he recognized as inviolable, and the internal borders between republics, suggested that a "moratorium" be placed on the latter. Although this may have been intended to signal a willingness to consider the opening of negotiations over borders as a means of bringing the fighting to an end, nothing came of the suggestion.

The working group on minority rights established at the London

Conference as part of the ongoing ICFY included a subgroup specifically devoted to Kosovo—the only regional minority nationality issue to receive such treatment. The EC/UN leadership resisted efforts by Serbian representatives at the conference to introduce a list of other regional minority issues deserving the same treatment. It also resisted the efforts of the Albanian delegates to elevate the Kosovo question from the rubric of minority issue to such a status as to require direct negotiations between Serbia and Kosovo. In doing so, the international community may have lost another opportunity to encourage direct negotiations between all parties and to introduce internally generated cross-pressures on the post-Yugoslav leaderships as a means of encouraging a comprehensive settlement.

The ICFY, which was based at the UN headquarters in Geneva and cochaired by Cyrus Vance (for the United Nations) and Lord David Owen (for the European Community), became the focus of coordinated international efforts to resolve the conflict. The London Conference appeared briefly to have gotten the ICFY process off to a positive beginning with an agreement on humanitarian actions signed by the leaders of the three warring parties: Radovan Karadzic for the Bosnian Serbs, Alija Izetbegovic for the Muslim-led government, and Mate Boban for the Bosnian Croats. This agreement committed the signatories to collaborate in efforts to deliver relief throughout Bosnia by road, secure humane conditions for those in detention, end unlawful detention of civilians, provide for the safety of refugees, comply with international humanitarian law including the Geneva Conventions, and bring undisciplined elements in their respective areas under control. Furthermore, all parties formally undertook commitments to establish an effective and durable cessation of hostilities throughout the former Yugoslavia, and in Bosnia-Herzegovina in particular. This was to include the lifting of sieges of cities and towns, the international supervision of heavy weapons, and the withholding of transborder military assistance. They agreed to cooperate in confidence-building measures, including a ban on military flights and the deployment of observers to monitor heavy weapons and borders; dismantle detention camps; consider the establishment of safe areas for refugees; and strengthen international support for the rigorous application of sanctions, for monitoring efforts, and for the enforcement of international humanitarian law. Ensuing events on the ground in Bosnia and the difficulty of negotiations in Geneva revealed that these were empty commitments.

The ICFY attempted, through diplomatic efforts, to find a solution to the multiple conflicts in the former Yugoslavia by balancing recognition of the sovereignty and territorial integrity of the Bosnian state (defined by former republic borders) with respect for individual rights, implementation of constitutional guarantees of the rights of minorities, and the promotion of tolerance. From the beginning, negotiators recognized that the views of the three parties diverged widely. The Muslim-dominated government preferred a unitary, centralized state. The Serbs opted for three independent states defined by ethnic identity. Since negotiators determined that there was no way to create three ethnically homogeneous states without enforced population transfers, they rejected this model. But they also rejected the unitary, centralized state model, opting instead for a decentralized state consisting of seven to ten provinces whose borders would be determined on the basis of ethnic, geographical, communications, economic, and other relevant factors. Negotiators attempted to address the concerns of ethnic groups by providing for the rotation of key offices among representatives of the groups and by incorporating extensive provisions for the protection of group or minority rights. As a security- and confidence-building measure, negotiators also provided for an indeterminate transitional period during which there would be extensive, direct participation in and oversight of domestic institutions by international actors.[87] The ICFY approach thus attempted to achieve de facto territorial and political separation of the three groups without formally partitioning territory.

The negotiations were carried out bilaterally, between the ICFY and each of the three parties. The Muslim-dominated government delegation continued to oppose the decentralization plans put forward by negotiators, as well as the emphasis negotiators placed on ethnic factors in shaping their proposals. But their negotiating position was weakened by a series of severe military defeats at the hands of the Bosnian Croats, suffered in October, which led President Izetbegovic to seek compromise and which split the more hard-line Muslim members of the government from him.[88] The Bosnian Croat delegation insisted on demilitarization of the state, the establishment of three "constituent units" composed of ethnically like provinces, and the introduction of decisionmaking in state institutions based on consensus among the three constituent groups. The Croats also opposed most of the provisions for international oversight of Bosnian state institutions. The Bosnian Serbs continued to propose the establishment of three distinct, sovereign, ethnically defined states with international legal status, loosely confederated to form the state of Bosnia-Herzegovina, which also would enjoy a more limited international legal status. The Serbs also sought to impose consensual decision rules and exclude international oversight.[89]

Although the parties remained far apart, all seemed to agree that a settlement would include some form of internal division of the republic. Negotiations became focused on defining these internal divisions. The ICFY cochairs came forward in January 1993, at the first joint meeting of all the delegations, with a map and proposals for the future constitutional and political organization of the postwar state, and an agreement for peace that included an ambitious schedule for the cessation of hostilities, separation of forces, demilitarization of Sarajevo, and opening of land routes to the city. The proposals were quickly labeled the "Vance-Owen Plan," after the cochairs of the ICFY.

Most international attention was drawn to the map proposed by the ICFY. It called for the establishment of ten provinces whose boundaries were drawn on the basis of ethnic, geographic, economic, and politico-military considerations. The map effectively created three "Serbian provinces," in territories where ethnic Serb majorities had been recorded in the 1991 census. Three were Muslim, and three were Croat. The tenth province, surrounding Sarajevo, was multiethnic. No province was to be given over to the exclusive control of one or another group. The plan called for the distribution of leading government offices among all three groups in each of the provinces for an interim period, in rough accordance with their proportion of the population in 1991. In Sarajevo province, each of the groups would enjoy equal representation. Interim governments would then be expected to draft local constitutions and prepare free and fair elections on the basis of proportional representation. While the final shape of the provincial and republic governments could be determined in important ways by decisions yet to be made about electoral laws and other important details, it was clear that negotiators were seeking to end the conflict through the application of principles of extreme devolution and consensual decisionmaking, or further "Yugoslavization" of the republic. By applying principles of proportionality to elections and to government offices, negotiators were seeking to establish "power-sharing" arrangements often cited by political scientists as effective means for ameliorating conflict over control of the state.[90]

The final arrangements also had to comply with international human and civil rights standards as defined by seventeen international conventions and agreements specifically enumerated in the "proposed constitutional structure for Bosnia and Herzegovina" proposed by the ICFY cochairs.[91] The plan called for extensive international involvement in local police and judicial institutions to instill popular confidence in their impartiality, as well as involvement in the reconstruction of infrastructure throughout the country.

The provisions of the Vance-Owen Plan represented an attempt to forge a compromise between contradictory international principles and values, as well as the conflicting interests of the warring parties. They also represented an attempt to create internal borders that might satisfy demands for ethnic autonomy yet make further attempts at secession more difficult. However, the warring parties were able to agree in Geneva only on the cessation of hostilities provisions and on the general constitutional principles for construction of the postwar state. They could not reach agreement on the number or boundaries of the provinces, the definition of their

Ten Provinces of Proposed Vance-Owen Plan

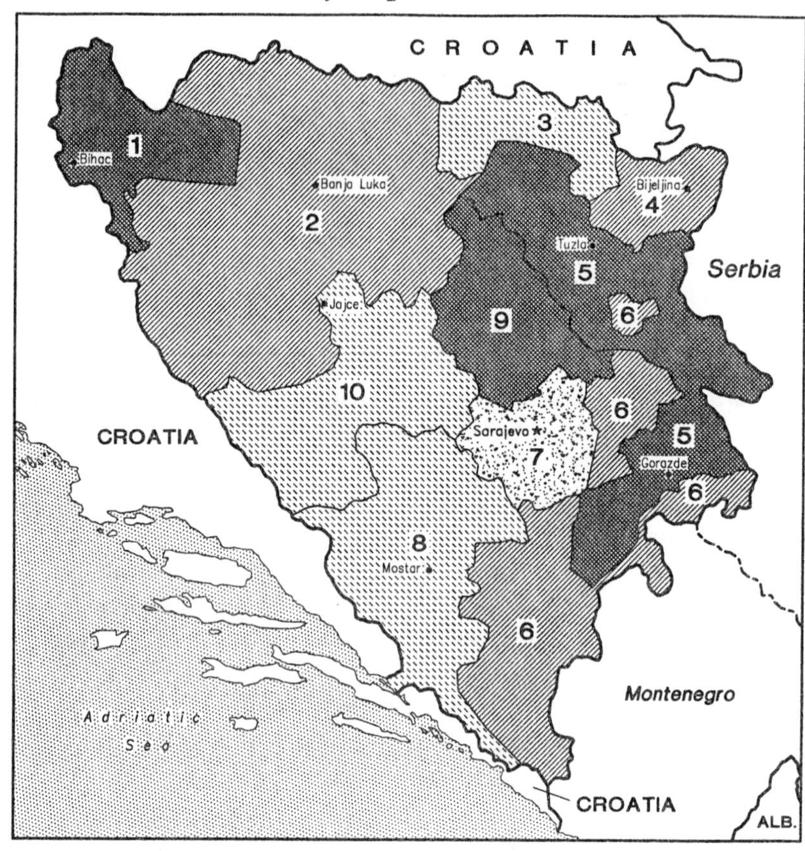

Proposed Administration of Provinces

Bosnian Government

Bosnian Serb

Bosnian Croat

Sarajevo District

Numbers for provinces correspond to those used in the Vance-Owen draft map.

Serbia and Montenegro have asserted the formation of a joint independent state, but this entity has not been formally recognized by the United States.

Names and boundary representation are not necessarily authoritative.

character, or the division of authority between them and the central government. The Serb delegation continued to press in Geneva for the simple partition of the republic into three ethnically defined units that enjoyed international recognition and would enter into a loose confederative relationship with one another.[92]

When the provisions of the plan became public, it was attacked in the United States for allegedly having given away too much to the Serbs. A former assistant undersecretary of defense for policy planning in the Bush administration, Zalmay Khalilizad, argued that the plan "amounted to appeasement." *New York Times* columnist Anthony Lewis warned Washington to "beware of Munich."[93] Although there were serious deficiencies in the Vance-Owen Plan, if there were parallels to the infamous Munich agreement of 1938 in the contemporary situation, they were to be found in European acquiescence to German insistence on the dismemberment of Yugoslavia, not in the Vance-Owen Plan. Some of the deficiencies of the plan could have been corrected through further negotiation, and some were.[94] But the most important deficiency was the continuing absence of any provision for enforcement of the territorial, institutional, and legal provisions of the plan against those who might not comply with them. This reflected negotiators' realization that the international actors capable of providing such support remained unwilling to commit themselves to intervention. Most of all, the negotiators remained hampered by the unwillingness of the United States to support any form of intervention—or even the Vance-Owen negotiation process itself.

Intensification of the international diplomatic effort to achieve a settlement in Bosnia took place during the prolonged period of transition in the United States between the November presidential elections, in which the incumbent was defeated, and the inauguration of Bill Clinton as president in January 1993. American policy, which opposed any use of force, thus became temporarily frozen in place. In an interview featured prominently in the *New York Times* in September 1992, the chairman of the Joint Chiefs of Staff, General Colin Powell, had effectively ruled out U.S. military involvement in

Bosnia.[95] In response to criticism of the Bush administration's inaction leveled by candidate Clinton, Powell argued that military force should be used only when a decisive victory is possible. He contended that it would be difficult to locate and destroy all the Serb artillery, that by intervening Washington would be seen as taking sides in the conflict, and that the warring parties might respond by retaliating against personnel carrying out the UN relief effort.

All these were legitimate concerns. But what General Powell failed to take into account was that by ruling out the use of force in advance he reduced the prospects of a political settlement. Les Aspin, then chairman of the House Armed Services Committee, responded to General Powell's interview by pointing out, "if we say it is all or nothing and then walk away from the use of force in the Balkans, we are sending a signal to other places that there is no downside to ethnic cleansing. We are not deterring anybody." His view was echoed by a former State Department official for human rights, who pointed out that "in order to get the Serbs to negotiate seriously, we and our allies have to be prepared to use force."[96]

A month later, the Bush administration reportedly considered providing the Muslims with additional arms as a means of counterbalancing Serb military superiority, but it could not do so unilaterally without violating the UN arms embargo that the administration had helped establish. The United States also sought Security Council authorization to establish a "no-fly zone" over Bosnia, but this was essentially irrelevant in view of the nature of the conflict on the ground. At the December 1992 meeting of the ICFY Steering Committee in Geneva, the United States called for the convening of a Nuremberg-like tribunal to prosecute war crimes committed in Bosnia and named several Serb leaders who might be tried as war criminals, including Slobodan Milosevic. However justified this move was on moral grounds, it complicated the ongoing negotiations still further and contributed to the difficulties confronting the Clinton transition team, which was already planning the incoming administration's responses to the conflict.

During the presidential campaign, Bill Clinton had argued for more forceful action in Bosnia-Herzegovina. Immediately upon taking office in January 1993, he therefore ordered a full policy review by his principal foreign policy advisors. The review was animated by doubt that the ICFY negotiations could, in the words of secretary of state-designate Warren Christopher, "find an agreement, find a solution that's peaceful that the parties would, in fact, agree to."[97] A long list of options—some new, most already considered and rejected—was considered.[98] In the end, the six-point plan announced by Secretary Christopher in mid-February did not substantially change American policy. Although the Clinton administration was clearly unhappy with the Vance-Owen Plan, it was reluctant to become involved militarily on the ground in Bosnia and could offer no viable alternative of its own.

The administration therefore had no choice but to support the Vance-Owen negotiations, although it carefully hedged its position on the crucial issue: according to Secretary Christopher, "the United States [was] prepared to do its share to help implement and enforce an agreement that is acceptable to all parties. If there is a viable agreement containing enforcement provisions, the United States would be prepared to join with the United Nations, NATO, and others in implementing and enforcing it, including possible U.S. military participation."[99]

The Clinton administration's stance contributed to a stiffening of the Bosnian Muslims' positions, which in turn compelled the negotiators to offer them territorial concessions. This ensured that the Serbs would reject the plan, despite the pressure brought to bear by Milosevic, who viewed quick settlement in Bosnia-Herzegovina as a means of consolidating Serb gains there and, more important, as providing the basis for ending international sanctions against Serbia. The Bosnian Serb parliament rejected the Vance-Owen Plan in April 1993 after an impassioned tirade against it by the Bosnian Serb military commander, Ratko Mladic.

Secretary of State Christopher's statement had made it clear that a major commitment of ground troops to Bosnia was contingent on the conclusion of a viable agreement acceptable to all the warring parties. Thus, Bosnian Serbs could prevent Western intervention by rejecting such a settlement. Indeed, despite reports in early March that the United States was urging NATO to prepare for a large-scale intervention,[100] no action was taken as the Bosnian Serbs mounted a new military offensive in March and April and overran besieged Muslim towns in eastern Bosnia.

Rejection of the Vance-Owen Plan led the Clinton administration to propose lifting the arms embargo against the Bosnian government and using airpower to strike at the Serbs and protect the Bosnians while they received the weapons and training necessary for them to defend themselves. This proposal, widely known as "lift and strike," was opposed by the British and the French, who were concerned that its implementation would not only expose their peacekeeping troops to retaliatory attack but also widen the war. If the proposed steps failed to deter the Serbs, or if they encouraged the Muslims to launch new offensives, this would prolong and escalate the conflict and increase the likelihood of spillover into neighboring countries. Outside powers, including NATO member states, might be drawn into the fighting. The European Community appeared willing to accept the status quo rather than become more deeply involved militarily or risk such escalation and spillover. The Europeans proposed instead to establish and defend "safe havens" in Bosnia-Herzegovina. This proposal seemed to retreat from efforts to solve the conflict; it appeared to acquiesce to partition on the worst possible grounds for the Muslim-led Bosnian government. It provoked intense opposition from the Bosnian government, Islamic countries, and nonpermanent members of the UN Security Council, as well as internal dissension among NATO member states.

In the face of the British and French opposition, the Clinton administration abandoned its attempt to win allied support for arming the Bosnian government. Instead, it shifted toward a strategy of containment and signaled its willingness to accept the territorial gains achieved by the Serbs, rather than impose a reduction in those territories as called for by the Vance-Owen Plan.[101] It also appears to have decided that, in the words of Secretary Christopher in a confidential letter to U.S. ambassadors, the conflict in Bosnia was "not central to our vital interests."[102] At the same time, the administration persisted in its halfhearted, and perhaps merely symbolic, support for arming the Muslims. In June, for example, the United States voted with the minority in favor of a failed Security Council resolution calling for the lifting of the arms embargo. Such actions undermined concurrent efforts to negotiate an end to the fighting.

International mediators had already shifted their efforts toward negotiating a partition of the republic intended to bring the fighting to an end. Despite diplomatic and political pressure from European states and the international mediators, as well as concessions from the Croats and Serbs, however, no agreement could be reached. Deep divisions within the Muslim-dominated Bosnian government between those willing to compromise and those who sought to reestablish control over the whole of Bosnia-Herzegovina by force made it impossible for the Bosnian Muslim leadership to agree to any settlement short of total victory on the battlefield. Those who believed that victory was possible drew sustenance from such statements of support as Security Council Resolution 836, adopted in early June 1993, which had commended the now-dead Vance-Owen Plan while at the same time reaffirming the UN commitment to establishing the full sovereignty, territorial integrity, and political independence of Bosnia-Herzegovina. (The United States had voted in favor of this resolution; Britain, France, and Russia had abstained.) The Muslims also based their hopes on the repeated resurfacing of the American proposal to lift the arms embargo and provide air support for the government, and on their continued success at securing weapons on the international arms market.[103]

The failure of U.S. efforts to win support for arming the Bosnian government, the apparent withdrawal of U.S. interest, and the signal that the Bosnian Serbs would not be compelled to give up territory they then controlled were followed by an initiative by Presidents Milosevic and Tudjman to move negotiations toward the de facto confederalization of Bosnia-Herzegovina on principles similar to those drafted as part of the Lisbon Agreement. On the basis of this initiative, ICFY negotiators reported, "the leadership for the three sides negotiated for the first time intensively, cordially and in a constructive manner,"[104] and "intense and detailed bilateral and trilateral talks" made "a great deal of progress"[105] on developing an agreement on de facto partition of Bosnia-Herzegovina into three units, including movement toward an agreed map. On August 20, 1993, the cochairs of the ICFY reported that the three sides had reached agreement on a complete set of documents, including a map defining the borders of the three "constituent republics."[106]

As was the case with the Lisbon Agreement negotiated in February-March 1992, however, the agreement negotiated in July-August 1993 fell apart as the result of the refusal of the Bosnian Muslims to accept partition. In the course of negotiations over the agreement, splits had developed within the Bosnian government, dividing Croats and Muslims willing to negotiate a partition from more hard-line Muslim members of the leadership.[107] President Izetbegovic presented the plan to an assembly of the remaining (mostly Muslim) members of the Bosnian parliament and several hundred Bosnian public figures, but opposed its adoption. Members of parliament voted 65–0 against accepting it.[108]

Resistance to the settlement was undoubtedly also strengthened by continuing American efforts to secure NATO agreement to carry out extensive air strikes against Serb positions around Sarajevo, driven by extensive Western media coverage devoted to the siege of Sarajevo.[109] President Izetbegovic returned to Geneva on August 31 with a set of demands for additional territories to be included in the proposed Muslim-majority constituent republic. These demands appear to have been couched in terms of specific towns that the government insisted were predominantly Muslim before the war or were economically or geographically essential to the viability of the proposed Muslim-majority republic.[110]

Muslim demands proved unacceptable to both the Serbs and the Croats. An ICFY proposal that the parties commit themselves to later negotiations over the possible exchange of territories between the Serb-majority and Muslim-majority constituent republics, and between the Serb and Croat republics, was rejected by Izetbegovic, who also rejected the settlement package as a whole.[111] Shortly thereafter, President Izetbegovic appeared before the Security Council to call for NATO air strikes and the lifting of the arms embargo against Bosnia-Herzegovina, and traveled to Washington to lobby Congress for more direct American military involvement in defense of his government.[112]

International efforts to mediate an agreement continued in the form of bilateral talks between some of the parties, as well as between the cochairs and each of the parties. Direct multilateral negotiations were resumed in September 1993 aboard the HMS *Invincible* in the Adriatic Sea. The *Invincible* negotiations produced an amended version of the August agreement, providing the Muslim-majority republic of the future Union of Republics of Bosnia-Herzegovina with access to the Adriatic Sea.[113] This required the Croats to grant the Muslim-majority republic guaranteed use of, as well as uninspected access to and transport from, a port to be constructed under a ninety-nine-year lease arrangement at the Croatian town of Ploce, located at the mouth of the Neretva River. It also required the Serbs to cede territory on the Neretva River to the Muslim-majority republic, previously slated for inclusion in the Serb-majority republic, for construction of a new, permanent port facility. These concessions, while significant, were far outweighed by the political gains to be achieved by the Croats and the Serbs as the result of the de facto partition still called for by the package. Like the immediately preceding agreement, however, this was rejected by an assembly of Bosnian public figures and by the remaining members of the 1990 parliament. Each group formally voted to accept the package but made its acceptance conditional on the fulfillment of additional territorial demands.

Refusal to accept this version of the ICFY plan could be attributed to several factors: its failure to accede to Bosnian government demands for the inclusion in the Muslim constituent republic of the cities and towns alleged by the government to have been predominantly Muslim in 1991; the reluctance of participants in the Muslim assembly and members of the Bosnian parliament to give up on the idea of a multicultural Bosnia; what one government minister called their unwillingness "to sign their own death sentence"; and the hope that "the tide in the war was beginning to shift."[114] But it could also be attributed to continuing American support for Muslim demands. The U.S. envoy to the ICFY, Charles Redman, for example, was reported to have attended the Bosnian parliamentary session that considered the package and to have expressed approval of the vote as "democracy in action."[115]

Additional negotiations took place over the next three months concerning possible exchanges of coastal territories among the three parties.[116] Additional Croatian, Bosnian Croat, and Bosnian Serb concessions tabled in Geneva in January 1994 partially addressed the Bosnian government's demand for access to the sea and for additional territory but failed to satisfy President Izetbegovic. He again demanded that territories in eastern and western Bosnia, where he insisted Muslims had been in the majority before the outbreak of fighting, as well as territory in central Bosnia, be included in the Muslim-majority republic. Earlier Serb proposals also were accompanied by some key demands. The map the Serbs proposed, for example, broadened the strategic northern "corridor" assigned to the Serb-majority republic, an element certain to be rejected by the Muslims.[117] Although both the Serbs and the Croats accepted an ICFY proposal to submit further territorial disputes to an arbitration commission that would make recommendations to the Security Council following implementation of the agreement and withdrawal of forces to provisional boundaries, this was rejected by the Muslims. Izetbegovic argued that this provision left the fate of too many important areas unresolved and that the Muslims were unwilling to allow Serb or Croat forces to remain in disputed territories. However, it was also clear that the Muslim-led government was pursuing a delaying strategy with respect to negotiation of a settlement.

As the negotiations dragged on, governments with peacekeeping troops on the ground were growing increasingly concerned about the vulnerability of these troops and the open-ended nature of their commitment. The fighting in Bosnia appeared to be escalating rather than winding down. Mounting evidence suggested that all three sides were preparing for new offensives. The prospect that Croatia and Serbia would be drawn into direct involvement in the war, with untold consequences in Kosovo, Macedonia, and beyond, also was increasing.[118] The Clinton administration was growing concerned that continued inaction would jeopardize the credibility and coherence of the NATO alliance and destabilize the fragile new democracies elsewhere in Eastern Europe.[119] Nonetheless, the NATO summit in January 1994 adopted a cautious and well-hedged approach to the use of force in Bosnia that reflected the continuing differences between the member states.[120]

The French government broke ranks with its allies, however, and began pressing for direct international military intervention, with American participation, to bring the fighting to an end.[121] Against the background of a renewed, contentious debate fought out in the media between Western policymakers over what should be done to end the fighting, the explosion of a mortar shell in the central marketplace in Sarajevo in early February 1994 sparked a public outcry for action. Worldwide coverage of this event, as well as the accompanying background reporting on the war and the failure of the international efforts to bring it to an end, intensified the pressure on Western policymakers and lent added urgency to the conclusion already reached by President Clinton's senior national security advisors: it was time for the United States to undertake a new initiative.[122] The president began to participate directly in his advisors' deliberations on Bosnia and to lobby other NATO leaders to take direct action—activities that he had for the most part declined to do up to this time.[123]

After extended debate, NATO issued an ultimatum in mid-February that reflected a compromise between the American and French positions. It ordered the Serbs to cease their attacks on Sarajevo and withdraw their heavy weapons from an exclusion zone around the city, or face NATO air attacks against them, and admonished Bosnian government forces not to launch assaults of their own from within the city. This latter was widely viewed as a cosmetic attempt at evenhandedness. But it reflected the reality of Bosnian government tactics of launching military assaults against Serb positions from protected areas. If the NATO effort was to achieve a meaningful cease-fire, the well-established pattern of attack and counterattack, or provocation and response, of which Bosnian tactics were an integral part, had to be broken.

Washington's choice of NATO as the venue for debating the use of force—a move designed to permit the United States to retain close political and military control over any eventual operations—effectively minimized the role of Russia in policy deliberations. This increased the resistance of the Russian government to extending Security Council authorization for any NATO action. NATO was thus obliged to justify its actions on the basis of existing Security Council resolutions, and despite the objections of the Russians, no effort was made to seek explicit Security Council authorization for the use of airpower. This reflected the Western powers' determination to use increased force against the Serbs in order to break the siege of Sarajevo while maintaining control over the decision to use force. However, at this point, Lieutenant General Sir Michael Rose, the UN commander in Bosnia, negotiated a cease-fire agreement between the Serbs and Muslims that included provisions for the interpositioning of peacekeeping troops. This placed significant constraints on the use of airpower against forward Serb positions and moved the conflict significantly closer to a Cyprus-like outcome.

The Serbs appeared to be pursuing precisely such an outcome when they negotiated a separate, simultaneous agreement with Russia that called for Russian troops to participate in the UN deployment. The Western powers, the United Nations, and the Bosnian government were compelled to accept this agreement, even though the deployment of Russian troops made the use of air power still more difficult and contributed to returning the ultimate authority for its use to the United Nations. Most important, the injection of Russian forces counterbalanced the U.S. support for the Muslim-led government and affirmed the importance of Russian participation in any international effort to achieve a settlement.

The creation of a NATO-enforced weapons exclusion zone around Sarajevo and a similar, later action applied to Gorazde and the four other "safe areas" established by earlier Security Council actions highlighted the differences in philosophy and practice between UN peacekeeping operations and the kind of coercive diplomacy advocated by NATO. The inclinations of peacekeepers to maintain strict neutrality and afford warring parties ample opportunities to "save face" in the interest of establishing voluntary compliance clashed with the inclinations of NATO countries, particularly the United States, to respond to force with counterforce, or at least with the threat of counterforce.

UN officials in Bosnia repeatedly clashed with NATO and Western leaders in their assessment of events and of the need for force. The secretary-general's personal envoy, Yasushi Akashi, was drawn into a particularly bitter dispute with the Americans, arising out of his inclination to negotiate a settlement rather than resort to force and his criticism of the Clinton administration's unwillingness to contribute troops to the peacekeeping effort.[124] Neither UN officials nor the NATO leadership, however, appeared to be guided by a coherent strategic concept for the settlement of the conflict. Rather than embarking on a coordinated effort to bring the fighting to an end and encourage the warring parties to make concessions in the interest of a durable settlement, individual NATO countries, the United Nations, and Russia worked at cross-purposes to one another.

Russia appeared to be motivated by a desire to thwart any Western effort to impose a settlement on the Serbs by force. UN officials, meanwhile, were bent on preventing NATO from using force out of concern for both the safety of UN personnel in Bosnia and the prospects for a negotiated settlement. Washington appeared to be motivated primarily by the desire to reaffirm the effectiveness of U.S. leadership in NATO and the broader international community, as well as by the wish to bring the war to an end. The American administration appeared unwilling, however, to undertake the military action required for any strategy of coercive diplomacy to succeed. The president repeatedly ruled out the use of U.S. ground troops to impose a settlement. It also remained clear that the United States was not willing to compel the Muslim-led Bosnian government to accept that it had been defeated and that it would have to agree to partition of the country.

The escalation of NATO, Russian, and American involvement in Bosnia highlighted the degree to which the warring parties were able to manipulate outside powers and international organizations, and the negotiations they sponsored, to advance their own political and military agendas rather than to move toward peace. American officials, for example, repeatedly defined their participation in ways that handed the Muslims veto power over U.S. proposals[125] and encouraged Bosnian government claims that were designed to ensure the failure of negotiations and draw the West into more direct military involvement. At the same time, Washington was unwilling to acknowledge publicly that no settlement could be reached without the participation of the Serbs, and that such an agreement could be achieved only by recognizing a substantial proportion of the Serbs' territorial and political goals. The American-brokered plan to create a federation of Bosnian Muslim and Bosnian Croat territories that would then enter into confederal relations with Croatia, for example—which was announced with much fanfare at a formal signing ceremony in Washington in March 1994—could not be meaningfully implemented without the participation of the Serbs.

The Washington Agreement left the most difficult territorial and political issues unresolved. It repackaged proposals put forth in the ICFY context, applying them to those areas of the republic in which the Bosnian Muslims (called "Bosniacs" in the documents) and Bosnian Croats constituted the majority of the population. It established a Yugoslav-like set of federal institutions, applied unspecified principles of proportionality to elections for representative office, established "consensual" principles of decisionmaking on unspecified critical issues, and allocated the federation access to the sea by adopting arrangements similar to those developed as part of the *Invincible* package. Most important, it made no effort to provide for the eventual inclusion of Serb-majority territories. Indeed, the whole initiative seemed to reflect an American decision to ignore Serb interests.[126] Following the signing of the Washington Agreement, the American national security advisor, Anthony Lake, chose to ignore the diplomatic record by characterizing the positions of Serbia and the Bosnian Serbs as intransigent.[127]

The main consequence of the Washington Agreement was to end, for the most part, Muslim-Croat fighting and establish a common Muslim-Croat military effort against the Bosnian Serbs. Croatia became more open to the Bosnian government's circumvention of the arms embargo, and Bosnian military commanders appeared to be encouraged further in the belief that they would eventually defeat the Bosnian Serbs. The Bosnian government came forward with a series of demands for an increasing share of territory. Tensions persisted, however, in the political relationship between Croats and Muslims in Bosnia, and between Croatia and the Muslim-led Bosnian government. Indeed, there was little reason to believe that the Croatian-Muslim federation would not disintegrate in the face of the next credible opportunity to partition Bosnia, just as every previous Croatian-Muslim alliance had disintegrated. Croatian president Franjo Tudjman, in an interview conducted at the time of the ceremonial signing of the agreement in Washington, made it clear that he conceived of the plan as the first step toward partition, to be followed by a "logical" agreement to permit confederation between Bosnian Serb territories and Serbia.[128]

Neither the establishment of a Muslim-Croat federation nor the halfhearted coercive diplomacy pursued by the United States and the NATO allies offered much hope of achieving an overall political settlement. Indeed, the NATO ultimatum produced a corresponding hardening of the Bosnian government's negotiating positions and the breakup of the ICFY talks in Geneva.[129] At the same time, UN-brokered talks appeared to be headed toward institutionalizing the status quo. On the same day that Washington unveiled the Croat-Muslim agreement, the United Nations announced that the Bosnian Serbs and the Bosnian government had agreed to reestablish limited movement of civilian populations and relief supplies across the

Sarajevo siege lines under UN supervision.[130] This brought Bosnia a large step closer to a de facto partition that, as in Cyprus, would be acceptable to neither side, perpetually a condition of "neither war nor peace." Bosnian president Alija Izetbegovic had indicated the previous October that this was the interim goal of the Bosnian Muslims and that such an outcome would simply mark the start of a prolonged period of guerrilla warfare and terrorist activity conducted across UN-monitored cease-fire lines. Indeed, Izetbegovic was reportedly influenced in this choice of strategy by his discussions with PLO leader Yasir Arafat, who had counseled him to accept any deal that legitimized Muslim control of territory and then to engage in guerrilla warfare from that base.[131]

The Clinton administration, frustrated by the lack of progress in the ICFY negotiations and by the opposition of UN officials to the use of force against the Serbs, forged an alternative approach, convening a "Contact Group" of American, Russian, French, German, and British representatives in late April 1994 to hammer out a solution that all could support and enforce, effectively circumventing the ICFY and ending its role as the focus of efforts to mediate a settlement.[132] Formation of the Contact Group transformed the international effort to achieve a settlement. The Contact Group would not attempt to arrange direct, multilateral negotiations between the parties themselves. Representatives of the group met with each of the parties separately for consultations and attempted to devise a plan that all members of the group would be willing to impose on the parties.

The group produced a map in July 1994 and presented it to all three parties along with a "peaceful ultimatum" to accept it.[133] The map expanded the territories assigned to the Muslims and Croats (now formally in federation) over those allocated to them under the August agreement. The additional territories appeared to be a direct response to the Muslim demands of August and September, which were rejected by the Croats and Serbs and thus scuttled hopes of an ICFY-mediated agreement. The political principles that would be imposed on Bosnia as part of this plan were not articulated publicly in any detail. Although the Muslim-led government remained dissatisfied with the territorial division, Izetbegovic made it clear that the government would accept it so as to throw the onus of rejection onto the Serbs. "If we evaluate that the Serbs will say no," he stated, "then we will say yes. So I emphasize that we will be saying yes, since the Serbs will be rejecting it."[134] Predictably, the Bosnian Serbs rejected the plan, and no credible threat of the use of force to compel acceptance of the plan by the Serbs was forthcoming, due to the continuing opposition of the Europeans and Russians.[135] The result was a continuing stalemate between the American-led Contact Group and the Bosnian Serbs.

In late October 1994, the Bosnian army launched a major offensive out of the Bihac pocket, scoring substantial territorial gains against the Bosnian Serbs. These were subsequently reversed by a combined Croatian Serb, Bosnian Serb, and antigovernment Muslim counteroffensive. Even the limited use of NATO airpower failed to protect the gains made by government forces. The events in Bihac made it clear that, in the absence of outside intervention, neither side enjoyed a decisive advantage over the other, and a very long and bitter struggle lay ahead. Confronted by this reality and by the onset of another winter, the Bosnian government and Bosnian Serb leaderships agreed in late December to a cease-fire facilitated through the mediation of former U.S. president Jimmy Carter and the United Nations. That cease-fire brought most of the fighting in the republic to a temporary halt.

The prospect that negotiations had reached a dead end in late 1994 increased political pressure in the United States to lift the arms embargo against the Bosnian government. But France, Britain, and Russia remained opposed to such action, making it unlikely that any effort to lift the embargo would pass the Security Council. The United States, for its part, would not be likely to act unilaterally, at least, not openly. As early as November, however, the United States was compelled to deny reports that it was secretly arming the Bosnians.[136] In February 1995, United Nations military observers reported flights of transport aircraft that suggested a major covert operation to supply arms to the Bosnian army at Tuzla airport was under way.[137] Media reports suggested that these were part of a larger covert American effort to supply the Bosnian army.[138] In April, the media revealed that Iran had for months, perhaps for more than a year, been delivering "hundreds of tons" of weapons and ammunition to the Bosnian army via Croatia, "with the Clinton administration's tacit acceptance."[139]

Fighting resumed in Bosnia in March 1995, six weeks before the scheduled expiration of the cease-fire, with an offensive by Bosnian government troops. Over the next several months, military and political conditions in Bosnia changed radically. With the formal expiration of the cease-fire in early May, Croatia moved immediately to retake the Serb-held UN-protected zone in western Slavonia by force. Muslim-led government forces launched offensive operations around Sarajevo in June. And in July, Bosnian Serb forces overran the Muslim-held enclaves of Srebrenica and Zepa, leaving only the enclave around Gorazde in government hands in eastern Bosnia.

Seizure of the eastern enclaves by the Serbs and evidence that these seizures were accompanied by large-scale atrocities against their civilian populations set off another policy debate between the Western allies, reported to have been characterized by a "sense of urgency verging on desperation."[140] The debate juxtaposed two options: withdrawal of UN forces to permit the warring parties to continue to fight on their own, versus a deliberate escalation of Western military involvement to end the war.[141] The Clinton administration, under increasing political pressure to take more decisive action from the Republican-controlled Congress and from the president's likely Republican opponent in the 1996 election, pressed for the use of airpower against the Serbs, despite continuing objections to such action from the Russians and the openly expressed reluctance of the British.[142] At the same time, it appears that the Americans made no serious effort to deter—and, according to some sources, may even have encouraged—the Croatian military reconquest of the Serb-held, UN-protected areas of Dalmatian Krajina.[143] The Croatian operation was concluded in a matter of a few days. Neither Serbia nor the Bosnian Serbs entered the conflict, and the Krajina Serbs offered no resistance, withdrawing instead. The recapture of the Krajina was followed by intensified joint Muslim-Croat military operations against the Bosnian Serbs.

These events raised the prospect that the Bosnian conflict might, indeed, be settled on the battlefield between the warring parties themselves. It also raised the prospect that the British and French might withdraw their UN forces entirely. This confronted the United States with the possibility that it might be called on by its allies to supply a large ground force to implement and ensure the safety of that withdrawal, and then be drawn into the military defense of the Muslim-led government.[144] The specter of escalating warfare and the potential involvement of American ground troops, as well as fear of Bosnia becoming a presidential campaign issue in the spring, led the Clinton administration to undertake a renewed effort to bring the fighting to a negotiated end.

The return of the Krajina to Croatian control and the elimination of Muslim-held enclaves in eastern Bosnia removed major and difficult issues from the negotiating table. American officials began to talk openly of negotiating a partition of Bosnia.[145] Despite resistance to the American initiative from all three sides, the Americans placed the blame for the continuing difficulties of negotiating such a settlement squarely on the Bosnian Serbs.[146] However, the most determined resistance to negotiating a partition appeared to come from the Bosnian Muslims. Bosnian army commander Rasim Delic, for example, openly rejected the American initiative, characterizing it as a plan "without a head and without a tail" and declaring that "we have only one direction and that is to continue fighting." Bosnian president Izetbegovic, meeting with American and French officials in Paris, declared that the government could not negotiate with "a pistol on our temple" and would not participate unless airpower was used against the Serbs.[147]

Thus, despite a decision by the Bosnian Serb parliament to accept the U.S. initiative, taken under pressure from Milosevic, and the assumption by Milosevic of personal control over Bosnian Serb negotiating positions so as to facilitate a settlement,[148] NATO launched a prolonged air campaign against Serb targets in Bosnia. Air attacks on the Bosnian Serbs were triggered by a mortar attack on a Sarajevo marketplace that, like the February 1994 attack, inflicted heavy civilian casualties. Although attributed to the Bosnian Serbs, its origin, also like the 1994 attack, was disputed.[149] Nonetheless, the air campaign attacked a wide range of Serb military resources across Bosnia, hitting command and control facilities, including especially air defenses. Variously justified as a specific response to the mortar attack, as an effort to put an end to the siege of Sarajevo, and as an effort to compel the Serbs to negotiate, the attacks inevitably had the effect of weakening the Serb military. They contributed to the success of a joint Croatian-Muslim offensive, carried out while NATO continued to attack Serb targets, that gained control over much of central and western Bosnia and threatened the largest Serb-held city, Banja Luka, until Bosnian Serb forces stiffened their defenses and ended—at least temporarily—the Muslim-Croat offensive.

As the air campaign unfolded, the foreign ministers of Croatia, Bosnia, and Yugoslavia (Serbia and Montenegro) met in Geneva under the sponsorship of the Americans to sign an accord calling for the mutual recognition of existing borders and for the Bosnian state to be composed of two "entities": the Muslim-Croat federation, created with American support in March 1994, and a "Republika Srpska" (Serb Republic)—the name used by the Bosnian Serbs to describe their self-declared state. Furthermore, each of these entities was granted "the right to establish parallel special relationships with neighboring countries."[150] This represented the first formal recognition by the Americans of the Bosnian Serb political claim to autonomous status, and thus brought the American position closer to that which had been pursued by international negotiators—and much maligned by the Americans— since 1992. Although this agreement amounted to a de facto agreement to partition Bosnia, it left unsettled the crucial questions of the division of territory, the status of Sarajevo, and the degree of autonomy to be granted to the

Serb entity. Moreover, it established no cease-fire, and both NATO bombing and fighting between Serbs and allied Muslim and Croat forces continued.

By September 1995, the warring parties had established another, more consolidated, but still unstable front line that divided Bosnia approximately in half between the Serbs and the Croat-Muslim alliance. The Bosnian Serbs had withdrawn their heavy weapons from the NATO exclusion zone around Sarajevo, leading to the end of the NATO air campaign. And the balance of military power had been shifted in favor of the Muslim-Croat alliance. But the attempt by the United States to use force to end the conflict had not produced a political settlement. Indeed, military success appeared once again to harden the Muslim-led government against making any further concessions, while the Croatian government appeared to be drawn toward the prospect of using its army to create a greater Croatian state.

LESSONS OF THE YUGOSLAV CRISIS

The wars in the former Yugoslavia have made it clear that the principles and practices that provided a stable framework for international security during the Cold War are no longer adequate for preserving the peace. The principles of state sovereignty, territorial integrity, human rights, and self-determination, which are embedded in the UN Charter and in the documents of the Conference on Security and Cooperation in Europe, have proven to be, if not contradictory, at least subject to conflicting interpretations. Moreover, the mounting human tragedy in Bosnia-Herzegovina has revealed the inadequacies of the decisionmaking principles, operational guidelines, and conflict management capabilities of the United Nations and such Euro-Atlantic institutions as the CSCE, NATO, and the European Community.

Appeals to national identity have proven central to the legitimation of new states and governments. Such nationalist patterns of legitimation have reinforced authoritarian tendencies in the domestic politics of several new states, which in turn have increased the tensions between the ethnic majority and minority populations within them. The nationalist concept of the state as coincident with ethnic identity has led politicians, not all of them extremists, to raise demands for the redrawing of international borders along ethnic lines.

New mechanisms must be developed to cope with demands for self-determination in ways that do not undermine the foundation of international stability: the system of sovereign states. The development of such mechanisms requires reconsideration of the meaning of self-determination and the principle that state sovereignty is indivisible. At the very least, it requires that we limit the ability of states to use their claim to sovereignty to defend their abuse of human rights against international inquiry. For any such mechanisms to be effective, however, democratic states—as well as the international organizations through which they may act together, affirm the legitimacy of their actions, and influence the actions of others—must become more proactive in their efforts to manage ethnic and other conflicts that threaten international peace.

Despite clear evidence that Yugoslavia was disintegrating and that its disintegration would lead to violence, few efforts were undertaken to address the underlying conflicts and thereby avert a crisis. In order to become more effective in preventing conflict, however, Western states will have to overcome their long-standing reluctance to become involved in the "internal affairs" of other states. This is especially true in disputes involving competing ethnic territorial claims. As the Yugoslav case clearly demonstrates, ethnic violence rapidly escalates and engulfs the civilian population. All members of an ethnic group become potential targets of attack by virtue of their ethnic identity.

In Yugoslavia, where ethnic identity is not associated with clear physical differences, early incidents of ethnic violence were characterized by the brutal disfiguring of victims, which served to mark the victims as different and as unworthy of the empathy that might otherwise be felt by members of the perpetrators' own group. Such violence undermines local interethnic solidarity and facilitates the mobilization of local populations for combat by extremist elements on both sides. This narrows the opportunities for negotiators—whether domestic or international—to reach and implement a settlement. The onset of violent conflict brings those willing to use violence to the political forefront and pushes nonviolent leaders and groups to the side. Advocacy of ethnic accommodation under conditions of violence becomes politically difficult and is often personally dangerous. The hostility generated by civilian casualties and the civilian population displacement that takes place once fighting has broken out make it very difficult for ethnic leaders to make the kinds of mutual concessions usually required to reach a stable settlement.

The Yugoslav experience argues, therefore, for the establishment of an international capacity to help defuse local episodes of ethnic violence against civilians before they escalate. It argues for the development of a corps of civilian investigators and judicial personnel who can be deployed in an effort to resolve ethnic incidents in a manner perceived as just by the local population. The early and rapid involvement of international investigators and judicial personnel would insulate the investigation of such cases from manipulation by local extremists. Direct international participation in identifying and penalizing individual perpetrators of violence would reinforce the perception of the fairness of the outcomes and prevent the assignment of guilt to whole groups. Such activities would represent the application of principles underlying such accepted international practices as electoral monitoring missions to new, more demanding tasks. They would constitute the strengthening of such capacities for preventive, nonmilitary intervention as are already emerging from the CSCE process.

The Yugoslav experience also suggests some important lessons for international negotiators. The cease-fire in Slovenia, the later agreement to establish a UN peacekeeping operation in Croatia, and the inability to reach agreement on a peace plan for Bosnia-

Herzegovina make it clear that local interests determine the success or failure of mediation efforts. Beginning with the EC Conference on Yugoslavia and continuing with the ICFY, international negotiations and the plans they produced were treated by the warring parties as instruments for advancing their respective military and political agendas rather than as means by which to end the war. Accession to the initial Vance-Owen Plan by the Bosnian government, for example, was explicitly seen as a way to gain political advantage in light of the calculation that the Bosnian Serbs would reject it.[151] Indeed, as early as January 1993 it was reported that government participation in such negotiations was motivated primarily by the desire to "avoid alienating the West," and that Muslim hard-liners hoped to continue the fighting until the West was compelled to intervene.[152] At each moment when a negotiated settlement appeared possible, the government side came forward with additional territorial demands or used some particularly egregious example of alleged Serb misconduct to shift international attention from negotiation to the use of force as a means of settling the conflict.

The unwillingness of Western states either to become directly involved in ground combat or to contribute to its escalation by ending the arms embargo was not matched by efforts to discourage Bosnian Muslim expectations of such developments. Indeed, repeated American efforts to secure allied support for military efforts to defend the government and to attack the Serbs worked at cross-purposes to European-UN efforts to convince the parties to negotiate a settlement. When the United States signaled, at least temporarily, its abandonment of efforts to arm the Bosnian government and its willingness to accommodate Serb territorial demands, ICFY negotiations began to make progress.

The prospect that agreement on a partition plan might be within reach in mid-1993 also contributed to the effectiveness of negotiators' pressure on the Bosnian Serbs and their Serbian supporters to come forward with a proposed map that addressed Muslim concerns. While Bosnian Serb demands for de facto partition had to be accommodated, it quickly emerged that accommodation of the political dimension of these demands could be used to extract territorial concessions that addressed some of the concerns of the Bosnian government. The initial success of the American initiative in August 1995 appears to have been based on recognition of the Serb demand for autonomy within Bosnia. But the difficulty of progressing beyond the initial stage of that negotiation must be attributed to the impact of improved military prospects on the Muslim-led government's positions. An approach that simultaneously disabuses all sides of the conviction that they can pursue a military victory, and compels each side to exchange or even relinquish key territories thus seems essential to any effort to reach a negotiated solution. The latter condition can be achieved, it seems, only if the political demands of each side are addressed.

The threat of force may have been an important factor contributing to Serb willingness to relinquish territories and enter into the agreement concluded in August 1993. Karadzic's initial acceptance of the Vance-Owen Plan in Athens in early May came against the background of a Clinton administration campaign that included open congressional testimony by military planners,[153] consultations with congressional leaders,[154] and leaks to the press asserting that the president had "decided in principle today to commit American airpower to help end the fighting in the Balkans."[155] These were clearly intended to add credibility to the threat that American airpower might be used against the Serbs. Following the American signal in May that Serb territorial gains would be substantially accepted, the Clinton administration mounted another public campaign, this time to increase the threat of NATO air strikes against Serb targets in the event that the Bosnian Serbs continued to interfere with UN operations and "strangle" Sarajevo. This threat was reflected in a formal NATO statement in early August and amplified by administration officials.[156] The NATO debate revealed, however, continuing divisions between the allies over the escalation of their involvement, and the procedures adopted for authorizing air strikes promised to limit their impact. UN officers in Sarajevo reported that the Bosnian Serbs concluded from these developments that the threat of air strikes had receded.[157] But their impact on Serb negotiating behavior cannot be entirely discounted.

At the same time, however, the record of negotiations under the auspices of the ICFY makes it clear that the Muslim-led government could not be encouraged to seek all its territorial goals simultaneously if a negotiated settlement was to be achieved. For the government to do so, especially for any international actor to encourage them to do so, would constitute a transparent attempt to prevent an agreement. Yet any settlement would have to address the legitimate demand to protect the rights of refugees driven from their homes. Thus, a negotiated settlement would seem to require both the imposition of limits on Muslim demands for territory and extensive implementation and enforcement guarantees with respect to the rights of all individuals, especially those whose homes wind up on the "wrong" side of ethnic boundaries. Settlement would seem to require, in short, an intrusive, extensive, and prolonged international involvement in the internal administration of the successor regime(s) in order to reestablish social peace.

The ICFY process constituted an attempt to bring warring parties largely uninterested in compromise to a negotiated agreement. It was an attempt to facilitate the discovery of an equilibrium point between their competing interests and goals. The record of that effort demonstrates that these warring parties could, in fact, be brought at least to the brink of compromise, as long as each believed it could not expect to gain support from outside forces for its maximalist objectives. If the ICFY was less than evenhanded, it was in its treatment of the Bosnian Serbs, upon whom negotiators exercised appropriate pressure in the interest of achieving agreement. Contrary to public excoriation of the process and of the cochairs personally, it is clear that the ICFY made considerable progress against great odds up until February 1994. After that date, the increased possibility that NATO military force might be used against the Serbs and the unmistakable U.S. diplomatic intervention in support of Muslim objectives ended Bosnian government interest in negotiations. The formation of the Contact Group ended the negotiation process, and the dramatic changes in the military-political balance in the summer and fall of 1995 pushed the Bosnian conflict toward an eventual, but distant, resolution on the battlefield.

It is self-evident that where there is no will to peace there can be no settlement. The record of negotiations even in the earliest stages of the Bosnian conflict underscores the importance of not allowing negotiations over the future of a disputed territory to be monopolized by the most extreme parties. From the very outset of international involvement in the dissolution of Yugoslavia, regional and nationalist leaders used their access to international actors to legitimate their claims to authority and exclude local competitors from the process of shaping a settlement. Future international mediation efforts undertaken as preventive intervention must therefore be constructed specifically to allow participation by domestic forces committed to peaceful solutions. Preventing the escalation of violence makes it easier to achieve this goal.

The war in Bosnia-Herzegovina demonstrates the extent to which the authority and control of local leaders become dissipated under conditions of ethnic war, the great difficulty leaders have in recapturing authority once it is lost, and the still greater difficulty they have in enforcing any agreement that might be reached. It is therefore in the interest of outside actors to engage local leaderships in negotiations before the stakes involved, especially the costs of making concessions to achieve agreement, are raised by the human toll of war. All these lessons suggest that preventive intervention must occur quite early in the evolution of a disagreement, certainly before violence has become sufficiently widespread so that civilian populations perceive themselves as probable targets of attack and become mobilized for conflict.

Some elements of a capacity for preventive intervention, at least within the Euro-Atlantic community, have already been established through the CSCE. However, for the CSCE to be effective, it must develop decisionmaking procedures that prevent conflicting parties from obstructing international action; it must also increase the pressure on states to support not only peaceful means for resolving conflicts but also the broader principles of democracy articulated in CSCE documents. The CSCE took the first tentative steps in this direction by adopting a consensus-minus-one principle of decision making at its Prague meeting in January 1992. It decided that "in cases of clear, gross and uncorrected violations of relevant CSCE commitments," appropriate peaceful action to protect human rights, democracy, and the rule of law may be taken "in the absence of the consent of the State concerned." This decision was prompted by the ongoing Yugoslav crisis and by concerns that the accession to membership of the post-Soviet republics made it likely that other, similar crises would arise in the future. However, the CSCE's actions were to be limited to "political declarations or other political steps to apply outside the territory of the State concerned." The Prague meeting avoided expanding CSCE authority to launch such activities as fact-finding or rapporteur missions without prior consent.[158] This would represent the next logical, and necessary, step in establishing an international capacity for preventive engagement.

Even if the international community had responded to the Yugoslav crisis as early as 1990, when U.S. intelligence estimates predicted the subsequent violent disintegration of the country, its actions would have remained futile so long as the Western states refused to support the redrawing of borders as a possible path to a peacefully negotiated solution to the crisis. The declaration of independence by a territorially compact ethnic community, such as that of the Serbs in Croatia or any other group in Yugoslavia, could have been recognized as a legitimate demand for self-determination. By recognizing the equal rights of all peoples in the country to self-determination, international mediators might have been able to lead local actors toward mutual concessions. Those who refused the opportunity to participate in such negotiations could then have been held accountable for their actions from the outset. The success of such negotiations, however, would have depended on, first, the recognition that international principles and the rights derived from them are equally applicable to all parties, and second, the willingness to try to renegotiate borders. In this, the international community failed.

Opportunities for the renegotiation of borders must be clearly linked to, and even made contingent on, the fulfillment of clearly articulated criteria that empower claims advanced by democratically legitimated groups and leaderships against states or governments that fail to conform to internationally recognized standards of democracy and the protection of human rights. These criteria must deny claims advanced by antidemocratic or violent groups against states or governments that do conform to international standards. In this way, ethnic competition to gain international recognition and support can be redefined; military- and force-based principles for resolving conflicts derived from realist theory can be replaced by political principles derived from theories of democracy and human rights.

The Yugoslav case demonstrates how insistence on territorial integrity and the preservation of existing borders may discourage democratic change and encourage the use of force. The early insistence by outside powers on the democratic legitimation of existing borders might have encouraged greater concern for the protection of human rights and avoided the escalation of ethnic tensions in Croatia and Bosnia. The communist order that held Yugoslavia together began to disintegrate as early as 1986 but reached crisis proportions only in December 1989. This left sufficient opportunity for international actors to influence events.

The importance of articulating—clearly, publicly, and early on—democratic and human rights criteria for recognition in such a situation cannot be overemphasized. By doing so in the Yugoslav case, international actors might have influenced popular perceptions and elite strategies and, through them, the development of domestic politics. The responses of the Yugoslav and Serbian leaderships to internal conflicts in Kosovo and elsewhere, or the fate of democratic proposals for reform of the economic and political systems, might have been different if it had been clear that international policies toward Yugoslavia would be affected by such considerations. Regional elections held in 1990 might have produced more moderate governments if the human rights standards of the potential ruling parties had been understood by all concerned to be a central determinant of Western policies toward them.

The existence of competing claims to territory complicated the Yugoslav crisis. But this in itself does not account for the magnitude of the human destruction that has occurred. The extreme violence in Yugoslavia must also be attributed to the establishment of ethnically defined governments that failed to provide democratic safeguards for the human rights of minority communities. This reinforces the conclusion that, if the international community is to facilitate the peaceful settlement of such conflicts elsewhere, it must devise instrumentalities for preventing ethnic domination and safeguarding human rights in such territories. In short, principles of sovereignty, territorial integrity, and national self-determination must be integrated into a single framework for determining the legitimacy of claims to political authority. And that framework must be based on the superiority of principles of human rights and democracy.

CHAPTER 3

From Nationalism to Democratization

THE ETHNIC CRISIS in the post-communist states reflects the inherent conflict between nationalist definitions of the state and the establishment of a civil order that protects diverse populations. The ethnic heterogeneity of the East European states, as well as the numerous actual and potential irredentist issues among them, means that the consolidation of democracy will require the accommodation of internal ethnic diversity. Two distinct strategies have characterized attempts to manage ethnic diversity in democratic systems: pluralistic integration and organizational isolation of ethnic communities, or consociationalism. Although consociational strategies are favored in much of the literature on ethnic politics, I argue here that such strategies are inherently destabilizing in ethnically divided societies and contribute to their breakup—whether peaceful, as with Czechoslovakia, or violent, as in Yugoslavia. I emphasize instead the importance of supporting the pluralization of society and ensuring that societal pluralism can find expression in political institutions.

Reliance on nationalism as an ideology of legitimation complicates the process of consolidating democracy. The assertion of collective identity and the institutionalization of privileges for the dominant ethnic groups inherent in nationalist legitimation make it difficult to establish and defend one of the essential characteristics of a democratic regime: the rights of minorities against the majority. However, there are institutional mechanisms that may be established to protect minorities, that do not introduce the fatal flaw embedded in consociationalism, and that contribute to preserving the pluralistic character of majority rule and thereby contribute to the consolidation of democracy.

For many post-communist governments, popular support consists predominantly of affective attachment to the state as the expression and guarantor of the ethnic identity of the majority, rather than instrumental, or pragmatic, support for particular governmental incumbents or their policies. Neither principles of individual liberty nor economic systems based on private ownership and markets, which might reinforce the importance of such liberty, are established firmly enough to generate instrumental support among the mass population. Nationalisms in the region have not yet been weakened by economic or other interests that introduce political differences within ethnic groups and establish commonalities across ethnic boundaries. Precarious economic conditions have slowed the multiplication and diversification of interests in society. This has made it difficult for newly established governments or opposition parties to displace appeals to nationalism with inclusive and pragmatic appeals to individual self-interest. Efforts to consolidate democracy in the post-communist states must therefore focus on encouraging the emergence of heterogeneous social and economic interests as well as the creation of political institutions through which such interests can act as constraints on nationalism.

INSTITUTIONS AND CULTURE

The relative importance of institutions, as opposed to political culture, is the subject of fundamental argument in the political science literature on democratization. Early attempts to understand the social foundations of democracy focused on the apparent importance of "civic culture" to democratic stability. In a classic empirical study of mass values and beliefs in five different democracies, Gabriel Almond and Sidney Verba argued that the civic culture was conducive to democratic development and that variations in democratic stability corresponded to variations in culture.[1] Since then, many scholars have acknowledged the close connection between institutions and culture. But it has remained unclear whether civic culture is a necessary precondition of democratic development.

In a recent influential study of what makes democracy work in

Italy, political scientist Robert Putnam argues that differences in political culture arising out of centuries of differences in the patterns of development explain current variations in the operation of regional political institutions.[2] But he acknowledges that democratic institutions themselves do affect behaviors. Others, such as comparative political scientist Terry Lynn Karl, survey researchers Edward Muller and Mitchell Seligson, and even the influential political philosopher/theorist John Rawls, have argued more forcefully in favor of the view that democratic institutions may be seen as instruments for creating democratic political cultures.[3] From this perspective, it would appear that democratization might best be achieved by concentrating on the identification of democratic institutions appropriate for conditions in the post-communist states and supporting their successful operation.

Perhaps the strongest evidence in support of this view is to be found in the Federal Republic of Germany. There, democratic political institutions were imposed on an authoritarian political culture and have contributed to the democratic transformation of that culture over a historically short period. Despite pessimistic early assessments, democracy itself has become consolidated in Germany, withstanding even the social dislocations associated with unification and the shock of renewed right-wing activity.[4] The strength of German democracy can be attributed to several social-structural factors, including generational change, the expansion of higher education, economic modernization that produced increased social differentiation and the multiplication of salient issues and interests, and the moderation of regional and religious cleavages that resulted from territorial truncation and population transfers associated with the postwar division.[5] But the design of democratic political institutions—including the adoption of such important characteristics as federalism, bicameralism, and administrative decentralization—as well as the successful institutionalization of electoral competition, expansion of opportunities for political participation, and the protection of individual liberties all preceded and contributed greatly to the democratization of German culture.

The impact of democratic institutions on the development of

political culture suggests that democratic regimes can be established and consolidated even where the civic culture associated with democracy is weak or absent. This suggests further that Western democracies intent on supporting the democratization of post-communist regimes, alleviating interethnic conflict, and securing international peace throughout post-communist Europe must work to foster those conditions that contribute to the successful functioning of democratic institutions. The German experience suggests that economic success, manifest in tangible improvements in the standard of living, may be an important criterion of political success in the minds of the populace, and a key to legitimating democratic institutions. This view is consistent with David Easton's widely cited theory of political support, which argues that pragmatic support arising out of material satisfaction is transformed over the long term into affective support for the system itself.[6] Thus, policies designed to encourage and support the establishment of democratic institutions seem to require simultaneous efforts to address the material needs of the population.

PREVENTING VIOLENCE

Neither pluralist nor consociational institutions can long survive the systematic resort to violence on the part of any group. If the establishment of democratic institutions is to stand any chance of success, violence must be precluded. The wars in the former Yugoslavia are an extreme example of the violence that can arise out of the failure to negotiate the resolution of outstanding ethnic grievances. But they are not the only examples: a similar pattern of violence has enveloped Nagorno-Karabakh for more than eight years, and the conflicts in Georgia and the North Caucasus—including the clash between Russia and its Chechen minority—do not appear likely to end soon. Violent conflict makes it very difficult for minorities to accept majority rule or for majorities to respect the rights of minorities with any degree of confidence in the stability of such arrangements. This in turn makes it difficult to establish social norms of political behavior that can contribute to the stabilization of a multiethnic democratic regime. Differences between conditions in Yugoslavia and Czechoslovakia suggest some of the factors that may affect whether interethnic conflict turns violent. Such comparison also suggests how factors that contribute to the onset of violence, if addressed in a timely fashion, might be altered by local or international actors, thereby making the peaceful resolution of conflicts possible.

The territorial settlement patterns of ethnic groups represent a structural condition not easily altered. In some respects, the distribution of groups in Yugoslavia and Czechoslovakia differed sharply; in other respects it was similar. Following World War II, Czechoslovakia was characterized by the distinct territorial separation of the Czechs and Slovaks and the effective elimination of the German minority as the result of forced population transfers.[7] In 1991, Czechs constituted 94.5 percent of the population of the Czech Republic, which encompassed over 99 percent of all Czechs. Only 3 percent of the population was Slovak. Slovakia was 85.6 percent Slovak and was home to 93.6 percent of all Slovaks in the country. Czechs constituted only 1 percent of the population of Slovakia. Thus, the ethnodemographic and territorial issues between the Czech and Slovak lands approximated those between Slovenia and the rest of Yugoslavia. In Czechoslovakia, as in Slovenia, territorial separation between the conflicting groups shaped the political debate in terms of whether distinct communities organized into their own national states could sustain common institutions. The alternative to such an arrangement was division into separate states defined by relatively clear ethnoterritorial borders.

The presence of more than 560,000 Hungarians in Slovakia, who constituted over 10 percent of the population, complicated the establishment of an exclusivist, national Slovak state in much the same manner as the presence of a large Serb minority complicated the establishment of a Croat nationalist state in Croatia.[8] With the disintegration of Yugoslavia and Czechoslovakia, ethnic divisions within the successor states took on additional salience. Nationalist leaders of the dominant groups in Croatia and Slovakia attempted to strengthen their control over minority-populated territories. In both Croatia and Slovakia, the minority population was supported by a larger and more powerful external homeland that provided a political—and in the case of Serbs in Croatia, a military—counterweight to the power of the dominant group. Under such conditions, an ethnic minority confronted with the prospect of political domination by the majority is likely to pursue a secessionist strategy.

In Bosnia-Herzegovina, territorial settlement patterns compelled large segments of each ethnic population to coexist in the same social spaces. Initial arrangements designed to continue the power-sharing practices established under the communists soon collapsed. In the struggle for control that ensued, ethnic group leaderships came into direct conflict over status and power. This conflict was intensified by the involvement of outside forces, namely, Serbia and Croatia, in support of internal actors. The failure of political negotiations to divide power and authority then gave way to military efforts to divide territory.

Whether ethnic groups are territorially distinct or intermingled, however, relations between them depend heavily on the political choices of their leaderships. In the case of Czechoslovakia, the Czech leadership made it clear that there would be no attempt to force the Slovaks to remain in a unified state against their will, thereby making a peaceful dissolution possible. As Yugoslavia broke apart, the Slovenian leadership was able to strike a similar agreement with the leadership of Serbia that sharply limited the scope and duration of violent conflict between Slovenia and Serbia. But territorial distinctiveness alone is insufficient to assure a peaceful political divorce. No such agreement could be reached between the leaderships of Azerbaijan and Nagorno-Karabakh.

Territorial intermingling only complicates the political challenge. The leaderships of the three ethnic communities in Bosnia-Herzegovina could agree neither to govern jointly in a multiethnic state nor to divide the republic peacefully into ethnically defined cantons.

Three-party conflict, as in Bosnia-Herzegovina, is inherently more complicated than conflict between two groups, and in this instance the intermingling of substantial portions of the ethnic populations made partition more difficult. The presence of powerful external forces supporting maximalist demands for territory made it even more likely that the Serbs and the Croats in Bosnia-Herzegovina would resort to violence.

Interspersed settlement patterns make disputes inevitable. But this need not lead inevitably to violent conflict. Ethnic tensions in Yugoslavia were aggravated by the actions of political leaders. Exclusionary behavior on the part of the leaderships of the regionally dominant groups raised fears among the Serb minorities in Croatia and Bosnia-Herzegovina of being relegated to the status of a permanent—and discriminated against—minority. An attempt to embed ethnic domination or discrimination in a state's constitutional and legal framework—as some Serbs were inclined to view Muslim efforts in Bosnia-Herzegovina to overturn a constitutional order based on interethnic consensus and replace it with one based on majority rule—undermines the confidence of the minority in its ability to defend its interests through peaceful, democratic means. It effectively delegitimates electoral competition, devalues political participation, and denies political equality to the minority. Thus, the political institutions and processes established early in the process of transition have a crucial effect on the willingness of minorities to recognize the authority of new regimes. The challenge for domestic elites and the international community of democratic states, therefore, is to encourage the establishment of democratic institutions and processes in multiethnic states that reflect the diversity of the population and reward ethnic cooperation.

Intergroup animosity, which is often characterized in the media as "age-old hatreds," is another important element contributing to the onset of violence. The legacy of ethnic suspicions and grievances in Croatia and Bosnia-Herzegovina, which arose out of the historical frustration of Croatian and Serbian national aspirations and out of the more recent violence of World War II, is not unique to Yugoslavia. Such suspicions and grievances are common among conflicting groups, as are past episodes of intergroup violence. But such grievances and past conflict do not necessarily have to engender contemporary violence. The role they play in contemporary politics is defined by the conscious choices of cultural and political elites.

The growing crisis in Yugoslavia was manifest early on in increasingly politicized and nationalistic cultural output. This was especially pronounced among the Serbs. The Yugoslav mass media were, with few exceptions, compartmentalized by region and language; these reinforced narrowly ethnic perspectives on contemporary issues. Media criticism of nationalist politics tended, for the most part, to be directed across republic borders at other national groups, rather than internally at the critics' own national leaderships.

The rise of nationalist leaders in both Croatia and Serbia in the post-communist era was accompanied by suppression of independent voices in the media. The seizure of power in Serbia by Slobodan Milosevic in September 1987 was followed almost immediately by purges of the editorial boards of major newspapers and newsmagazines. Television in Serbia was transformed into the outright propaganda arm of the Milosevic regime. Later, the Tudjman regime moved in similar ways to suppress media criticism in Croatia. Thus, the capacity of opponents of the nationalist tendencies in Serbian and Croatian politics to mobilize mass support was progressively restricted. In Czechoslovakia, in contrast, the media did not fall under the control of a single political force in the post-communist era. The struggle between the Czech and Slovak leaderships over the nature of the political order was subjected to continuous, critical scrutiny. Not surprisingly, the emergent nationalistic regime in Slovakia has attempted to restrict the independence of the Slovak media and thereby reduce the ability of its opponents to mobilize sentiment against the government. An independent, critical media is an important factor in limiting the ability of nationalist leaders to manipulate legacies of mistrust and to impose nationalist interpretations on contemporary conflicts, thereby generating ethnic animosities.

In Yugoslavia, the turn toward violence must also be attributed to the willful action of extremists intent on escalating intergroup tensions. Violence was introduced into the Yugoslav conflict through a series of violent incidents and the responses to these incidents. The Yugoslav government was unable or unwilling to investigate and adjudicate individual incidents of ethnic violence in ways that were perceived by the populace as fair and legitimate. Nor did it possess the instruments for implementing and upholding any decision that would be perceived as neutral. The Yugoslav military, for example, was seen as an essentially Serbian institution. By 1991, elements within the military had already been compromised by their support of Serbian nationalism.

In Czechoslovakia, in contrast, the enormous moral authority of President Vaclav Havel as a voice of reason and fairness cannot be overestimated as a factor contributing to the peaceful dissolution of Czechoslovakia. Havel's early public assurances that force would not be used to hold the Czechoslovakian federation together, despite attempts by Slovak extremists to provoke an authoritarian response,[9] permitted political leaders on both sides peacefully to negotiate a dissolution agreement. It is also important to note that although the Slovak leaders were at times confrontational in their approach to the issues, they never threatened, supported, or condoned violence toward the Czechs. The contrasting behavior of political leaders in the former Yugoslavia underscores the importance of elite behavior in such situations. Milosevic and other Serb leaders, for example, made clear their intention to use force to implement the Serb nationalist agenda, thereby strengthening their opponents' resolve not to compromise.

One explanation for this contrast in behavior may lie in differences in the sources, distribution, and legitimation of power in the two cases. Croatian and Serbian leaders relied heavily on appeals to mutually exclusive nationalist agendas to build popular support, and they won decisive electoral victories on this basis. They were not compelled to share power, nor were they under threat of electoral defeat by domestic opponents of their secular political agendas. In

Bosnia-Herzegovina, each of the major parties secured decisive support within its own ethnic constituency and had little hope of winning support outside it. In none of these cases, therefore, were political leaders under pressure to broaden their political appeal to additional sectors of the electorate or other ethnic groups by moderating their positions. In Czechoslovakia, in contrast, several parties and political personalities competed for support in each of the republics from the outset of democratic electoral politics. In both the Czech Republic and Slovakia, the 1990 election results distributed electoral support among several parties. Even after a sharp realignment of parties and personalities, and a year of increasing national discontent in Slovakia, the 1992 elections again resulted in a distribution of power across several parties in Slovakia. Thus, the political leadership in Slovakia remained under constant pressure to broaden its support in the electorate.

An alternative explanation for the resort to violence in Yugoslavia and the preservation of peace in Czechoslovakia might be based on the differences in the political cultures of the two countries. Armed confrontation plays a lesser role in the histories of the Czechs and Slovaks than in that of the Serbs. And there are similarities in the Slovenian and Czech political traditions arising out of their common experience in the Austrian empire. There has been no systematic analysis of Czech or Slovak political cultures, especially not of the role of violence as an instrument of political struggle.[10] But a recent, careful analysis of the role of political culture in the Czech-Slovak conflict contains no suggestion that either culture is prone to violence.[11]

In the Yugoslav case, however, there is an enormous literature on the multiple political cultures of the former state, ranging from the insightful observations of foreign travelers to careful statistical analyses of mass survey data by foreign and domestic social scientists.[12] Sharp cultural distinctions between the nationalities have been widely noted, and narrative accounts of the contemporary conflict commonly cite the importance of armed traditions among the Serbs for understanding the onset of violence. Journalist Misha

Glenny, for example, cites the "warrior consciousness" of the Krajina Serbs in explaining the conflict between Serbs and the Croatian state.[13]

Nonetheless, political culture must be translated into mass behavior through example. Hence, differences in the behavior of the Czechoslovak and Yugoslav elites are central to any explanation of the different outcomes in these two cases. This is significant because although the international community, and democratic states in particular, may have little opportunity to affect mass behaviors in states in transition, they do have many opportunities and substantial resources for affecting the behavior of elites. Moreover, while cultures may be difficult to change even in the long run, the institutional and procedural arrangements under which elites compete for power, adopt authoritative decisions, and implement policy are subject to alteration in the short term. Thus, institutional arrangements represent a potentially important means by which to constrain elite behaviors.

The distribution of resources and patterns of economic activity are also important factors affecting the degree of conflict between groups. Regional differences in the distribution of resources and economic activity may result in mutually beneficial economic interdependence. But they may also give rise to intergroup competition and resentments.[14] Such competition is a powerful stimulus for ethnic conflict in the contemporary world.

Structural differences between the Slovak and Czech economies, for example, played a large part in the growing conflict between Slovak and Czech leaders and contributed to increasing electoral support for nationalists in Slovakia.[15] As a result of these differences, economic conditions worsened more rapidly in Slovakia than in the Czech Republic following the collapse of the communist regime. Industrial production and real wages declined and the cost of living increased more rapidly in Slovakia. The unemployment rate was almost three times greater in Slovakia than in the Czech Republic.[16] Under these conditions, it is not surprising that some Slovak leaders sought to protect their republic from the further dislocations that would result from the rapid privatization and marketization schemes advanced by Finance Minister (and later Prime Minister) Vaclav Klaus.

In Yugoslavia, interregional competition to maximize resources was an important stimulus to ethnic tensions in the communist period.[17] The Yugoslav economy went into a sharp decline in the 1980s. Standards of living fell and interregional economic differences widened. Per capita national income in Slovenia was about six times greater than in Kosovo and about three times greater than in Bosnia-Herzegovina and Macedonia in the 1960s and 1970s. Per capita income in Croatia was about four times greater than in Kosovo and about twice that in Bosnia-Herzegovina and Macedonia. By 1988, per capita income in Slovenia was more than eight times, and in Croatia about five times greater than in Kosovo.[18] The perceived opportunity costs of the transfer of resources from the more developed Slovenian and Croatian republics to the less-developed southern regions, carried out as part of the communist regime's attempt to equalize economic development among the regions, became a source of particular dissatisfaction. In Slovenia, such dissatisfaction was compounded by the relative economic independence of the region from the rest of Yugoslavia.[19] In Croatia, it was compounded by resentment of alleged Serbian economic penetration of the Croatian economy and exploitation of Croatian resources.

The dynamics of ethnoregional conflict in Czechoslovakia can be traced to similar structural forces. Much of the popular support for greater Slovak autonomy could be attributed to the widespread belief among the Slovak population that the existing federation worked to their economic disadvantage. According to data published in October 1991, 70 percent of Slovaks believed that the Czechs enjoyed a more advantaged position in the federation. Only 24 percent of Slovaks viewed the republics as equals. As in Yugoslavia, however, those in the more developed region also resented existing economic arrangements. Sixty percent of Czechs believed the Slovaks gained disproportionate advantage from the federation; only 35 percent viewed the two republics as equals.[20] Other survey data revealed that 73 percent of Slovaks viewed the Czech Republic as gaining an advantage from the existing system, and those who expressed this view were far more likely to support separatism (37 percent) than those who did not (14 percent).[21] Such linkage supports the view that nationalist movements gain strength under conditions of ethnic competition for benefits.

Czechs and Slovaks differed not only in their evaluations of the past and present, but also in their preferences for the future socioeconomic development of Czechoslovakia. Among Czechs, 52 percent favored a market economy and 39 percent favored a mixed economy. In Slovakia, almost precisely the opposite results were obtained: 53 percent favored a mixed economy and 33 percent favored a market economy.[22] Moreover, each calculated that separation—which would allow the pursuit of distinct economic strategies—promised certain economic benefits. This popular perception of mutual benefits to be obtained through ethnoterritorial separation may be sufficient to explain the peaceful character of the Czechoslovak breakup. Such a perception was not present in Yugoslavia.

Other factors moderating the Czechoslovak conflict, and absent in Yugoslavia, were the salience of economic policy issues for both the leadership and the electorate, the progress toward economic reform achieved before and during the dissolution crisis, and the mass perceptions of the shared benefits that might be derived in the future from a successful reform effort. The progress toward economic transformation in Czechoslovakia, especially the fact that the voucher-based privatization plan proceeded without interruption, diversified the public agenda and focused popular attention on the promise of longer-term material gains. The continuing participation of Slovak citizens in the distribution of ownership of former state assets created substantial incentives for the leaderships on both sides to limit the economic significance of the emerging border between the new states. Joint participation in an emerging market and the anticipation of benefits from that participation moderated the conflict arising out of the differential impact of reform on Slovaks and Czechs.

As the crisis in Yugoslavia unfolded, in contrast, bases of interest formation other than nationality proved relatively weak. Economic and ideological interests were most developed in Slovenia, where the relative ethnic homogeneity and higher level of development of the republic, as compared to the rest of Yugoslavia, paralleled the difference between the Czech Republic and Slovakia. In both Slovenia and the Czech Republic, economic development may have contributed to the pluralization of internal politics, but it did not develop into interests that bound either republic to the rest of the country. In the case of Slovenia, the lack of any prospect for the rapid economic reform of the Yugoslav economic system eroded regional support for it. Moreover, the Serbian leadership purposefully cut off economic relations between the two republics in December 1989, further undercutting the moderating influence of shared economic interests on the behavior of the two republic leaderships.

Economic development alone does not eliminate ethnic conflict. Although such conflict is generally expressed more peacefully in developed states, this fact can be attributed to the level of democratic political development, rather than to the level of economic development, of these states.[23] The inability of extremists in Quebec or the Basque country of Spain to provoke either popular violence or a violent reaction by the government, for example, may be due in both cases more to the democratic character of the overarching regime than to the level of economic development of the country or region.

In Yugoslavia, the emergence of a political alliance between elements of the military and the Serbian nationalist leadership was an important factor contributing to the escalation of violence. The army conducted limited, conventional military actions in defense of a reduced definition of Yugoslavia and provided material and direct combat support to Serb nationalist and extremist groups attempting to drive ethnic aliens from this territory.[24] With the onset of war, the military leadership was subjected to intensified political pressure from the Serbian nationalist leadership. Officers associated with the "Yugoslav" orientation of the old regime were replaced by adherents to the Serbian nationalist perspective. In Czechoslovakia, in contrast, the military played no such political role and submitted peacefully to division between the republics. Military culture, especially the relationship between civil and military authorities, thus plays an important role in defining the nature of ethnic conflict.

External factors also played an important role in encouraging violence in the former Yugoslavia and discouraging it in Czechoslovakia. International actors failed to support potential peaceful alternatives in Yugoslavia and, by supporting the status quo for too long, may have encouraged the use of force against the secessionist republics. In the case of Czechoslovakia, the European Community made it clear that dissolution was possible but that neither side would be permitted to benefit from relations with the EC in the absence of a peaceful settlement that conformed to Community standards. Such pressure may have played an important role in stimulating agreement on preserving Czech and Slovak economic relations.

Both the EC and the Czech and Slovak leaderships may also have benefited from the extreme negative example of nearby Yugoslavia, which provided an additional incentive not to allow events in Czechoslovakia to get out of hand. The influence of such negative examples may, however, be contingent on territorial proximity or the prior predispositions of leaders. Neither the prolonged violence in the Caucasus nor the political failure of the Soviet attempt to use force against the Baltic states in January 1991 deterred Yugoslav leaders from resorting to the use of force in their own country.

Among the Yugoslav republics themselves, Serbia functioned as an external base of support for armed resistance among Serbs in Croatian Krajina and for Serb extremists in Bosnia-Herzegovina. Such cross-border support has also played a role in Nagorno-Karabakh and Georgia. Russian military support for the self-declared Dniester republic in Moldova parallels the support given by the Yugoslav army to Serb irregular forces.

The impact of such external supply channels has serious implications for future conflict between Serbs and ethnic Albanians in Kosovo. Because Kosovo shares a mountainous border with Albania, were the conflict between Albanians and Serbs in Kosovo to become militarized, Albanian fighters would likely be able to secure the delivery of military and other supplies necessary to sustain a prolonged and violent struggle, and perhaps even to carry that struggle to the neighboring Sandzak region of Serbia and Montenegro, as well as into western Macedonia.

Thus, while peaceful resolution of conflict may require early diplomatic and political intervention by actors committed to safeguarding human rights and securing international peace, it also requires continued support for principles of military nonintervention. External military support—either direct or indirect—for parties engaged in ethnic conflict must be prevented through such devices as monitoring missions and more restrictive enforcement arrangements to stem the flow of arms across borders.

External factors that contribute to the onset of violence may be among those most susceptible to control by international actors. But, absent fertile internal conditions, they may be among the least important in determining the course of events in a developing domestic conflict. If international actors are to prevent violence and encourage democracy, they must address the kinds of internal structural and political factors that reinforced intergroup conflict in both Czechoslovakia and Yugoslavia and led to violence in Yugoslavia. They must come to grips with the territorial dimension of ethnic conflict, the centrality of elite behaviors to political development, and the linkage between economic interests and political behavior at both the mass and elite levels.

PARTITION VERSUS DEMOCRACY

The territorial dimension of ethnic identity and the centrality of claims to self-rule or autonomy to the political mobilization of ethnic identities often lead to proposals for partition as a means to solve ethnic conflicts. In discussing partition, we must distinguish between partition arrived at as part of a negotiated solution and partition imposed by force, whether internal or external. The Slovene and Czechoslovak cases suggest that the peaceful negotiation of dissolution between regions of a multiethnic state whose populations can no longer agree on remaining together may be an important means of avoiding violent conflict. But the example of Croatia cautions that, to the degree ethnic nationalism remains the dominant basis of a secessionist region's claim to autonomy, and if the international community chooses to recognize such claims, peaceful secession may require the renegotiation of existing internal administrative borders and realignment of territory if violent conflict between nationalist majorities and their ethnic minorities is to be avoided. The example of Bosnia-Herzegovina demonstrates the enormous difficulties likely to be encountered in any effort to redefine boundaries in heterogeneous regions and the still greater difficulties of doing so once a cycle of ethnic violence has been initiated.

Peaceful partition may represent a viable solution only where ethnic populations are separated and territorially compact, as in both the Czechoslovak and Slovenian cases. Patterns of intermingled ethnic settlement and competing claims to exclusive control over common territory, which are most often at the center of violent conflict, make partition difficult to achieve by peaceful means. In the former Yugoslavia, the number and complexity of competing claims offered at least the possibility of negotiating a peaceful comprehensive settlement before the onset of violence. Once the fighting began, however, the number and complexity of claims became a stimulus to escalation. Even where conflicting groups are more or less territorially distinct, the territories to which they lay claim may not necessarily be homogeneous. In the case of the former Czechoslovakia, partition has set a precedent to which ethnic Hungarians in Slovakia may turn to buttress future demands for autonomy in response to continued cultural pressure by the Slovak government.

In cases of ethnic war, partition—including both the division of territory and the segregation of ethnic groups—is sometimes proposed as a means of ending the fighting. In Bosnia, for example, independent American analysts proposed partitioning the republic into three independent, ethnically homogeneous states as a means of bringing the fighting to an end in 1993.[25] The proposed settlement negotiated under international auspices in the summer and fall of 1993 represented a de facto plan for partition, as did the so-called Contact Group proposal of 1994. The settlement that appeared to be emerging in the fall of 1995 also called for de facto partition, but along the lines of a military standoff established, at least temporarily, between the warring parties. For external actors to impose such a partition in the absence of such a standoff would require substantial military pressure on all three warring parties.

Even if achieved by negotiation, however, partition would require the transfer of ethnic populations to their designated states. Such transfers would inevitably require substantial coercion, generate additional conflict, and fail to achieve homogeneity. This may be one reason why, as conditions appeared to be moving toward negotiations in 1995, the Bosnian Serbs failed to resist the takeover by combined Muslim and Croatian forces of territories likely to be relinquished to them as part of a settlement: the outrage of the Serb population ousted from these lands could later be directed against the enemy. Some elements of the populations displaced during the fighting or as the result of partition would continue to press for their return to their home villages, cities, or regions. The example of the increasing pressure being placed on the Czech Republic by Sudeten Germans suggests that, even in the long term, and when peaceful interstate relations have been reestablished, exiled populations do not easily give up their claims to former territories or properties or to restitution for their losses.

Even more important for the development of democracy, partition and population transfers legitimate the de facto ethnic definition of regimes on all sides of the conflict, thereby placing the minority populations that will inevitably remain on each side of the partition lines at continued risk. A Muslim rump state in Bosnia-Herzegovina, for example, would almost certainly be characterized by a militarized form of nationalism, while similar nationalist-extremist forces would continue to dominate Bosnian Croat and Bosnian Serb politics. The appeal of nationalist extremism on all sides of a Bosnian partition is also likely to be strengthened by the insecurities arising out of claims by displaced ethnic populations for the return of property seized by newly settled populations.[26]

The Muslim-led state that would be established in central Bosnia under the several proposed plans for partition would likely face continued pressure from Serbs intent on regaining "lost" territory and from Croats intent on establishing their own ethnic domination over territories under their control. It would face a prolonged struggle over internal political relations and require long-term external military support to assure its survival. At the same time, displaced Muslims would inevitably seek to wage a guerrilla war for the return of lands assigned to the Serbs or Croats, as anticipated by President Izetbegovic in October 1993. Extremist elements on both sides would use each terrorist attack or incident of abuse of their conationals in the neighboring state to legitimate retaliatory measures. The states that would be created as the result of partition, therefore, would be unlikely to remain at peace. International forces deployed to police such arrangements would inevitably confront opposition from all sides.

The application of a partition principle in response to group demands is thus unlikely to end the violence associated with the most difficult cases of intergroup conflict. In the former Yugoslavia, the partition of Bosnia-Herzegovina would, from the perspective of Kosovar and Macedonian Albanians, establish a precedent for the partition of both Serbia and Macedonia and increase the likelihood of more violence between Serbia and its ethnic Albanian population, and between Macedonia and its Albanians. Ibrahim Rugova, the popularly elected president of the opposition shadow government of Kosovo, who has resisted escalating tensions in the hope that moderation will lead to increased external support for the peaceful recognition of regional autonomy, has warned that the partition of Bosnia-Herzegovina along ethnic lines would require the Kosovar leadership to "take new measures."[27] In Croatia, opposition parties criticized Tudjman's support for the partition of Bosnia-Herzegovina precisely because it would set a precedent for the partition of Croatia. Such an outcome was precluded only by the use of force by the Croatian government not only to establish its control over the territory of the Krajina, but also to expel most of the local Serb population. The leadership of Serbia might very well decide, in the face of a partition of Bosnia, to take the same sort of preventive measures the Croatians did.

Thus, any partition of Bosnia-Herzegovina intended to stabilize the Balkans would have to be accompanied by comprehensive efforts to address other, related ethnic conflicts. The example of partition in the Balkans might further destabilize the Caucasus and lend new urgency to conflicts with ethnic dimensions in the Baltic states and Ukraine, as well as in Romania and Slovakia. Separatist sentiments among Russians in the Crimea, in particular, might be reinvigorated by the ethnically legitimated partition of Bosnia-Herzegovina. Advocates of partition in any one part of the post-communist world must therefore give careful consideration to its likely consequences elsewhere.

The adoption of partition in response to the current and potential ethnic conflicts among the post-communist states would lead inevitably to the proliferation of microstates whose economic weakness would undermine the appeal of democratic development and strengthen the attractions of authoritarian politics. For the economically weak states of Eastern Europe, membership in the European Community, which formally became the European Union (EU) in November 1993, represents an attractive solution to the problems of economic weakness and small size. The EU has already extended assistance to some of these states and entered into association agreements with them. But membership in the European Union is restricted to democratic regimes. The post-communist states therefore cannot rely on EU membership as a means of consolidating weak domestic democracies. Austria, Finland, and Sweden, states with stable democratic regimes and healthy economies, have already entered the EU, and applications have been made by Cyprus and

Malta. The EU is engaged in efforts to "intensify" relations with Turkey, an associated state since 1964.[28] The large number of probable and potential members relative to the existing membership, especially if the claims of East European states are included, may delay further expansion of the Union.

At present, each member state exercises considerable influence over EU policy decisions. Within the Council of Ministers, voting powers and rules of decisionmaking balance economic, political, and population factors. Until new policymaking arrangements are established within the Union that take into account the relative size, wealth, and power of member states, some members may be reluctant to dilute their influence over EU policy still further by admitting additional states.[29] Moreover, all EU member states share a common interest in opposing the admission of economically weak states that would introduce new and greater regional inequalities into the Union. Their presence would likely increase the costs to wealthier states of EU equalization policies and dilute the benefits to poorer ones. Such considerations may delay the admittance of the East European states for many years. Indeed, the EU leadership noted at Copenhagen in June 1993 that the Union's "capacity to absorb new members" was "an important consideration" with respect to the Central and East European states.

The policy of "strengthened dialogue and consultation" with Eastern Europe adopted by the EU in Copenhagen establishes membership for these states as its explicit goal. Nonetheless, the Copenhagen decisions reaffirm that the new states of Eastern Europe must have "achieved stability of institutions guaranteeing democracy, the rule of law, human rights and respect for and protection of minorities, the existence of a functioning market economy as well as the capacity to cope with competitive pressure and market forces within the Union" before they will be accepted for membership.[30]

The successor states of Eastern Europe cannot afford, therefore, to allow internal ethnic differences to become a barrier to the growth of their domestic markets and economies. Nor can they afford to turn their backs on the potential benefits of regional cooperation.

For the successor states of the former Czechoslovakia, Yugoslavia, and Soviet Union, in particular, regional cooperation will involve reviving many economic relationships that existed in the past. The expansion of economic relations across ethnic groups and state boundaries is an important step toward establishing interests that can moderate ethnic conflicts and lay the foundation for peaceful relations between states as well as between ethnic groups.

Thus, the partition of successor states in response to ethnic conflict would more often than not weaken democracy, undermine economic recovery and reform, and delay economic and political integration with the West. Alternatives to partition as a means of resolving conflicts and avoiding violence must be sought in strategies that assure the inclusion of minorities, the consideration of minority interests in the authoritative decisionmaking processes of new governments, and the protection of minorities against discrimination at the hands of dominant majorities. The advantages of economic integration and cooperation must be preserved, even as the legitimate demands of ethnic groups for self-determination are addressed. Little progress can be expected in any of these areas, however, until the principle of national self-determination is understood to mean the right to democratic participation in government rather than the right to create separate state entities.

DEMOCRACY AND DIVERSITY

Pluralist integration and consociationalism represent two broadly differing approaches to securing the inclusion of distinct ethnic groups and the protection of their interests in a democratic polity. A pluralist strategy of ethnic integration depends on contact between individuals of diverse ethnic identities who share certain functional interests that lead them to cooperate. Such cooperation may be manifest in the formation of groups to pursue interests that cut across ethnic divisions or in the establishment of mutually beneficial exchange relationships, as in a market. The integrative power of economic, or functional, interests, for example, is widely viewed as having provided the foundations for elite-led efforts to achieve the postwar integration of Western Europe.

Proponents of pluralism argue that crosscutting lines of social, economic, functional, and other cleavages give rise to multiple, voluntary, competitive, nonhierarchical, and overlapping groups.[31] Pluralists view the political process as the product of both conflict and shifting alliances among groups as each pursues its own self-interest. Conflict is institutionalized through the activities of broadly aggregative, and therefore integrative, political parties. Because individuals usually belong to more than one group, they feel conflicting cross-pressures that moderate their identification with any one group, their position on any single issue, and their behavior. These cross-pressures, it is argued, lead to moderation in individual political attitudes and in the behavior of both individuals and groups. The aggregation of numerous, and often conflicting, group interests, in turn, leads to moderation in the ideology and policies of political parties. It is this moderation, finally, that accounts for the stability of liberal democratic systems, or pluralist democracies.[32] Pluralist theory thus posits a causal relationship between the character and distribution of social cleavages among the masses and the stability of political democracy: to the degree that social cleavages are distributed in a crosscutting pattern, the political system will be stable.

Pluralist theory emphasizes the existence of common interests that cut across lines of cleavage that might otherwise divide a system into separate communities. Such interests are assumed to derive, most of all, from economic activity, or function. The history of the scholarly debate over the relationship between economic development and democracy is a long and contentious one. However, it is clear that the development process is accompanied by social differentiation, functional specialization, and professionalization, as well as the emergence of a more broadly and more highly educated population. These factors multiply the interests in society, increase social demands for participation and democracy, and improve the ability of groups to organize around their interests and articulate their demands. To be sure, the proliferation of skills provides the basis for effective ethnic group politics and nationalist movements. But the simultaneous proliferation of functional interests provides the basis for group formations that cut across ethnic identities and establish the basis for pluralist politics.

The existence of distinct cultural communities within a single state is, from a pluralist perspective, a threat to democratic stability.[33] Ethnic divisions are often associated with differences in territory, economic activity and well-being, and social status. Such differences give rise to distinctly different group interests. Linguistic and cultural barriers to communication, for example, reinforce intergroup isolation by making it difficult to mobilize political support across groups. In short, ethnic diversity suppresses the salience of crosscutting cleavages. Moreover, because ethnic identity almost invariably includes a territorial dimension, it often coincides with, and therefore reinforces, cleavages based on the territorial distribution of economic resources.

One response to territorially distributed political cleavages, including ethnic cleavages, has been the devolution of authority among such territories according to federal or confederal formulas. But such arrangements require agreement on the divisibility of sovereignty and its allocation between central and regional authorities. They succeed where politics within the territorial communities is pluralistic and the territories are held together by economic or other forces. As political scientist Daniel J. Elazar points out, "Federalism is a democratic middle way requiring negotiation and compromise. All aspects of society fostering uncompromising positions make federalism more difficult, if not impossible." He concludes that "ethnic nationalism is probably the strongest force against federalism."[34]

Absent other ties that bind ethnic populations together, federalization of a previously unitary state is unlikely to ameliorate separatist tendencies. Rather, it is more likely to be seen only as a partial step toward independence. Political leaders intent on holding their countries together may also be dissuaded from offering federal solutions to ethnic conflict by the decision of the international community to extend recognition to the previously internal borders of the Yugoslav federal republics. Federalization thus appears to be a viable strategy of conflict resolution only where a separatist impulse is counterbalanced by the political legitimacy of, and popular support for, the overarching political community.

Contrary to the expectations derived from pluralist theory, mutually reinforcing lines of cleavage have not destabilized democratic regimes in Belgium, Switzerland, and the Netherlands. These countries are divided into distinct cultural communities by combinations of such factors as language, religion, ideology, and economic activity. Although they may vary in the extent to which they are divided along territorial lines, the communities defined by these cleavages are segregated organizationally. Each cultural community "produced competing networks of schools, communications media, interest groups, leisure time associations and political parties" that effectively insulated their members from contact with other communities.[35] Moreover, the defining identities of each community are strongly and mutually incompatible. The multiple political parties characteristic of these systems each represent the interests of only one of these communities. They do not aggregate interests across cleavage lines.

The combination of such deep divisions and democratic stability contradicts the pluralist view that crosscutting cleavages are an essential condition of stable democracy. Analysts explain this apparent contradiction primarily in terms of elite behavior and rules for common decisionmaking. Organizational segregation of the communities, they argue, maintains and reinforces group coherence, reduces the opportunities for intergroup conflict at the mass level, and establishes the structured predominance of political elites. This permits these elites to negotiate intercommunal differences and, especially, to exchange concessions while maintaining political power.[36] Indeed, "deliberate joint effort by the elites to stabilize the system" represents "the essential characteristic" of these systems. Systems in which such practices prevail are labeled consociational democracies.[37]

Consociational decisionmaking practices, it is argued, redress the problem of the permanent electoral minority. Consociational arrangements include electoral systems that favor proportional systems over first-past-the-post or simple majority systems as a means of ensuring the effective representation of all groups. All significant groups participate in government, and each communal leadership is granted an effective veto in the policymaking process. Such systems are held together by a degree of internal pluralism within the communities, the existence of shared interests that lead communal leaders to cooperate for mutual benefit, and the existence of a sense of common identity.

Because ethnically divided states share many of the characteristics of states divided into distinct cultural communities, much attention has been devoted to consociational approaches to managing conflict. The stipulation that such approaches require the existence of a sense of common identity might, however, be seen as rendering them irrelevant to the kinds of conflict characteristic of ethnically divided states. As political scientist Brian Barry has suggested in his criticism of consociational theory, there is a qualitative difference between conflicts over "how *we* are to get along together" and conflicts over whether the existing state should be a single country at all.[38] For the Baltic states, Nagorno-Karabakh, Czechoslovakia, and Slovenia, the latter perspective appeared to predominate from the beginning. But for Croatia, Bosnia-Herzegovina, and much of the rest of Eastern Europe, the early stages of intergroup conflict—before the onset of widespread violence—focused on the former question. Indeed, the territorial intermingling of populations requires that it be asked. Thus, the early stages of ethnic conflict often do present opportunities to negotiate agreements for living together.

Far more serious objections to the use of consociational strategies for securing democracy in ethnically divided states are to be found in the requirements that ethnic communities remain organizationally segregated and that communal leaderships be granted an effective veto over joint decisions. Approaches based on ethnic segregation are fundamentally flawed. Ethnic populations frequently are characterized by regional and economic differences that introduce inequalities between them. To reinforce these inequalities by establishing ethnically segregated social, cultural, and political organizations would block the emergence of shared interests and force all lines of conflict to converge around ethnic identity, making it more difficult for the elite leaderships of ethnic communities to engage in deliberate joint efforts to stabilize the political system. This was the experience of both the former Yugoslavia in the late 1980s and Bosnia-Herzegovina in the period following the 1990 elections.

Both the Yugoslav and the Czechoslovak experiences suggest the disintegrative potential of building a multiethnic political order on consociational principles in the absence of forces that bind the ethnic communities together. Furthermore, they alert us to the acute danger inherent in formulas that grant ethnic elites unconstrained veto power over common decisionmaking processes while insulating them from the influence of their mass constituencies.

From the 1970s on, Yugoslavia was an extreme example of the devolution of power to federal units and decisionmaking among regional representatives based on consociational principles.[39] Cooperation between the regional leaderships stabilized the system in the period immediately after the death of Tito in 1980. But by 1986, the clash of regional economic interests and inequalities, perceived as ethnic issues, had eroded that cooperation. Consociational principles of decisionmaking gave each regional leadership a veto over federal policy. The result was the political paralysis of the center.

Extensive devolution gave each leadership the ability to pursue independent development strategies in its own region. This resulted in the erosion of cross-regional, integrative economic interests. With the already-noted exception of Slovenia, there were few pluralistic political tendencies within the regions to moderate the rise of authoritarian, separatist nationalisms. In effect, to the degree that the structural characteristics of the Yugoslav system approximated the consociational model, they hastened that system's demise by preventing the emergence of economic and political counterweights to nationalism among the dominant population in each of the regions, thereby eliminating incentives for elite cooperation across regions.[40]

In Czechoslovakia, the federalization of the state carried out by the communists in 1969 had given extensive veto power over the legislative and constitutional decisionmaking processes to each of the republics. All legislation affecting the interests of the republics and all constitutional changes could be vetoed by as few as twenty-six representatives of either republic in its chamber of the upper house of the federal parliament. Members of the Slovak chamber of the House of Nations exploited these provisions, for example, to prevent the adoption of federal legislation that would have established a referendum procedure by which the growing stalemate between regional elites might have been circumvented by a direct appeal to the mass population.

Thus, in both Yugoslavia and Czechoslovakia, the combination of federal institutions and consociational decisionmaking arrangements placed enormous power in the hands of regional leaders and left little room for the participation of multiethnic or nonethnic political forces. It also insulated political leaderships intent on secession from popular sentiments against it.

In Yugoslavia, the growth of a nonethnic "Yugoslav" identity suggested the emergence of a shared civil identity in the country. Unpublished results from surveys conducted in all the Yugoslav republics in 1988 revealed widespread popular belief that the growth of such feelings deserved support as a means of resolving ethnic issues. But this was ignored, and even opposed, by political leaderships wedded to ethnically defined constituencies. Similarly, in Czechoslovakia, all public opinion survey data indicated that the majority of the populations in both republics favored preserving the unified state.[41] A September 1991 poll, for example, indicated that 48 percent of Czechs and 35 percent of Slovaks would "definitely" have voted yes in a referendum on maintaining the federation, while only 4 percent of Czechs and 10 percent of Slovaks would "definitely" have voted no.[42] However, elites determined to achieve the dissolution of the union exploited their veto power over the federal decisionmaking process to prevent this question from being decided by popular referendum.

In short, strategies of devolution appear not to be effective for securing democracy in ethnically divided states in the absence of other cleavages that cut across the ethnic division(s), establish interests that unite ethnic populations, and act as constraints on elite behavior. This suggests that under conditions of ethnic diversity, leaders may best encourage democratization by legitimating common institutions through democratic electoral processes and fostering the emergence of interests that cut across ethnic cleavages before embarking on devolution or the democratization of local elections.

BUILDING DEMOCRATIC INSTITUTIONS

Whether they are consociational or pluralistic, democratic regimes must be inclusionary in character. Yet many of the post-communist states have adopted constitutional provisions and citizenship and language laws that have the effect of excluding minority populations from political life and reinforcing the power and privileges of the ethnic majority.[43] In Estonia, the potential political power of ethnic Russians has been legally voided because the leadership simply declared an unbroken legal continuity between the post-Soviet and prewar states. Estonian citizenship was extended by laws adopted in late 1991 and early 1992 to all individuals who were citizens in 1938 and their descendants. This was done regardless of ethnicity but was clearly intended to negate the citizenship of the vast majority of Russians, who migrated to, or were born in, the republic after 1938. Those excluded were granted three years in which to apply for citizenship. Applicants must pass an Estonian language examination, and they must have been resident in Estonia for two years. There is a further one-year waiting period for citizenship.

The citizenship law restricts the right to vote in national elections to citizens only, thereby disenfranchising large proportions of the non-Estonian population until they have completed the naturalization process. The Estonian constitution limits the right to hold public office, to be employed in the upper civil service or police, and to be a member of a political party to citizens only. Such disenfranchisement, even if only temporary, reinforces the political dominance of ethnic Estonians in their own state during the critical period in which a new political order is being institutionalized. Moreover, legislation adopted by the Estonian parliament in 1993 calling for an end to the use of Russian as a language of instruction in public secondary education by the year 2000 and legislation requiring all noncitizens to apply for registration and work permits increased the pressure on ethnic Russians to leave the republic, despite the fact that the first legislation was blocked by Estonia's president and the second was partially moderated in reaction to criticism from the Council of Europe.[44]

The laws of Latvia and Lithuania are similarly exclusionary. The Lithuanian citizenship law passed in December 1991 grants citizenship to all residents of the republic prior to June 1940 and their descendants, and to all residents of the present territory of Lithuania from 1919 to June 1940, so long as they are not citizens of another country. Naturalization requires knowledge of Lithuanian, permanent residence in Lithuania for the previous ten years, legal employment in the country, and a loyalty oath. The Latvian law also grants citizenship to citizens of the interwar republic and their descendants. The guidelines for naturalization include a sixteen-year residency requirement, proof that an individual is not a citizen of another country, a language examination, and a loyalty oath. The guidelines also declare ineligible broad categories of people who served the communist regime in various capacities. The exclusionary character of the Latvian citizenship laws is clearly discriminatory with respect to the Russian population in the republic. It has imposed significant economic disadvantages on resident Russians and has contributed to their political alienation.[45]

Laws establishing the language of the majority as the official language of the state have been adopted in several states in Eastern Europe. In Slovakia, the adoption in October 1990 of a law declaring Slovak the official language of the republic contributed to the escalation of tensions between the majority Slovak population and the substantial Hungarian minority. The legislation entitles citizens to use Czech in official dealings but restricts the official use of other minority languages to those cities in which the minority population constitutes at least 20 percent of the total. This represents a step backward from conditions under the old regime, when minorities were entitled to use their own languages, regardless of their number. The Slovak legislation exempts public officials from having to achieve proficiency in minority languages and directs that public documents are to be prepared in the official (Slovak) language. Moreover, it mandates the use of Slovak in state and local institutions, thereby undercutting the already limited rights of minorities to use their own language.[46] More radical nationalists had sought to ban the use of any language other than Slovak in official communications.

The language law in Slovakia is symptomatic of a deep hostility toward the Hungarian minority among the Slovak majority. Legislative debate on the language law was the occasion for angry street demonstrations and counterdemonstrations between nationalists and supporters of minority rights.[47] These demonstrations were a clear signal of the potentially disruptive consequences of official discrimination against the Hungarian minority. Nonetheless, the Slovak leadership proceeded to adopt a new constitution for the republic in September 1992 that gives the Slovaks privileged status. The new constitution locates sovereignty in the Slovak nation rather than in the citizens of the republic. More ominously, it restricts the civil rights of ethnic minorities in instances when the exercise of such rights might "endanger the sovereignty and territorial integrity of the Slovak republic or cause discrimination against the rest of the population."[48]

Similarly, the constitutions of the Yugoslav successor states affirm the right of their dominant ethnic groups to self-determination, identify the state as the expression of ethnic sovereignty, and assert the "official" status of the national language.[49] In Croatia, these provisions are reinforced by a citizenship law that discriminates against non-Croats by linking citizenship to ethnic origin and requiring non-Croats to accept Croatian culture.[50]

If the post-communist governments of Eastern Europe and the former Soviet Union are to move from nationalist to democratic bases of legitimation, such exclusionary practices will have to be replaced by attempts to integrate minorities into political life on an equal basis. The approach of the new government of Ukraine to questions of minority rights, for example, is based on careful attention to inclusiveness and equality. Ukrainian language legislation adopted in 1989 and affirmed in 1991, for example, establishes Ukrainian as the state language of the republic and establishes Russian as the language of interethnic communication. But it also guarantees the free development of all national languages, including their "active and equal use in various spheres of life."[51] This inclusive approach to the use of languages other than Ukrainian helps explain why the large Russian population of Ukraine has continued to support the new regime. A recent survey of minority policies in Ukraine concludes that such liberal treatment has contributed to preventing ethnic conflict.[52]

In democratic political systems, political parties and party systems are among the most important vehicles for the institutionalization of mass political participation. The nature of the electoral system is an important factor determining whether parties that aggregate interests across ethnic groups, moderate the behavior of political leaders, and encourage interethnic accommodation can be established or sustained in a multiethnic state. On issues highly salient to communal identity, the mass electorate in a multiethnic state is likely to vote along strictly communal lines. Simple majoritarian or plurality-based systems would thus reduce elections to little more than a reflection of the ethnic demography, leaving minority groups with little hope that their interests could be safeguarded against abuse at the hands of the majority.

This was precisely the outcome of the elections in Bosnia-Herzegovina in 1990. Electoral support for the ethnically based parties reflected the relative demographic strengths of their respective ethnic constituencies. The Muslim-based Party of Democratic Action, with 36 percent of the popular vote, won 86 out of the 240 seats in the two chambers of parliament. The Serbian Democratic Party, with about 30 percent of the vote, won seventy-two seats. The Croatian Democratic Union secured 18 percent of the vote and forty-four seats. The reformed Communists secured nineteen seats, and the Alliance of Reform Forces, twelve. The remaining seven seats were split among five parties.[53] Similarly, in the referendum conducted at the end of February 1992 to satisfy EC demands for a demonstration of popular support for independence, Muslims and Croats voted for independence, while Serbs boycotted the referendum out of the certain knowledge that a simple majority vote would reduce them to the status of a permanent minority.

While simple majoritarian and plurality-based electoral systems display inherent deficiencies with respect to the representation of minority populations, proportional representation systems vary widely in their potential effects. In the absence of carefully constructed thresholds that preclude the representation of small parties, for example, proportional representation systems encourage fragmentation rather than interest aggregation, and political polarization rather than alliance building.[54]

Political scientist Donald Horowitz has rightly observed that, so far as interethnic cooperation is concerned, "absent incentives, politicians will not engage in intergroup compromise in a severely divided society."[55] He argues that incentives to interethnic compromise and cooperation can be created by the adoption of an electoral system that allows moderate candidates to appeal across ethnic boundaries and voters to apportion their support on the basis of political, as well as ethnic, considerations. Horowitz proposes a system in which voters cast ballots for individual candidates (rather than for party lists) in order of preference. Votes for each candidate in excess of those necessary to secure election would, in his system, be transferred to the candidates next in line according to voter preferences.

Extremist parties or extremist candidates cannot extend their appeal beyond their ethnic constituencies and usually do not even enjoy the support of all members of their own group. Moderates, in contrast, can appeal for votes across ethnic lines. The system proposed by Horowitz would allow moderate candidates from different ethnic groups to pool their votes and thus maximize the scope of their electoral support. They could enter into agreements with other ethnic moderates to encourage their respective supporters to choose moderates from other ethnic groups as a second or third preference over extremists from their own group. The importance of second and third preferences, Horowitz points out, is increased if an electoral majority is required for victory. This increases the chances that electoral victory will depend on a candidate's ability to secure the second or third preferences of voters. Such dependence on broad electoral support to achieve power would create a clear incentive for individual candidates and parties to negotiate interethnic compromises.[56]

For such an electoral system to produce moderation, however, several conditions appear to be necessary. Where one group constitutes a clear majority of the population, support in that group for moderation must be sufficient to prevent an extremist party or candidate from securing an electoral victory on the basis of first preferences. Even then, the votes to be gained by moderate candidates through interethnic cooperation must be sufficient to establish an electoral majority. This suggests the importance of ethnically heterogeneous constituencies. It was in ethnically heterogeneous counties of Yugoslavia, for example, that the phenomenon of "Yugoslav" identity was strongest in 1981.

In the end, however, such a system "depends on the willingness of voters to think in terms of second and third best."[57] Under such conditions, Horowitz argues, "the need for interparty agreements to exchange votes" would produce "a pull toward the center of the system that would help counter polarization."[58] Even in Bosnia-Herzegovina, it is important to remember that in the 1990 elections, prior to the onset of violence, significant proportions of the electorates in the counties voted for moderate, nonnationalist, and interethnic parties. If electoral rules are drafted with moderation in mind, it might be possible to strengthen the role of such forces in an ethnically divided system—at least when elections are carried out in advance of escalating conflict. Electoral rules and the definition of electoral districts are thus important means for creating incentives to interethnic cooperation. One must acknowledge, however, that once identities have become politicized, electoral competition is likely to contribute to their mobilization by competing leaderships and, hence, to the intensification of conflict.

Not only the timing of elections is important. The sequence of elections to different levels of the political system may also establish incentives to ethnic cooperation. In Yugoslavia, for example, competitive elections were initiated at the republic level, where appeals to nationalism offered immediate benefits. No democratic elections to federal office were held. Prior or simultaneous elections for federal office might have offered the opportunity to democratize and legitimate the federation. Moderate leadership might have been encouraged if national candidates had been required to secure concurrent electoral majorities in a majority of the regions. Simultaneous federal and regional elections might even have moderated the power of nationalist forces in the republics. In Czechoslovakia, the simultaneous elections for federal and regional offices demonstrated the different dynamics of such elections. Simultaneous elections contributed to the dispersion of power among several parties and the pluralization of politics in each of the republics, as well as at the federal level.

The problem of the permanent minority may also be addressed through innovative approaches to decisionmaking rules in representative institutions. Political scientist James Coleman, for example, has suggested a system of organizing parliamentary voting that is designed to allow numerical minorities—such as the representatives of ethnic minorities—to outvote majorities on some, but not all, issues.[59] He proposes a cumulative voting scheme in which each member of parliament would be provided with an equal number of fungible votes, any number of which could be voted on any issue. When a bill is passed, those who voted against it are compensated by the return of their votes for later use. Those who supported the bill relinquish the number of votes they allocated for it. When a bill is defeated, compensation is reversed. Coleman argues that "legislators who represented minority interests would not be subject to continual oppression from the majority. By building up their accounts on issues where they have some interests and bid those interests but lose, they come to be in a position to employ their [votes], with a good likelihood that they will win, on an issue on which they have very strong interests and the majority interest is less strong."[60]

Such an approach to legislative voting avoids the institutionalization of a minority veto inherent in consociational systems. It does not allow representatives of a minority group simply to exercise a blanket veto and thereby paralyze the political system. In cumulative voting schemes at the mass level, minorities could logically be expected always to cumulate their votes, but the fact that members of parliament must vote on many issues ensures that the act of cumulating votes entails clear political costs. It compels representatives to weigh the relative importance of particular issues and increases the incentive to bargaining across the minority-majority divide.

If implemented against the background of an electoral system structured to increase incentives for cooperation, it might prevent ethnic considerations from overwhelming other interests in the political process. This is an especially important consideration for many of the post-communist states. The rapid collapse of the old regimes left little time for local actors to build organizations based on economic and other nonethnic interests or for politicians to build links to them. Such interests are underrepresented in many of the post-communist legislatures.

No single formula can be expected to work in all countries. Democratic electoral and decisionmaking rules and procedures must be adapted to suit local conditions. But each variation must be constructed so as to include populations on the basis of full political equality.

TOWARD POLITICAL PLURALISM?

The abstract issues that dominated the initial politics of the successor states, such as "democracy" and "participation," offered little basis for political opposition. Nor were they easily translatable into policy outputs by which the success or failure of an incumbent leadership or party might be measured. Issues surrounding economic transformation, especially the performance of governments with respect to securing the material well-being of the population after several years of incumbency, offer stronger bases for the emergence of differentiated interests.

Protecting the interests of the industrial workforce in the transition to private ownership and a market-based economy represents the most obvious basis on which to organize interest-based politics. Historically, class-based parties provided the most powerful alternative in West European political development to parties based on ethnic, religious, or cultural identities. In some post-communist states, nationalist forces have sought to occupy this political space themselves by substituting the collectivist appeals of nationalism for those of class. Elsewhere, former communist parties have exploited popular dissatisfaction with the material consequences of economic change to secure electoral support and, in Lithuania, Poland, and Hungary, to secure governmental power. Pensioners and public employees, a larger proportion of the electorate in some post-communist states than in the West, as well as private farmers are also hard hit by the effects of reform in some states and have expressed their discontent at the polls. Thus, interest-oriented politics based on the aggregation of interests through modern political parties is developing in some of the post-communist states.

In Czechoslovakia, the June 1992 elections reflected the breakup of the anticommunist coalition that had dominated the first free elections in 1990. They produced a clear differentiation between right-of-center and left-of-center parties in each republic. The simultaneous victories of the democratic right in the Czech Republic and the national left in Slovakia hastened the breakup of the federation.

In Slovenia, the coalition of prodemocracy forces that took power in the initial free elections in 1990 also succumbed to internal divisions. The collapse of the Demos coalition under Prime Minister Lojze Peterle of the Christian Democrats in December 1991 led to a successful parliamentary vote of no confidence in the government and the establishment of an interim government under Janez Drnovsek of the Liberal Democrats. The results of the first postindependence elections, held in December 1992, were inconclusive.[61] After several months of negotiations, the Liberal Democrats forged a five-party governing coalition with the right-of-center Christian Democrats, the Unity List (a coalition of center-left groups and former communists), the Social Democrats, and the Green Party. Drnovsek remained as prime minister and Peterle became deputy prime minister and foreign minister. Although this coalition commanded a majority of sixty out of ninety seats in parliament, it united two parties with heretofore incompatible ideological and political perspectives and competing leaders.[62]

Slovenia thus successfully crossed a number of thresholds in the transition to democracy. A democratic opposition successfully gained power in the period of authoritarianism. It carried out the functions of a ruling government and submitted to the legitimate authority of parliament by relinquishing power to a loyal opposition following a vote of no confidence. Moreover, free and fair competitive elections have confirmed the transfer of power from one coalition of parties to another. However, although political parties appear to be coalescing around ideological and programmatic distinctions, the governing coalition remains internally divided and, therefore, inherently unstable.

The threat of nationalist authoritarianism also remains very real in Slovenia. The extreme nationalist Slovenian National Party gained almost 9 percent of the vote and ten seats in parliament in 1992 by exploiting difficult economic conditions. Unemployment was approaching 12 percent at the time of the elections, and the standard of living had dropped to below 1972 levels. The party mounted an ethnocentric campaign, alleging that foreigners were taking jobs

away from Slovenes and advocating discriminatory measures against them.

The National Party appears to have lost its appeal in recent years (it polled only 4 percent of the popular vote in local elections held in December 1994), but nationalism has not.[63] Discussions with a broad cross-section of Slovenian political figures, activists, intellectuals, and citizens in Ljubljana in June 1994 revealed a strong desire in many quarters to protect sectors of the Slovenian economy, especially agriculture, from outside competition. Similarly, there was widespread concern—understandable among a people who number less than two million—over the effects of outside influences on Slovenian culture. The presence of large numbers of Bosnian refugees was repeatedly noted as "a problem," as was the presence of refugee/émigré populations from "the south" more generally. One opposition political leader pointed out that Slovenia's citizenship law—notable for its liberal character in comparison to those adopted by other formerly communist states, especially neighboring Croatia's—had produced a 10 percent increase in the number of "new citizens," and he suggested it should be made more restrictive. Declining economic conditions in the country may reinforce these ethnocentric attitudes and make them a more important political force. This leader's party, the Slovenian People's Party, secured 12 percent of the December vote. A significant improvement in economic conditions may therefore be necessary to protect democratic tolerance against ethnocentrism in Slovenia.

The elections in Lithuania in late 1992, in Hungary in May 1994, and in Estonia in March 1995 exemplified the power of economic issues in mobilizing support for nonnationalist parties once independence has been secured. In Lithuania, the Sajudis coalition of opposition forces had won an overwhelming victory over the Communist Party in the 1990 elections and assumed control of the government. It led Lithuania to full independence in September 1991. But, following a period of increasing fragmentation among the factions within the coalition, parliament decided in June 1992 to call early elections. By this time, the reformed communists had reori-

ented themselves toward social democratic positions, attracted new noncommunist supporters, and renamed themselves the Lithuanian Democratic Labor Party (LDLP). Combining support from both the Lithuanian and the minority populations, the LDLP won a decisive electoral victory, securing an absolute majority of seats in the parliament.[64] Thus, by the end of 1992, Lithuania, like Slovenia, had achieved an important milestone in the consolidation of a democratic regime: the transfer of power from incumbents to opposition through the electoral process. Material interests had begun to play a central role in defining the patterns of political support, and cross-ethnic alliances had produced an electoral majority. Moreover, the shock of electoral defeat led some elements of the Sajudis coalition to form a more traditional political party.[65]

The Hungarian elections of May 1994 produced an overwhelming electoral victory for the Socialist Party, which was built on the former reformist wing of the Communist Party. The Socialists won 209 of 386 seats in parliament and therefore the opportunity to govern alone. However, they chose instead to enter into a coalition with the liberal, center-left Alliance of Free Democrats, which had won seventy seats and was the second largest party in parliament. The former ruling party, the center-right Hungarian Democratic Forum (HDF), which had previously achieved a dominant position by winning 164 seats in the 1990 elections and forging a coalition government with the more conservative and nationalist Christian Democratic and peasant parties, suffered a crushing defeat, winning only 37 seats. Only three of these were the results of victories in individual districts. Even more striking, an extreme nationalist party formed by a breakaway faction of the HDF failed to win even one seat. Although these results reflected the Hungarian electorate's overwhelming dissatisfaction with the economic performance of the first democratic government, they also demonstrated its unwillingness, for now, to turn to extremist alternatives. As one political observer explained in an interview in Budapest in June 1994, nationalist leader Istvan Csurka "was good at posing questions, but his answers were catastrophic." Simply put, economic issues appear to

have dominated other considerations in the minds of Hungarian voters.

While the victory of the Socialists and the defeat of the nationalists in Hungary offer hope for the emergence of a more pluralist, interest-based politics, these developments also suggest caution with respect to any prediction about the future. The electorate in Hungary has proven highly volatile. In an interview conducted in June 1994 in Budapest, one Hungarian survey researcher reported that a third of the electorate had voted for center-right or rightist candidates in 1990, switched to the radical opposition in 1992 local elections, and voted center-left or leftist in 1994. If domestic economic conditions worsen, or if external stimuli contribute to the politicization of Hungarian national identity, nationalist politicians may yet be able to secure power by appealing to collectivist, authoritarian, and economic egalitarian inclinations in the population.

The apparent progress in the Czech Republic, Slovenia, Lithuania, and Hungary toward institutionalizing democratic, competitive party systems based on the representation of material as well as national interests may reflect the greater internal homogeneity of these countries and the relatively more peaceful international contexts in which they are located compared to other parts of the post-communist world. The influence of internal divisions and external pressures is reflected in the still central role of national issues in the politics of Slovakia, Latvia, Estonia, Croatia, and Serbia. Croatian and Serbian political developments underscore the important role territorial conflict and ethnic violence play in sustaining the appeal of extreme nationalist positions and in preventing the transition from nationalist to democratic bases of legitimation.

In the September 1992 elections in Estonia, the electorate spread its support among several parties. With the ethnic Russian population effectively excluded from the electoral process, nationalist issues were subordinated to questions of economic policy, and the elections produced a clear victory for supporters of economic reform.[66] Nationalist concerns were revived, however, by the results of the local elections held in October 1993.[67] Noncitizens were permitted to participate in the local elections, and the Russian population took advantage of this opportunity, turning out in greater proportions than Estonians to capture twenty-seven of sixty-four seats on the city council of Tallinn. These results might have stimulated Russian demands for political equality and possibly increased separatist tendencies in Narva. They did produce an immediate escalation in the nationalist rhetoric of Estonian leaders. But the fact that the Russian population split its support between moderates and nationalists raised the possibility that political equality for the Russian population of Estonia might produce an alliance between the nonnationalist Estonian population and Estonia-oriented Russians.

This possibility was further enhanced by the results of the March 1995 elections in Estonia, which produced a shift in voter support away from extremist politics and toward the politics of interest.[68] Plummeting support for the parties of government reflected the political salience of hardships imposed by its radical reform policies. The largest share of the vote went to parties representing the interests of farmers and pensioners, two groups hit hardest by the elimination of state subsidies. With only 41 out of 101 parliamentary seats, however, the Coalition Party-Rural Union was compelled to form a coalition government with the Estonian Center Party, whose support for continued economic reform ensures that the new government will attempt only to soften the effects of reform, not abandon it. The elections also produced a significant diminution of nationalist politics. Radical, exclusivist Estonian nationalist forces are no longer represented in parliament, while a moderate coalition of pro-Estonian Russian groups gained five seats. The Estonian electorate thus also appears to be moving toward a politics of interest, but without turning toward the former communists.

Politics in Croatia in the period following the 1990 elections was dominated by the conflicts surrounding the collapse of Yugoslavia. From the outset, President Tudjman and the ruling Croatian Democratic Union (CDU) displayed a strong tendency toward authoritarianism. The government purged Serbs and others it alleged to be representatives of the old order from positions of public responsibility, harassed political opponents, and sought to suppress criticism in the media. Its efforts to establish tight central control over local communities led it almost immediately into confrontation with the rising nationalist separatism of the Serbs in the Krajina region.[69]

The de facto loss of almost a quarter of the republic's territory to the Krajina Serbs as the result of the ensuing war and the establishment of the UN-protected areas appeared to strengthen the most extreme nationalist, and even fascist, elements in Croatian politics. However, Tudjman and the CDU reaffirmed their domination of Croatian politics by calling and winning early elections in August 1992.[70] Tudjman and the CDU benefited from the prestige and nationalist appeal of having guided Croatia to independence and having led the nation in war. They also benefited from structural characteristics of the electoral system that favored the CDU as the largest of Croatia's political parties. Sixty of the 138 seats in the lower house of parliament were allocated proportionally among national party lists. This weighted the electoral process heavily in favor of the CDU. Sixty additional seats were allocated on a first-past-the-post basis in individual districts, further weighting the process in favor of the CDU. The CDU won 43.7 percent of the vote for national lists and secured thirty-one of the sixty seats allocated proportionally, and it swept fifty-four of the sixty seats allocated in individual electoral districts. These results gave it a dominant, 85-seat majority out of a total 120 seats. However, the CDU, a coalition of several distinct political groupings, is almost certain to share the fate of the Civic Forum-Public against Violence coalition in Czechoslovakia, the Sajudis coalition in Lithuania, and the Demos coalition in Slovenia.

In the short run, the successful military reconquest of the Serb-occupied Krajina will reinforce nationalism and strengthen the CDU in Croatia. In the longer run, and especially following the de facto partition of Bosnia-Herzegovina and the creation of a "greater Croatia," Croatian politics will inevitably become focused on issues arising out of economic reconstruction and social and political reconciliation between Croats and Serbs. These are tasks for which the CDU is ill suited. Indeed, President Tudjman's policies have already alienated key sources of Western economic assistance.[71]

Signs of fragmentation within the CDU were already apparent in the spring of 1994, when two prominent members occupying leadership positions in the party and the parliament broke away to form their own opposition party. An overall realignment of political forces in the republic could increase the importance of the ethnic Serb population that remains in the urban centers of Croatia in the construction of an effective democratic opposition alliance and provide the impetus for Croat-Serb reconciliation within Croatia.

In Serbia, the strength of nationalist-authoritarian forces is even more pronounced and the prospects for democratic changes weaker and more distant. As the war continued in Bosnia and the ravages of war and international sanctions produced worsening economic conditions in Serbia, popular support for nationalist extremism increased between the elections held in 1990 and those held in December 1992. By the spring of 1993, the democratic opposition had been completely marginalized, and there was little hope that it would assume a significant role in Serbian politics until the wars in Croatia and Bosnia-Herzegovina and international economic sanctions are brought to an end. Even as these developments drew closer in the fall of 1995, however, there were few signs that Slobodan Milosevic's grip on power in Serbia would soon be broken.

OR ONE-PARTY DEMOCRACY?

Ethnic exclusion and ethnic violence are not the only obstacles to democratization in the post-communist states. The successor regimes have inherited social orders heavily dominated by the state. While most public attention in the West has been focused on the institutionalization of electoral competition and the privatization of ownership, another important part of the effort to democratize the post-communist states must be an attempt to break the dominance of established elites over a country's economic, cultural, and political institutions and to establish a genuinely pluralistic social order. Studies of one-party dominant regimes in the West make it clear that a party that controls government over long periods is able to use the powers of incumbency, even in an institutionalized democracy, to "reshape society in its own image, to reward its adherents, and to deny such rewards to its opponents."[72] Under conditions of transition, when the most fundamental characteristics of the socioeconomic and political systems are being established anew, the opportunities to use incumbency to perpetuate the power of a coherent ruling group are multiplied. The ability of a newly elected party to perpetuate its power is further strengthened if it establishes cooperative relations or a political alliance with the bureaucratic elites of the old regime. Such an alliance makes it even more difficult to create either a civil society or a liberal democratic political culture. Elite continuity between old regime and new is characteristic of several of the post-communist states.[73]

In Hungary, for example, the policies of the first post-communist governing party, the Hungarian Democratic Forum, contributed to the recentralization of power in the state bureaucracies, rather than its dispersal through pluralization of the socioeconomic order. In June 1992, the government established a government-run company to manage those enterprises in which the state will retain 25 percent to 100 percent ownership. The company's directors were to be appointed by and responsible to the prime minister rather than to parliament. Some enterprises in the state's portfolio were to be run directly by state ministries or the prime minister's office.[74] These arrangements afforded the government great leeway in the management of a large share of the country's most important economic assets, including control over appointments to thousands of managerial positions that might easily be dispensed as patronage to party supporters. Indeed, opposition leaders argued that the government was using these resources in precisely these ways to advance its own political agenda. State control over banks and industrial enterprises allowed the government to direct ostensibly private capital toward the funding of projects and activities, including the establishment of sympathetic media, that enhanced its support.

Such structural arrangements reinforced the party leaders' intolerance of opposition views. In September 1990, for example, Hungarian foreign minister Geza Jeszenszky "declared dissent in general, but social democracy and liberal politics in particular, un-Hungarian, and defined the notion of 'Hungarian' in only Christian terms."[75] Such intolerance of pluralistic tendencies is further reinforced when there is extensive continuity between the socioeconomic elite of the old regime, with its authoritarian political culture, and that of the new. In Hungary, the new regime relied extensively on existing bureaucratic organizations.[76]

The combination of such elite continuity with state domination of the economy is far more likely to lead to the establishment of new authoritarian party-states than to the consolidation of pluralist democracies. Too great a role for the state across too many arenas of social life suppresses the process of pluralization that is essential to democratic politics. In a multiethnic environment, widening the scope of state activity reduces opportunities for the expression of ethnic identity independently of involvement on the part of public authorities. Extensive state penetration of society converts private activities into objects of public policy, leading inevitably to their politicization. An important part of the process of democratizing post-communist states and depoliticizing ethnic identities, therefore, must be to create broad areas of cultural and other activities usually associated with the preservation of ethnic identities that are free from control by the state. In effect, the private sphere must be expanded, while the public is reduced.

In Hungary, the assumption of governmental power by the Socialist-Free Democratic coalition promised to bring a number of important policy initiatives to reduce the role of the state. The most dramatic of these was the expected freeing of the media from government control. In interviews conducted in Budapest in June 1994, while the coalition was still being negotiated, well-informed observers reported that the Socialists also intended to remove the privatization agencies from the direct control of the cabinet, subordinating them instead to parliament. This would reduce the vulnerability of the privatization process to political manipulation by the ruling party. Both moves could have been expected to contribute to democratization in Hungary.

Unfortunately, the Socialist-led government has failed to make progress in either of these two important areas. Legislation to free the media remains stalled as the government has proved unable to reach agreement on draft legislation, either internally or with the other political parties.[77] Privatization remained subject to political intervention. In early 1995, for example, the prime minister intervened to prevent the conclusion of an agreement to sell ownership of a major hotel chain to American investors, ostensibly because he considered the properties undervalued, but probably because of increasing popular resentment of foreign ownership.[78] Since then, the privatization process has been streamlined and concentrated in a single agency, but little additional progress has taken place.

But the new Hungarian government continues to face a daunting economic task. With the economy in decline, it confronts the need for price increases, devaluation, tax increases, and reduced domestic consumption. In short, it must impose austerity measures on a population that elected it as a protest against economic decline. In order to avoid social disruption, the government may seek to establish a "social pact" with employers and trade unions, relying on the close connections between the Socialist Party and the formerly communist unions, as well as on the presence of many former communists among the managerial elite. While such a pact might enable the government to impose the austerity measures necessary to achieve economic stabilization and recovery, it could also represent a direct threat to the development of a pluralist democracy. It raises the potential for Hungary to develop in the direction of a more corporatist state. And it carries the potential for institutionalizing the domination of the Socialist Party.

CONCLUSION

The consolidation of democratic regimes in the post-communist states will thus entail both processes of integration and processes of differentiation. The internal differentiation of ethnic communities can be achieved if the interests that cut across ethnic lines are multiplied, and if the representation of such interests in the political process is facilitated. The integration of formerly warring states into a single European community after World War II represents the most successful example of such integration. The success of this process depended on the existence of a multiplicity of autonomous interests throughout society, the ability of transnational organizations to deliver benefits to their constituencies, and the existence of political leaderships committed to transnational integration in each of the member states. The material benefits of cooperation contributed to the emergence of popular support for the EC and lent it a political legitimacy that moderated the appeal of ethnic, or national, identity as a basis for mobilizing interests.

The establishment of a new basis of political legitimation that can compete with the emotional appeal of national loyalties and that is rooted in the pragmatic desire for material benefit is essential to the European integration process. Individuals with established interests that cut across ethnic boundaries are likely to be concerned about the potentially costly material consequences of establishing barriers to economic activity, and to be less supportive of divisive political action, especially secession. Like Western Europe after World War II, Eastern Europe now faces a prolonged period of economic recovery and redevelopment. Domestic political leaders, as well as international actors prepared to support them, can encourage ethnic integration by shaping economic development projects at all levels so as to foster the growth of material interests that cut across ethnic boundaries. Some projects, such as improving environmental conditions, require large-scale cooperative efforts that lend themselves naturally to this goal. Others, however, must be consciously constructed with this goal in mind. Economic assistance to the post-communist states, especially future postwar reconstruction projects in the former Yugoslavia and the Caucasus, can be used to encourage ethnic cooperation, just as the United States used the Marshall Plan to encourage cooperative relations between West European states.

The historical pattern of democratic development in the West has involved the spread of private ownership, the proliferation of interests, the concomitant development of bargaining and negotiating cultures associated with the operation of markets, the gradual mobilization of mass participation through political parties and other institutions, and improving regime performance to meet the increased material demands of the population. The democratic states of the West faced the challenges inherent in the development of these capacities serially, rather than simultaneously. Although the precise sequence varied from state to state, the establishment of markets and the pressures for moderation and compromise inherent in the pursuit of material interests through exchange relationships generally preceded the onset of mass participation. Thus, it can be argued that the social and economic characteristics of society shaped the development of national political institutions in the West.

The integration of nation-states into a broader, multinational European community, however, reflects in large part the opposite process: the power of institutions to shape societies. The institutions of the European Community were designed by elites. Their successful operation over time—especially their effectiveness in supporting economic recovery and expansion—led nongovernmental actors to view them as important arenas for the pursuit of their material interests, and national governments to depend on them to achieve their own performance goals. European leaders came to realize "that a doctrine of 'naive sovereignty,' that is, [keeping] all policy instruments in their own jurisdiction, [was] counterproductive." The development of effective common institutions offered individual governments "access and influence where decisions with real effects are made."[79] Thus, where common or trans-state institutions have proven effective instruments for the pursuit of national interests, European governments and political leaders have proven willing to compromise sovereignty.

The consolidation of a multinational European community and the successful democratization of West Germany suggest some important factors for the establishment of democratic regimes in the post-communist states. First, both processes benefited from the purposeful cooperation of political elites determined to overcome the past. Second, both processes suggest the importance of institutions for achieving social change. It might be argued that in the period after the end of World War II, when the West European states confronted heavy demands for performance with only limited capacities, the sociocultural foundations of civil society remained intact in most of these states. Yet the transformation of political culture and the role of institutions in achieving this have been the most dramatic in Germany, where the challenge was greatest. Third, both German and European experiences underscore the importance of material success—and external material assistance—for building pragmatic, or instrumental, support for new institutions. And finally, German and European experiences support the views expressed by political theorist David Easton, who argues that instrumental support engendered by the material outputs of specific institutions and governments can itself, over a long period, give rise to emotional, or affective, support for the political system in general.[80]

Clearly, the fact that the European and German cases are characterized by the operation of capitalist, market economies based on private property has played an important role in creating the web of material, or functional, interests that cut across ethnic, political, and even state boundaries. But as European history makes clear, market-based, capitalist economies do not by themselves guarantee the development of democracy. Moreover, the rapid establishment of a capitalist market economy entails social dislocations that have already produced volatile electorates and aggravated ethnic tensions. To secure the short-term stability of the formerly communist countries, therefore, and to de-escalate ethnic tensions and encourage long-range economic revival, we must view the consolidation of political democracy as a means of hastening the establishment of market economies, rather than rely on the latter to secure democracy. A genuinely democratic, pluralistic political order creates the means by which to establish a mixed-market economy with extensive private ownership, and thereby ensures the development of social forces that will constrain the power of the state.

CHAPTER 4

Conclusion: Toward an American Strategy for Peace

As the Yugoslav crisis has so clearly demonstrated, a stable framework for international peace in the post-Cold War era must include an institutionalized capacity to deal with the challenges to both domestic and international stability arising out of mobilized ethnic identities. The domestic challenges to post-communist states can be met through efforts to support democratization. The challenges to international stability can be met by the development of clearer and more effective multilateral mechanisms for responding to potential crises before they happen and for expanding peaceful international involvement in the resolution of conflicts as they escalate.

The international response to escalating conflict may include the use of force when its use can bring about the end of violence and redirect a conflict toward a negotiated solution. But the use of international force does not represent a long-term solution to the problem of ethnic conflict. Such solutions must be found instead in efforts to broaden the scope and character of Western influence on the internal development of post-communist political systems; the redefinition of principles of international legitimation; and the adaptation of existing multilateral military and security institutions to the tasks of preventive engagement.

America's strategic objective with respect to the post-communist states of Eastern Europe and the former Soviet Union must remain the consolidation of democracy. Economic transformation cannot be allowed to create domestic social conditions leading to the consolidation of nationalist, authoritarian regimes. Moreover, the precise path of economic change in each instance must reflect local economic, political, and social conditions, including the dynamics of interethnic relations. Nor can the United States ignore the threats to internal democracy and international peace inherent in ethnic conflict. Its policies toward the region must not only address the legitimate grievances of ethnic groups, but also contribute to constructing positive incentives for these groups and their leaders to conform to democratic norms, while establishing severe sanctions against those who violate these norms.

The Yugoslav crisis should stand as a clear reminder of the importance of American leadership for the articulation and execution of a coherent Western strategy for ensuring the spread of democracy and international peace. If the United States is not to be left to shoulder such burdens alone, however, American leadership must be applied to strengthening the capacities of multilateral Euro-Atlantic organizations and institutions to carry out the tasks of preventive engagement. In order to do so, however, American leaders must first persuade their own electorate of the economic, political, and security interests that are at stake in the region.

SOCIAL AND POLITICAL RECONSTRUCTION

In urging the adoption of a new Marshall Plan, many of those who advocate increased American involvement in and aid to the post-communist regimes of Eastern Europe and the former Soviet Union draw an analogy between these regimes today and Europe in the immediate aftermath of World War II. There is no doubt that these states need help in making the transition to market economies and political democracy. But the Marshall Plan model cannot simply be adapted to present circumstances. Nor can Western assistance be focused exclusively on economic transformation.

Western assistance has up to now concentrated on measures designed to secure the establishment of free market economies in the post-communist states in the shortest possible time. Multilateral economic institutions and individual governments have provided much-needed economic and technical assistance. But they have also demanded changes in the structure and operation of economies for which there is only limited domestic social support. The rapid imposition of strict market criteria and the privatization of economic resources have been motivated by purely economic calculations and by the belief that such a transformation is best achieved by implementing as much change as possible as quickly as possible. However, such calculations do not take into account the political consequences of the social dislocations that result from such strategies. Radical economic transformation alone will not secure democratic governments against popular discontent arising out of material hardship; nor will it protect them against internal violence between ethnic groups or the threat of renewed authoritarianism.[1]

A narrowly economic perspective based on the Marshall Plan analogy generates goals that are impossible to achieve. If economic assistance were to be provided to the post-communist states on a scale proportionate to that provided West European states under the Marshall Plan, Western assistance would amount to approximately $23 billion a year over a four-year period.[2] However, one team of international financial analysts has calculated that even under extremely optimistic assumptions about economic growth, it will take between eighteen and forty years for the successor states to "catch up" with even the least economic developed West European states. Moreover, such an achievement would require the transfer of more than *two trillion dollars* in capital investment from the West.[3] As these analysts pointed out, capital transfers of such magnitude would expose the Western economies themselves to "unbearable" dislocations. They concluded, therefore, that funding from governmental and multilateral financial institutions "can act only as catalyst in this process."[4]

Some funds may be found if a portion of the hard currency transferred from East to West each year, in repayment of debts incurred under the Communists, is earmarked for reinvestment in the region. At present, much of the hard currency assistance provided to the post-communist regimes is simply being recycled back to the West in the form of debt payments. Even if such a recycling program were to be instituted, however, the bulk of the required capital will have to come in the form of direct investment by private entities. In Eastern Europe, as elsewhere, such investment is stimulated by the promise of attractive returns on capital.

Unlike the economies of postwar Western Europe, however, the economies of the post-communist states cannot be revitalized through the infusion of capital resources alone. For such investments to take place, the successor states must institutionalize the basic cultural, political, economic, and especially legal foundations of private property and the market economy. Where these have existed before, they have been lost as the result of suppression for more than a generation; in Russia and Ukraine, they have never existed at all. Disagreements over the character of the political regimes and economies to be created, the means by which to proceed, and the consequences of actions already undertaken have produced domestic turmoil throughout the region. Such disputes over basic policy have been further complicated by demands for national self-determination on the part of ethnic groups that raise the specter of further disintegration.

These uncertainties suggest that American policy must be shaped with two assumptions in mind. First, the economic reconstruction of the post-communist states is a long-term, and perhaps very long-term, task. Second, it would be unrealistic, given the fragmentation of local political cultures and the dependence of economic outcomes on internal political forces, to expect that reconstruction of the post-communist states will reproduce American, or even West European, capitalism. The most likely outcome is the emergence of a great variety of solutions to the problems of social, economic, and political development.

The character of these solutions as well as the rate of change may vary not only from country to country, but even within individual states. The Russian Federation, for example, is especially likely, because of its enormous size and the significant regional differences in conditions, to evolve into a highly "mixed" economic, social, and political system, with continuing regional variations in the level of development. Allowing for such a multiplicity of regional outcomes may represent an effective means for governments to respond to ethnic differences.

Market-based economic development can be achieved in any number of ways, and there are a great variety of institutional arrangements among successful market-based economies. The experience of Japan and the newly industrialized countries of Asia suggests that the successor states of Eastern Europe might achieve sufficiently rapid development to stave off social disorder and, in the process, build legitimacy for the political order by allowing state institutions to play a far greater coordinative and directive role in the economy than is characteristic of the American system. As Amartya Sen, the Harvard economist and analyst of development strategies, has pointed out, "neither the purely market approach nor the relentlessly bureaucratic solution works with automatic ease" when it comes to dealing with such public goods as education, public health, and the environment. Rather than focusing on the degree of state involvement per se, Sen stresses instead "the importance of an active democracy and of a vigilant public in fostering efficiency and equity in the delivery of health care, nutritional attention, basic education, and so on and in effectively devising environmental policies."[5]

The dramatic failures of the communist regimes in these areas, he argues, "would seem to be more closely connected with the absence of democracy than with the absence of a market." Under communist rule the population was severely limited in its ability to express its dissatisfaction with the performance of state institutions charged with the responsibility for producing public goods. Poor performance produced few negative consequences for these institutions and the bureaucrats who ran them. "Adversarial pressures that a practicing democracy can generate," Sen argues, "would have given governments and public enterprises significant political incentive to deal with several important problems, including environmental protection. While democracy is rightly seen as *intrinsically* valuable . . . [it] also has an important *instrumental* role in fostering efficiency and safeguarding equity."[6] The establishment of a competitive democratic political system may thus be seen as a means not only to redress political grievances, but also to ensure that economic success produces material benefits for the population.

The challenge for American policymakers, and for those of the democratic West more generally, is to find ways to support the emergence of conditions that will encourage the stabilization of democratic regimes. The push for marketization and especially privatization cannot be allowed to undermine the flexibility new leaderships require to deal with the many uncertainties of transition. Defining the limit of state participation in the economy, for example, may be contingent on the existence of a competitive, pluralistic political system. Where a single party dominates, it may be desirable to encourage governments to draw that limit as narrowly as possible to prevent the reconsolidation of a statist, authoritarian order. Where competitive party systems are more strongly established, that limit may be drawn more widely.

The strategic importance of democratization for stabilizing international relations may require changes in the priorities assigned by Western policymakers, particularly those in the multilateral financial institutions, to the various components of economic development. A recent review of thirty years of research on the relationship between development and democracy, for example, concludes that "it is not . . . mere economic growth that is the most important developmental factor in promoting democracy. Rather, it is the dense cluster of social changes and improvements, broadly distributed among the population, that are vaguely summarized in the term '*socio*economic development.' Most important here are improvements in the physical quality and dignity of people's lives."[7]

This finding has important policy implications. As its author suggests, "Giving priority to basic human needs is not only sensible from the standpoint of economic development policy and intrinsically more humane, it is also more likely to promote or sustain democracy than more capital-intensive strategies that view basic health and literacy needs as 'consumption' that must be deferred."[8] Where the population is diverse, it is especially important to ensure that the basic human needs of all ethnic groups are being met, and that public goods are delivered equitably. Discontented or culturally threatened ethnic populations and economically disenfranchised groups resentful of the emergence of a new entrepreneurial class represent potential social bases for authoritarian movements opposed to economic and political reform. The establishment of democratic institutions would introduce important domestic incentives for governments dependent on popular electoral support to invest in socioeconomic development and prevent widespread alienation. Competitive politics, especially the transfer of power from incumbents to opposition, encourages the wider distribution of socioeconomic benefits. Political scientist Adam Przeworski, in his study of the relationship between democracy and the market in the process of reform, draws similar conclusions about the instrumental advantages of democracy for the success of economic reform in a transitional regime.[9]

One area in which the United States can take unilateral and effective action to support the growth of market economies and private ownership in the post-communist states without impinging on the flexibility of local governments is in the regulation of access to the American market. By lowering or eliminating barriers for privatized enterprises in the East, the United States can support local initiative in Eastern Europe and encourage direct investment by American companies in the region. The establishment of extensive trade relationships with emerging private enterprises in the East European economies offers longer-range strategic benefits to the United States as well. As economic recovery proceeds, these countries are certain to become important markets in which American companies will be faced with stiff European competition. The establishment of strong trade relationships now will secure American access to these markets as they revive. If these countries gain entry into the European Union, long-standing trade relationships with the United States may lead them to become proponents in EU policymaking processes of improved trade relations with the United States.

Given the central importance of preserving the dignity of East

European leaders, governments, and social groups receiving aid from the West, current programs could benefit by emulating at least one important practice under the Marshall Plan: the direct participation of the recipient countries in defining the allocation of resources. East Europeans should be understood and treated as partners in the decisionmaking processes associated with the transfer of resources from West to East. It is especially important, under conditions of scarcity, for decisions affecting specific groups—ethnic groups as well as other groups—to be made with their direct participation and under rules of procedure that have been agreed to or at least are understood in advance. The greater the role of local institutions and organizations in setting Western governmental investment and assistance priorities, the greater will be the contribution of such efforts to the pluralization and democratization of East European societies.

The Marshall Plan model can be emulated in at least one other respect: East European participants should be required to establish common priorities and forge specific agreements for the allocation of resources prior to their distribution. The successor states might even be encouraged to establish common institutions along functional lines, where appropriate. By encouraging the multilateral participation of East European states in policymaking and planning efforts, the West can contribute to the intraregional efforts at cooperation that are already under way. By supporting development projects that integrate the economies of the post-communist states, the West can foster the emergence of transnational interests. By targeting social and economic investment at projects that serve multiple ethnic communities, the West can support pluralistic approaches to intergroup integration. One of the bitter ironies of the destruction wrought by ethnic war in the Balkans is that it also creates opportunities to shape eventual recovery efforts in ways that may contribute to social reconciliation and the construction of a civil order.

Although the United States and its European allies can provide only modest levels of financial capital to the post-communist states relative to the requirements for achieving Western levels of development, they can provide higher levels of human capital and assure its availability over a longer period of time. The United States is rich in human capital. The financial resources required to make additional human resources available to Eastern Europe are relatively small, and the potential benefits of doing so are many. In addition to the direct economic benefits for Eastern Europe of American participation in local economic activities, such participation may also contribute to changes in the local political cultures. Positive, constructive, mutually beneficial contacts will expose the East European partners to American democratic values. When such contacts are sponsored or supported by Western governments, multiethnic or multicultural Western delegations can demonstrate the compatibility of diversity, democracy, and economic development.

The direct participation of Americans in the reconstruction of Eastern Europe also promises other important benefits for the United States. It will sustain and expand American expertise with respect to changing conditions in the region, a valuable resource for both government and private enterprise. The participation of Americans in the reconstruction of Eastern Europe will create a corps of professionals experienced in managing social and economic change in ways that may prove useful at home. It will broaden the bases of direct American access to the region and strengthen political ties between emergent social forces in Eastern Europe and the United States.

American expertise may be especially valuable for the establishment of what one analyst has called the "infrastructures" of a market economy.[10] These include the legal protection of property rights, business and labor law, banking and other specialized financial institutions, regulatory institutions and enforcement capabilities, information collection and distribution networks, and educational and research capacities, among others. Although American participation in this effort is already extensive, it should go further. By calling attention to the need to protect individual rights and freedoms, American business, academic, legal, and political leaders participating in the construction of the infrastructures of the market economy can contribute to the institutionalization of norms that support both democracy and free markets.

The early and sustained involvement by legal and constitutional experts from the United States and Western Europe—especially experts on the accommodation of diversity—may lead the newly established post-communist states' governments to adopt principles and procedures for the inclusion and protection of minorities. Western experts must demonstrate to these governments that by giving minority populations the hope that their interests will be accommodated, they may turn these populations into supporters of the new order.

American efforts to support the development of democratic political cultures in Eastern Europe can be strengthened further by the expansion of programs for bringing East European business, cultural, and political elites to the United States for extended exposure to American democracy. If provisions are made for ensuring that graduates return to their home countries, expanding the opportunities and funding for East Europeans to acquire higher education, especially postgraduate training, in the United States will aid democratic development in Eastern Europe and encourage closer American-East European ties. By supporting the direct participation of American faculty and students in the reconstruction of East European universities, the United States can contribute to strengthening institutions that encourage critical thinking and contribute to the pluralization of society. The Central European University in Prague and Budapest and the Inter-University Center in Dubrovnik, for example, represent precisely the kind of multiethnic, transnational efforts in support of freedom of inquiry and discourse and mutual understanding among emerging ethnic elites that deserve strong support from the United States.

For democratization to succeed, the post-communist leaderships and their populations must identify with, and adhere to, the principles of pluralism that are at the core of Western liberal democracy. It is especially important, therefore, for the United States and other democratic countries to make certain that expertise with respect to the organization and operation of competitive political parties, electoral systems, parliaments, and other democratic institutions is easily available to those social groups and national political leaders who seek it. Careful attention to the construction of representative institutions and electoral systems can contribute to interethnic cooperation and the adoption of policies that de-escalate intergroup tensions. A broad array of American initiatives on constitutionalism, democracy, and the rule of law are already under way throughout Eastern Europe.[11] These initiatives must be expanded if the social, cultural, and organizational underpinnings of a democratic order are to be secured.

A free press is centrally important to democratic development. The importance of establishing and protecting a marketplace of ideas in the mass media—that is, television and radio—is amply demonstrated by the effectiveness with which authoritarian leaders have used control over these resources to suppress criticism and deny access to alternative movements and ideas to the population at large. The continuation of government control over the mass media in Hungary, for example, has helped sustain state domination of Hungarian society and delay the consolidation of a pluralist political culture. The spread of modern communications systems, including telephones, fax machines, personal computers, and the networks they require will make it increasingly difficult for any regime to suppress the free exchange of ideas. This fact underscores the mutually supportive connections between the goals of supporting economic and technological development of the region, creating markets for American products, and encouraging the pluralization and democratization of East European societies and politics.

Western support for the large-scale reconstruction of modern communications networks, coupled with efforts to ensure the availability of communications technology, represents a powerful means by which to advance economic, social, and political change simultaneously. The almost certain involvement of state agencies in the construction of nationwide communications systems lends additional weight to the importance of supporting diverse forms of economic organization as part of the overall recovery of the region. Privatization of such strategic sectors of the economy could well be deferred until a later stage of recovery. But such state-controlled economic agencies must be staffed with economically and technologically competent leadership and subjected to the critical scrutiny of parliamentary oversight.

Successful economic reform on the scale required in the post-communist countries demands a coherent government of the sort usually made up of well-defined political parties or coalitions that enjoy a stable parliamentary majority. But it also demands the presence of other organizations and institutions, especially trade unions and professional groups, capable of producing social consent and encouraging compliance with the demands of reform, motivated by concern for their self-interest. Thus, policies that contribute to the development of the organizational attributes of a civil society contribute to both the political and economic dimensions of transformation in Eastern Europe.

Some of these recommendations might be seen as culture-bound. The application of West European and American political principles and practices to entirely distinct societies, it has been argued, represents a new form of imperialism.[12] But powerful arguments in support of the universality of human rights suggest that resistance to the cross-cultural transfer of political institutions and practices may have less to do with a reaction to cultural imperialism than with the political interests of local leaderships.[13] Indeed, authoritarian leaders, as well as democratizing leaderships, are to be found on both sides of the alleged cultural divide between Catholicism and Orthodoxy in the Balkans. Wherever national political leaderships commit themselves to democratic government, Western support can contribute to economic recovery and the pluralization of society, the construction of parliamentary and electoral institutions, the organization of democratic political parties and interest groups, and the institutionalization of safeguards for human rights without coming into conflict with local cultural values.

Little has been said here about direct assistance to the governments of the new democracies. Such assistance has been an essential element of American policy, especially with respect to support for privatization and marketization efforts and the creation of national financial institutions. But it cannot be allowed to become the exclusive, or even dominant, instrument of American efforts. Support for incumbent governments is an inherently partisan act. With few exceptions, the incumbent governments in Eastern Europe are unlikely to retain power for very long. Close support for incumbents, as distinct from support for the democratic order itself, risks alienating domestic political opponents who may later assume power. It is especially important to avoid linking aid to individuals. The fate of Mikhail Gorbachev and the results of American efforts to support him stand as clear lessons in the futility of personalized policies in an era of immense political fluidity. Even if we assume complete good faith and the best of intentions on the part of individual leaders, it may become necessary for Western governments to distance themselves from their acts when these are inconsistent with democratic government. Individual leaders cannot on their own guarantee democratic outcomes. It is far more important to concentrate on the institutionalization of social changes, direct improvements in the quality and dignity of people's lives, and the pluralization of social institutions, which can introduce powerful constraints on the reversion to authoritarianism in the post-communist states.

NATIONALISM, SELF-DETERMINATION, AND DEMOCRACY

Social and economic changes are long-term processes. The challenges to democracy in Eastern Europe are immediate. The threat of domestic violence arising out of ethnic conflict and escalating into internal war represents the most powerful of these challenges. The ability of the United States, acting through the multilateral institutions of the Euro-Atlantic community, to encourage the democratic resolution of such conflicts before they turn violent must be enhanced. Preventive engagement on the part of the United States and other stable democratic states to strengthen democratic institutions and accelerate popular socialization to democratic values in the successor states may allow emerging democracies to weather the hardships of social and economic transformation. However, such engagement requires the Euro-Atlantic states to resolve the contradictions inherent in the Cold War principles of international order, create the capacities to act in support of agreed-upon principles, and find the political will to do so.

For policymakers in both the United States and Europe, the Yugoslav crisis revealed the great difficulty of addressing the challenges of nationalist unrest and democratic transition within the framework of the existing principles of international order that were adopted in an era of superpower competition and commitment to the preservation of the status quo. Yugoslavia, for example, had long been the object of special interest and concern to American foreign policymakers because of its perceived "geostrategic value" in containing Soviet power, its political importance as an example of "reform" for other communist regimes, and its role in sustaining ethnic peace in the Balkans. With the breakup of the Soviet Union, however, Yugoslavia no longer offered any of these benefits to the West, and there was no coherent substitute for the policy of "containment" as a basis on which American and European policymakers might formulate their responses to the crisis.

International responses to the ethnic conflicts plaguing post-communist Europe, especially efforts to prevent the outbreak of violence, have been complicated by the contradictions inherent in the principles of sovereignty, territorial integrity, and national self-determination as they have been applied in the postwar era. As the Yugoslav crisis unfolded, the United States and some European states chose to focus their actions on support for the territorial status quo. Some supported the sovereignty of the Yugoslav state, while others opted to support the right of the republics to self-determination. But none appeared to focus their efforts on discovering new arrangements that might lead to the conclusion of a peaceful agreement among all parties.

By supporting principles that legitimated the position of one side or the other, Western actors reduced the incentives to compromise on all sides of the Yugoslav conflict. Interpretation of the right to self-determination as a right to independent statehood, as well as the application of this right to the federal republics of the Yugoslav state rather than to their populations, encouraged intransigence on the part of secessionist regional leaderships. Support for the right of a state to secure its territorial integrity was offered without sufficiently strong warnings—and concrete actions to back them up—that such support was contingent on adherence to the international standards of democratic legitimation that had been articulated in the context of the Helsinki process. This encouraged local supporters of the status quo to use force against their opponents. However, the insistence on the status quo failed to prevent the breakup of either the former Soviet Union or Yugoslavia. Moreover, application of the principle of self-determination to boundaries over which there was no underlying political agreement contributed to the onset of war.

The situation in Yugoslavia was especially volatile because of the nationalist alliance between Serb leaders in Croatia and Bosnia-Herzegovina and leaders of the Serbian republic and the Yugoslav army. But such cross-border and military-civilian alliances cannot be viewed as exceptional. They are also present, for example, in the Nagorno-Karabakh, Abkhazia, and Transdniester conflicts. Hungarians in Romania and Slovakia, or Russians in the Baltic and other former Soviet republics, may seek to forge cross-border alliances in the future, especially if more nationalist governments come to power in Budapest and Moscow, or the governments in Bratislava and Bucharest turn more repressive. There is already evidence that Russian military forces have provided support for, or become directly involved in, ethno-secessionist movements in the Caucasus. In all these cases, as in Yugoslavia, the status of borders imposed by communist or other authoritarian regimes without popular participation, as well as the rights of ethnic populations established under the policies and politics of the old regime, have been called into question. Strong principles must be found, other than support for the discredited status quo ante, by which to settle such questions before they turn violent.

This is not to argue, as others have,[14] in favor of subordinating principles of territorial integrity and the inviolability of borders to the right of ethnic groups to self-determination through the establishment of ethnically defined states. Precisely this approach to the former Soviet, Czechoslovak, and especially Yugoslav multiethnic states has already strengthened the international legitimacy of nationalist and exclusivist approaches to state formation. The former Yugoslavia in particular has established troublesome precedents for the several European states—West and East—that still confront local movements for ethnic autonomy or independence. Rather than supporting this process any further, the United States and other international actors, if they are to prevent the outbreak of ethnic violence and the rise of secessionist movements among the many ethnic populations of Europe and North America, must affirm the moral and political superiority of principles of human rights, and especially the rule of law, over the claim of ethnic groups that the right of self-determination demands the establishment of an independent state.[15] As ambassador Max Kampelman, a principal American participant in the CSCE process, argues, self-determination "does not include the right to change boundaries at will. . . . Within every majority seeking secession," he cautions, "there is another minority that may want to secede."[16]

A right to create a sovereign state legitimated solely on the basis of its ethnic identity does not guarantee individual freedom. On the contrary, nationalist bases of political legitimation often subordinate the individual to the collective and lead to ethnic exclusivity and political privilege. Legitimation of states based on the establishment and protection of individual human rights, in contrast, makes possible the free expression of linguistic, cultural, and ethnic identities by individuals exercising their rights in community with one another, without privileging one group over another.

Support for those who uphold human rights should therefore take priority over support for those who advance narrowly ethnic claims to self-determination. Authoritarian movements that seek to legitimate their claims to power through appeals to nationalism do not deserve the support of the international community, nor do nationalist movements that offer no greater democracy than what has already been established under an existing regime. Democracy, which may be seen as that political order which both produces, and results from, the institutionalization of individual human rights, should be treated as superior to ethnic affinity as a basis for sustaining the claims by political regimes and movements to sovereignty. Such a principle corresponds closely to that devised by Robert Dahl, the democratic theorist, in consideration of the contradictions between majority rule and minority rights in pluralist democracies.[17]

Similarly, the principle of territorial integrity should be subordinated to the principle of preserving or advancing democracy. Institutionalized protection for the internationally recognized human rights of the population—not the existence of coercive power prepared to enforce existing borders—represents the limiting criterion by which secessionist claims should be denied. International actors should refrain from extending support to any group that rejects participation in a democratic or democratizing state solely on the basis of ethnic difference. In this way, the creation of an increasing number of microstates that contribute little to the advance of human rights, and may stand in the way of economic and material development, may be avoided. The adoption and articulation of such a perspective will encourage leaderships seeking to legitimate and secure their authority over territory to do so by democratic means. When a pattern of human rights abuses by an existing political authority remains uncorrected, efforts to change the status of that authority in order to improve the human condition should be recognized and supported.

The consolidation and survival of democratic regimes in the post-communist states require the leaderships to moderate the nationalist urges of majority populations in order to meet the cultural, economic, and political demands of domestic ethnic groups. Political leaders must encourage the development of constitutional and statutory frameworks that make possible the democratic participation of ethnic minorities—understood as individuals acting in community with one another—on a fully equal basis with ethnic majorities, similarly understood. And they must ensure the protection of such equality against encroachments on the part of nationalist majorities.

This is not an easy task. The rights of individuals to act in community to advance their own culture or religion and use their own language are enshrined in the 1966 United Nations Covenant on Civil and Political Rights. These were further specified in the Copenhagen Document of the CSCE, adopted in 1990, and affirmed in the 1992 UN Declaration on the Rights of Persons Belonging to National or Ethnic, Religious and Linguistic Minorities. But the precise obligations of state authorities with respect to the expression of these rights have been in dispute from the beginning of these efforts. While the 1966 covenant includes, in Article 1, the statement that "all peoples have the right to self-determination," India introduced a formal reservation that reflected the concerns of all governments of multiethnic states: it sought to prevent the application of this principle to "sovereign independent States or to a section of a people or nation—which is the essence of national integrity."[18] The 1992 UN declaration includes the stipulation that nothing in it "may be construed as permitting activity contrary to . . . sovereign equality, territorial integrity and political independence of states."[19] Thus, the precise obligations of states remain in dispute. While it is clear that member states of the United Nations and the CSCE are expected not to discriminate against minority populations, many states oppose any requirement actively to encourage, support, or subsidize the activities of national minorities out of fear that, by strengthening minority group distinctiveness and cohesion, they will make the tasks of political integration more difficult.[20] This apparent dilemma can be resolved only by the adoption of an ethnically neutral, or civil, definition of the democratic state.

Movement toward a civil definition of the state does not mean that East European political development should be expected to converge around American concepts and practices. Indeed, it is far more likely that the East European states will develop European-style parliamentary systems or mixed parliamentary-presidential systems. The American system will, for good reasons, remain exceptional. However, certain aspects of the American political order seem particularly well suited to East European conditions. Incorporation of an explicit bill of rights in the constitutional order and the separation of powers, institutional characteristics of the American system not necessarily present in the European parliamentary systems, offer protection for individuals against arbitrary state power, safeguard the fundamental social and political conditions of a pluralist order, contribute to the rule of law, and guard against the establishment of a monolithic state in the absence of a deeply embedded culture of rights.[21] These are all important elements of the transition to democracy in Eastern Europe.

So long as the state retains the power to determine the prospects of group survival, ethnic identity will remain salient in the political struggle for control over state institutions. The depoliticization of ethnic identity therefore requires an end to the exclusive claim of the state to authority over issues affecting the survival of group identity. The state must share or relinquish control over educational curricula, cultural production, religion, and other activities associated with the preservation of group identity in order to remove such issues from political contention. East European leaderships might do so by devolving authority over, and responsibility for, such matters onto the ethnic communities themselves. The Belgian example of establishing cultural communities and granting them enhanced decisionmaking authority over issues they deem central to their identity and survival represents an important precedent in this respect.[22] Carefully constructed institutions and procedures such as cumulative voting schemes that allow representatives of minority populations the opportunity to satisfy the need to act in community in defense of their interests must, however, avoid introducing the potentially paralyzing group veto advocated by proponents of the consociational approach.

In the East European context, where ethnic and political boundaries often intersect, such an approach might be enhanced by developing new forms of interstate relations that permit ethnic communities to draw on the support of their national states to satisfy communal needs. By widening the opportunities for cultural interaction between minority ethnic populations and their national states, while simultaneously empowering such populations through democratization of the domestic political order, East European leaderships may further encourage the depoliticization of ethnic identity and defuse irredentist issues in interstate relations. The former Yugoslavia and the Federal Republic of Germany, for example, established conditions that permitted the Yugoslav government to provide a host of services to the Yugoslav *Gastarbeiter* population in Germany.[23] Although these arrangements were motivated by very different considerations, that is, the desire of a host country to ensure that a "guest" population remain attached to its homeland, similar arrangements may serve as a useful starting point elsewhere for the development of new relationships between the post-communist states of Europe.

Indeed, the right to establish cross-border contacts is included among those specified in the 1990 Copenhagen Document of the CSCE and reaffirmed in the 1992 UN declaration. However, concern on the part of governmental leaders in Eastern Europe for ethnic brethren outside their own state must be expressed first and foremost through bilateral and multilateral contacts with the host government and through support for efforts to achieve or consolidate democracy in the host state. Concern to secure the equal protection of human rights in the host country cannot be allowed to justify irredentism.

Comparison of the Yugoslav and Czechoslovak experiences suggests that partition and the adjustment of borders through peaceful negotiation may, in certain circumstances, represent an effective means of ending ethnic conflict and avoiding violence. It is certainly the case that by denying the opportunity to alter borders peacefully in response to persistent patterns of abuse, the international community may inadvertently encourage their alteration by force. But border changes or partition schemes must be considered a means of last resort.

Only the persistent failure of a host country to protect the rights of an ethnic minority, not the simple existence of an ethnically distinct community, can be accepted as justification for demands to redraw boundaries. As one Hungarian analyst argued in anticipation of the collapse of both Yugoslavia and the Soviet Union, "If territorial claims are based on historic justifications, the whole European order is immediately threatened by collapse—every country in Europe could argue for a revision of its borders by reference to some historic 'golden era.' "[24] Thus, border changes may be appropriate only in the course or the immediate aftermath of the collapse of a multiethnic state, when the shape of the successor states has not yet been determined.

What one observer has characterized as "the turmoil among theorists and political leaders as the world community copes with the precarious balance between the sovereignty of nations and the collective human rights of their peoples"[25] demands action. But national leaderships are understandably reluctant to permit consideration of any arrangements that threaten to limit national sovereignty over state territory. Such an approach can be exploited for purposes that undermine rather than contribute to the peaceful settlement of disputes. Yet, as West European experience suggests, states may be willing to share or pool their sovereignty if, by doing so, they stand to make important gains.

The pooling of sovereignty in social and economic arenas by West European states enhances their capacities to deliver social welfare benefits to their populations. For West European governments, socioeconomic performance is an important determinant of electoral support. In Eastern Europe, the pooling of sovereignty in cultural arenas on bilateral and multilateral bases as part of a broader strategy of democratization may allow governments not only to expand their electoral support but also contribute to the legitimation of the existing state itself. Such pooling of sovereignty must be achieved through bilateral negotiation, perhaps assisted or facilitated by third party or multilateral actors, but motivated by mutual self-interest on the part of the states directly involved.

The establishment of regimes on each side of a border that guarantee individual liberties will make state borders increasingly irrelevant for the preservation and expression of group identity. Conscious policies to multiply economic and other forms of interstate cooperation that meet the material needs of local populations will help foster the processes of pluralist integration. Simultaneous democratization and cross-border economic cooperation may contribute to the emergence of a sense of community, founded not on the ethnic and cultural identities that differentiate these populations, but on the benefits of membership in a democratic community of nations.

CONFLICT PREVENTION AND MANAGEMENT

Former United Nations secretary-general Javier Pérez de Cuéllar, speaking in April 1991, noted that "we are clearly witnessing what is probably an irresistible shift in public attitudes towards the belief that the defense of the oppressed in the name of morality should prevail over frontiers and legal documents." He called for prudent and bold responses to the challenge of securing human rights: "In a prudent manner, because the principles of sovereignty cannot be radically challenged without international chaos quickly ensuing. In a bold manner, because we have probably reached a stage in the ethical and psychological evolution of Western civilization in which the massive and deliberate violation of human rights will no longer be tolerated."[26] Prudence requires that the international community strengthen existing capacities and procedures for responding to conflict. Boldness demands that the international community develop new capacities to secure human rights, especially the human rights of minority populations, before their abuse gives rise to crisis.

NATO and the Limits of Military Action

The Yugoslav wars revealed the inadequacies of existing arrangements within the Euro-Atlantic community for dealing with violent conflict, especially conflicts within sovereign states, that threaten to destabilize the wider international community. The CSCE mechanisms for the peaceful resolution of disputes proved ineffective for bringing the violence to an end. With the outbreak of fighting, UN peacemaking, peacekeeping, and peace enforcement capacities also proved inadequate. Because NATO had provided a powerful and effective organizational and political framework for establishing political cohesion and constructing a unified military response to Cold War threats to the security of Western Europe, the Yugoslav crisis focused attention on the opportunity to adapt NATO to the new challenges of the post-Cold War era.

Some steps toward adapting the NATO mission and widening the scope of NATO activities to meet the post-Cold War challenges had already been taken before the Yugoslav crisis. Meeting in London in July 1990, NATO opened the door to the discussion of mutual security issues with the East European states by granting them "diplomatic liaison" status. This led to the creation of the North Atlantic Cooperation Council (NACC) as a forum for East-West political consultation and to the participation of the "liaison countries" in NATO diplomatic meetings, committees, and other bodies. The Yugoslav crisis and the collapse of the Soviet Union heightened concerns about the need to strengthen the conflict management and prevention capacities of NATO. These were reflected in the new NATO strategy adopted in Rome in November 1991, as well as in proposals to strengthen the relationship between NATO and the CSCE.[27] The delegates to the Rome meeting echoed earlier calls for the suspension of the CSCE unanimity rule with respect to measures taken against states violating CSCE principles, and this change was adopted by the CSCE in January 1992.

NATO is at present considering how to proceed with expansion of its membership. Some member states, including Germany, have long favored such expansion.[28] In October 1993, the United States put forward an alternative proposal to establish a "partnership" with states seeking to join NATO. According to the U.S. secretary of defense, Les Aspin, the Partnership for Peace would focus on bringing the military organization, weaponry, training, tactics, and philosophy of these states into line with NATO's, in order to lay the foundations for eventual joint operations under NATO command.[29] While the partnership could be expected to have important effects on military culture and civil-military relations in these countries and prepare them for participation in operations under NATO command, it does not extend a NATO security guarantee to these countries.

The Central European states have been pressing for full membership since at least 1991.[30] In October 1993, Czech president Vaclav Havel offered a clear, public articulation of the arguments often made in favor of extending membership to selected post-communist states immediately.[31] NATO, he argued, constituted "one of the guarantors of the internal stability of a democratic Europe," represented "an instrument of collective defense against any outside aggressor," and provided the means "to support freedom and democracy elsewhere in Europe and even to defend it." The Czech Republic, Hungary, Poland, and Slovakia were "prime candidates for early membership," as were Austria and Slovenia, because all were "in the Western sphere" and were "contiguous and stable." President Havel thus viewed NATO as a primarily political organization. Others who have considered this issue also identify primarily political arguments in favor of expansion.[32]

However, NATO is primarily a military organization. The political solidarity among its members derives primarily from their common democratic cultures and the absence of conflicts between them. Long-term military cooperation and coordination contribute to this solidarity. But there is little reason to believe that—as presently constituted—NATO is any better able to resolve ethnoterritorial and political conflicts between its members now than it was at the time of the Cyprus conflict. The inclusion of Havel's candidates or other post-communist states raises the prospect of bringing unresolved conflicts, such as those between Hungary and Slovakia or Hungary and Romania, inside the organization. Membership must be restricted, therefore, to states that have stabilized their relations with one another. The coherence of the NATO alliance was derived not only from the clarity of the external threat to its members, but also from the strength of member states' adherence to shared democratic values. To admit states in which the strength of such values remains uncertain would only weaken the alliance.

Thus, an independent task force of experts considering this issue recommended that prospective entrants first establish themselves as "stable, market-oriented democracies," establish "mechanisms to protect the rights of minorities," and "settle all outstanding border issues" *before* being considered for membership.[33] In effect, they recognize that international peace requires simultaneous military-security integration, economic integration, and convergence around democratic norms.

Even in military-security terms, expansion of NATO can be seen as a double-edged sword. The admission of any subset of states, such as those suggested by President Havel, would imply that NATO had made a judgment about the relative instability of other states in the region. It would suggest an unwillingness on the part of the organization to be drawn into conflicts in them. At worst, it would suggest the division of post-communist states into "friends" and "foes." Admitting the Central European states into NATO while leaving Ukraine outside it, for example, might be seen as a signal of the West's lack of interest in supporting the peaceful resolution of the outstanding issues in Ukraine and between Ukraine and Russia. Perhaps even more serious, expanding NATO eastward while continuing to exclude Russia could lend an anti-Russian character to the alliance. The prospect of such a development has already led to new tensions in relations between Russia and its neighbors, as well as between Russia and the West. In November 1993, the director of the Russian Intelligence Service, fearing that a decision for expansion would be taken at NATO's January 1994 summit meeting, warned that expansion would trigger "a fundamental reappraisal" of Russian military security interests.[34] In short, a premature decision to expand NATO entails the risk of once again dividing Europe and initiating a new Cold War.

In this light, internal democratization and the stabilization of international relations that results from democratization must be seen as necessary preconditions for, rather than consequences of, NATO membership. There has been a strong tendency in the Western responses to uncertainty in the post-communist East to view membership in NATO, the European Union, or other Western organizations as an inducement to conform to Western political standards, in the apparent belief that membership affords an opportunity to exercise greater influence over the behavior of newly admitted states. In the absence of strong enforcement capacities and the willingness to use them on the part of the EU, the Council of Europe, the CSCE, and other multilateral organizations, this is a dubious assumption at best.

Slovakia, for example, has been subjected to consistent diplomatic pressure from Council of Europe and CSCE member states to equalize the political status of ethnic Hungarians since it was granted membership in these organizations, but there is little evidence to suggest that such pressure has been effective.[35] In March 1995, Slovakia and Hungary concluded a treaty on good neighborly relations and friendly cooperation in conjunction with a Council of Europe conference in Paris on European stability. The Slovak cabinet later issued a statement affirming the treaty as mutually acceptable, guaranteeing inviolability of state borders, barring territorial claims, and creating the opportunity to protect legal rights of persons belonging to ethnic minorities. However, in a statement delivered to the Hungarian cabinet, it rejected the Hungarian interpretation of the treaty as acceptance of the council's call for autonomous minority self-governments.[36] Moreover, as of September 1995, the Slovak government of Prime Minister Meciar had delayed submitting the treaty to parliament for ratification. The difficulty of resolving the tensions between Slovakia and Hungary suggests that it would be better to withhold the full benefits of membership in NATO until applicants have demonstrated their ability to resolve the political conflicts that divide them, as well as their readiness to participate in joint military operations.

In the interim, however, NATO must find ways to extend its stabilizing and protective influence eastward without weakening its own internal cohesion or introducing new instabilities to the east. In June 1992, NATO agreed to support and contribute to peacekeeping operations authorized by the CSCE, but only "on a case by case basis" and according to its own procedures. In December 1992, it made a similar commitment with respect to the United Nations. The NACC endorsed the concept of NATO peacekeeping and adopted a work plan to develop the capacity to carry out such operations. Under the pressure of events in Bosnia-Herzegovina, NATO undertook contingency planning for the support of an eventual peace settlement there.[37] There are, however, inherent limitations on the ability of NATO to perform such functions.

Efforts to use military force to compel conflicting parties to reach a political agreement are potentially costly operations, and once initiated, they run the clear risk of an escalating involvement. Efforts to bring the fighting in Bosnia-Herzegovina to a halt through the use of a combination of threats and limited air strikes only demonstrated that NATO is unable to act decisively when its member states differ in their assessments of a situation, especially when the United States does not provide clear political and strategic leadership. Membership in NATO does not in itself guarantee the cohesion necessary for undertaking such a task. This was amply demonstrated when American proposals in May 1993 to lift the arms embargo on Bosnia and to use airpower against the Serbs fell on deaf ears: differences between France, Britain, and Germany on the one hand, combined with irresolution on the part of the United States on the other, perpetuated NATO inaction. Any NATO action requires the active participation, agreement, and even leadership of the United States. The adoption of the February 1994 Sarajevo ultimatum and enforcement of the weapons exclusion zone in September 1995 came only after the Clinton administration, responding to the political pressure of congressional action to lift the arms embargo on Bosnia-Herzegovina and the fear that irresolution in Bosnia would represent a political liability in the upcoming presidential campaign, resolved its internal differences and took up leadership of an effort to bring the war to a negotiated solution.

For its part, the United Nations was reluctant to authorize even the limited use of force by NATO. When NATO appeared ready to embark on the use of airpower to break the Serb siege of Sarajevo in August 1993, UN officials on the ground worked assiduously with the secretary-general to retain control over the initiation of such action. As the NATO commitment, or at least its rhetoric, expanded, the UN commanders and the UN political hierarchy continued to resist ordering the use of force and continued to seek a negotiated settlement. Part of this resistance could be attributed to acute awareness on the part of UN officials that, while NATO might be willing to use airpower against the Serbs, NATO members, including the United States, remained unwilling to undertake the greater risks of the large-scale intervention with ground troops that would be necessary to impose peace by force.

In any event, military intervention to suppress armed conflict and protect the civilian population represents only part of the effort necessary to restore ethnic peace. Even the apparent success of the NATO bombing campaign of September 1995 in forcing the parties to the negotiating table required both U.S. negotiators and the parties themselves to address important political issues in order to make any progress: the United States was compelled to negotiate with Slobodan Milosevic; both the U.S. and Bosnian governments were compelled to recognize the claim of Bosnian Serbs to their own autonomous political entity; and Milosevic and the Bosnian Serbs were compelled to recognize the existence of Bosnia-Herzegovina.[38] Whether these developments will lead to a settlement that brings the fighting in Bosnia-Herzegovina to an end remains uncertain. It is quite clear, however, that the establishment of genuine peace will have to be accompanied by systematic, comprehensive efforts to reestablish a civil order. This will likely be a more complex and longer-lasting task than establishing military control over territory. The process of establishing civil order cannot even begin until the parties to the conflict have signed a political agreement commanding substantial popular support. Simply put, the Yugoslav conflict has demonstrated that, while the capacity and willingness to use force in the service of peace may be an essential element of any security framework for the Euro-Atlantic community, the use of force alone is no substitute for political solutions. Indeed, when the North Atlantic Cooperation Council agreed on principles for peacekeeping operations in June 1993 it excluded peace *enforcement* missions—the attempt to impose peace in the absence of a political agreement between the warring parties—as a matter of policy.[39]

As the humanitarian relief efforts in Bosnia-Herzegovina make clear, under conditions of armed conflict even humanitarian missions require either strong military engagement in support/defense of relief efforts or the prior agreement of the conflicting parties. The former, however, risks transforming such a mission into an armed intervention. The latter represents the condition that might allow successful peacekeeping.

The difficulties of mounting a successful peacekeeping mission are multiplied in the politically heterogeneous context of the United Nations. The difficulties are even greater in the case of a peace enforcement mission. The rare combination of circumstances that made possible the broad political coalition in support of the UN-authorized effort to reverse the Iraqi invasion and occupation of Kuwait are unlikely to be reproduced in cases of internal conflict between groups with competing claims to sovereign control over the same territory. Under such circumstances, even the definition of aggression is subject to dispute. In the case of the former Yugoslavia, for example, differences between Security Council members, especially the five permanent members, have made it impossible to develop such a consensus. Even if the United Nations had already acquired the enhanced military capabilities called for in the secretary-general's *Agenda for Peace*,[40] disagreements that undermined the effectiveness of Western responses to the crisis would have made it impossible for the Security Council to have authorized their use in the former Yugoslavia.

Thus, the success of peace enforcement efforts and peacekeeping and humanitarian relief operations ultimately depends on the success of political processes in creating a basis on which the conflicting parties can come to agreement. Western, especially American, policymakers must therefore devote substantial attention and resources to developing mechanisms to foster such political agreements. Within the Euro-Atlantic community, the CSCE member states encompass all the loci of potential threats to international security arising out of ethnic conflict. At the same time, the CSCE provides an arena within which the political agreements essential to conflict management and prevention may be developed. Even more important, the United States has already devoted a substantial effort to ensuring that the CSCE establish a useful set of principles articulating the standards of human rights and political democracy against which the policies and practices of all member states, as well as groups asserting claims to self-determination, may be judged.

The CSCE and the Politics of Prevention

Some efforts have already been undertaken to correct the inadequacies of CSCE institutions and procedures revealed by the Yugoslav crisis. In January 1992, the CSCE adopted a "unanimity-minus-one" rule to facilitate the adoption of peaceful measures in response to violations of CSCE principles by a member state without the consent of that state. The rule was applied for the first time at an emergency meeting of the Committee of Senior Officials in Helsinki to exclude the new "Yugoslavia" (Serbia and Montenegro) from CSCE decisionmaking until June of that same year. At the follow-up meeting in July, Yugoslavia was excluded. The July 1992 meeting also established a high commissioner for national minorities in an effort to improve the CSCE's capacity to prevent threats to peace arising out of ethnic conflict.[41]

The high commissioner on national minorities (HCNM) engages in what the current incumbent, Max van der Stoel, has characterized as early preventive diplomacy. This includes "provision of skilled assistance through good offices, mediation and the like" so as "to encourage and support efforts by contenders to seek accommodation" and thereby "resolve disputes well before eruption into armed conflict appears likely." The HCNM attempts to provide an impartial and confidential process through which information about a conflict may be gathered, assessed, and distributed to the parties in an effort to promote dialogue, mutual confidence, and cooperation between them in the search for a solution.[42] In order to succeed in these efforts, each party to the conflict must be committed to a good-faith effort to find a peaceful, mutually agreed upon solution. To date, the HCNM has addressed the conflicts over citizenship laws in Estonia and Latvia, as well as the law on aliens in Estonia. He has traveled to Slovakia to study the situation of the Hungarian minority and, in an effort to ensure support for his efforts from both of the states concerned, he has traveled to Hungary to study the status of the Slovak minority there. In Macedonia, the HCNM has attempted to facilitate a peaceful solution to the growing conflict between Macedonians and the ethnic Albanian minority.[43]

The creation of a CSCE capacity to respond to crises militarily had been discussed as early as the Paris Summit of 1990.[44] Although agreed to in principle at the Helsinki meeting in 1992, the concept of CSCE peacekeeping, the complexity of the authorization process, the conditions imposed on such authorization, and the narrow definition of the mission of such operations virtually ensure that CSCE peacekeeping will represent only a marginal contribution at best to the security of the Euro-Atlantic community. Authorization requires consensus among all the member states. CSCE personnel cannot be dispatched without the establishment of "an effective and durable cease-fire," guarantees for the safety of CSCE personnel, an explicit political agreement between the parties concerned, and their consent to such a mission. As this makes clear, CSCE peacekeeping is intended to serve as a means of maintaining an existing peace, not as a means to establish peace. Indeed, enforcement activities are specifically forbidden.[45]

The inherent limits on CSCE peacekeeping capabilities are not to be lamented. Military-security issues more properly belong in the NATO-NACC context. Attempts to convert the CSCE into a pan-European military-security framework led by France and Germany threaten to divert attention from the basic mission of the CSCE in the post-Cold War environment: to support the democratization of the post-communist member states and aid in securing the human rights of all individuals within the member states.

This leads to an important unresolved political debate within the CSCE. Some member states, such as Hungary, in advocating the concept of collective rights for national minorities, are attempting to advance the collective rights of their brethren living in other countries. Others, led by the United States, oppose this concept and support the principle of individual rights.[46] The United States must devote substantial attention and effort to this issue to ensure that the latter view is firmly established as the community standard. At the Helsinki meeting in 1992 the West European delegations resisted the suggestion that the CSCE undertake careful review of the extent to which its established principles of human rights have been implemented. They also opposed the strengthening of CSCE institutions for their implementation. The United States maintained its support for continuing implementation reviews and for strengthening the CSCE institutions devoted to implementing human rights principles. It must continue to do so.

CSCE member states are also beginning to grapple with some of the basic principles of the international order that underlie many ethnic conflicts. Through the Forum for Security Cooperation established in July 1992, the CSCE states have developed a "code of conduct." Preliminary reports of the discussion suggest that the early draft repeated one of the central mistakes of the Yugoslav crisis: extending international protection to internal borders. If adopted, this principle would have effectively shut off one means of encouraging peaceful negotiation of conflicts that threaten to end in a country's dissolution. Moreover, it would have increased the disincentives, created by the Yugoslav example, for the adoption of preventive measures to avoid ethnic conflict growing out of federal or regional autonomy arrangements. The text adopted at the December 1994 Budapest meeting includes instead a commitment to the territorial integrity of states. The code avoids affirming a right to self-determination, and it affirms the importance of protecting human rights and fundamental freedoms as a means of preventing conflict. While a preliminary draft appears to have singled out the rights of national minorities, the final does not do so, thus avoiding the internal contradiction characteristic of earlier CSCE documents concerning issues of ethnicity, human rights, and democracy.[47]

The consolidation of democratic regimes in the post-communist countries cannot be achieved in the absence of strengthened protections for the human rights of individuals in all Euro-Atlantic states. The formal acceptance of CSCE principles or Council of Europe human rights legislation means little in the absence of careful, consistent efforts to assess actual compliance and a willingness to penalize failure to comply. Recent reports on human rights and democratization in Croatia and Slovakia by the U.S. Helsinki Commission, for example, document the continuing abuse of the rights of minorities, along with a disregard for the principle of freedom of the press, by the nationalist governments in these two states, despite their membership in both the CSCE and the Council of Europe. The U.S. commission has also issued reports detailing its concerns over the treatment of Russians in Latvia and Estonia.[48] It is essential, therefore, that the United States maintain its efforts to establish the institutional capacity and mobilize the commitment necessary to ensure member states' compliance with CSCE principles.

The most effective path to ensuring such compliance is a political one that combines direct and indirect forms of political assistance with both positive and negative economic incentives. This is also the most effective path to the peaceful settlement of disputes. Just as the means to compliance cannot simply be reduced to the threat of force, the means to peaceful settlement of disputes cannot be simply reduced to legal arbitration. Many of the current cases of violent ethnic conflict revolve around conflicting interpretations of international principles that are themselves in dispute. This means that all decisions taken to resolve such conflicts are inherently political. Moreover, as the divergent Yugoslav and Czechoslovak experiences make clear, policies that succeed in one context cannot be expected to succeed in all contexts. The insensitivity to the need to accommodate ethnic minorities and avoid their delegation to permanent political minority demonstrated by the arbitration commission headed by the French jurist Robert Badinter (author of a proposal to establish a CSCE court of arbitration) demonstrate the counterproductive results that can be expected from a legalistic approach to intensely political questions. Such an approach should be resolutely opposed by the United States.[49]

Principled solutions to the conflicts within the Euro-Atlantic framework cannot be achieved without attention to external influences. Ethnic conflicts at the periphery of the CSCE, such as the ongoing conflicts in the Caucasus, affect the interests of neighboring non-CSCE states and may draw them into involvement. In instances where conflicts cut across regional boundaries, UN institutions provide a broader framework for negotiations and peacekeeping operations.

The United Nations also has a useful role to play when the peaceful means of negotiating the settlement of a dispute within the regional framework have been exhausted, and the CSCE turns to discussions of the use of force. The United Nations provides a ready framework for subjecting the regional peacemaking effort to additional political scrutiny. It offers an opportunity to advance political negotiations between conflicting parties by moving the discussions from the regional level to the global arena, and by introducing new participants with fresh perspectives and additional resources.

Although the usefulness of multiple institutional and organizational resources in resolving conflicts should not be neglected, the present proliferation of attempts by Euro-Atlantic organizations to address questions of nationalism and democratization has produced a counterproductive duplication of effort and a competition for authority. There is a clear and growing need to coordinate national policies and institutional activities to assure that the most effective action is taken. The effectiveness of any policy depends on follow-through and enforcement. Organizations or institutions unable or unwilling to act on agreed-upon principles must not be allowed to interfere in the operations of those that are willing and able to do so.

TOWARD A STRATEGY OF PREVENTIVE ENGAGEMENT

As the Yugoslav experience suggests, the capacity to mount peacekeeping operations and, if necessary, the capacity and will to deploy a peace enforcement mission are necessary components of any overall strategy for the management of conflicts that threaten international peace. But these, like most existing CSCE mechanisms and UN institutions, represent capacities for responding to rather than preventing conflict. The Yugoslav crisis demonstrates very clearly that the effectiveness of such responses is severely limited once ethnic conflicts escalate.

The EC-sponsored Conference on Yugoslavia, the UN negotiations that led to the establishment of protected areas in Croatia, and the Vance-Owen Plan negotiated by the International Conference on the Former Yugoslavia each came too late in the cycle of ethnic conflict to be effective. The escalating violence on the ground and the lack of interest on the part of the warring parties in a negotiated settlement precluded a traditional peacekeeping operation and raised the potential costs of an enforcement operation to unacceptable levels. Indeed, the central lesson of the Yugoslav experience is that the international community must undertake efforts to prevent, by political means, ethnic conflict from turning violent. Once such violence occurs, international actors must undertake efforts to prevent it from escalating. Unchecked, ethnic conflict escalates rapidly, and the international community is then faced with the unhappy choice of using force, with little prospect of immediate success, or acquiescing in assaults against a fundamental principle of international order: that borders cannot be changed by force.

If Western states do not develop capacities for preventive engagement, the moral outrage felt by at least some of the witnesses to the excesses of ethnic violence will continue to force policymakers to confront demands for interventions that pose unacceptably high risks. In the face of such demands, policymakers will again have to argue, as U.S. secretary of state Warren Christopher did in June 1993 (and as the Bush administration did earlier), that challenges to the principles of pluralist democracy inherent in efforts to establish ethnically nationalist regimes do not involve the strategic interests of the United States. In so doing, American policymakers will contribute to the contraction rather than the "enlargement of the world's free community of market democracies," the foreign policy goal articulated by the Clinton administration in September 1993.[50]

The development of mechanisms for the prevention of violent ethnic conflict requires that democratic states, working in concert and through multilateral institutions, overcome their reluctance to become involved in the internal affairs of other states. The first steps in this direction have already been taken. In order to gain admission to the Council of Europe, the post-communist states must accept the right of their citizens to appeal directly to the European Court on Human Rights. In an attempt to encourage, if not pressure, post-communist states to uphold human rights standards articulated through the CSCE, the EC added a provision to its association agreements permitting it to suspend such agreements if the associated state fails to uphold these rights. Within the CSCE, decisions adopted since 1989 have legitimated inquiry and involvement by member states in the ostensibly internal matters of other member states with respect to CSCE principles. With the establishment of a high commissioner for national minorities, the Euro-Atlantic states have created a first, although still limited, capacity for taking an active approach to ethnic issues before they turn violent or threaten international security. The high commissioner has already undertaken efforts to de-escalate the conflict between Hungary and Slovakia over the status and treatment of their respective minorities.[51] Both the European Court and the high commissioner legitimate direct international inquiry into, and assessment of, the treatment by states of their citizenry.

The tragic consequences of uncontrolled escalation of ethnic tensions in Yugoslavia make clear the need to construct a much broader array of peaceful, nonmilitary means by which members of the Euro-Atlantic community may prevent such escalation and avert the threats to international security inherent in the mobilization of ethnic identity. The institutionalization of a capacity for preventive engagement to facilitate the peaceful resolution of issues will require changes in the fundamental vocabulary of international relations. *Intervention*, because it has become irrevocably associated with *military* action, is too strong and too threatening a term, for both the executors and the objects of such efforts, by which to describe efforts to construct peaceful solutions to conflicts before they threaten international peace.

Preventive engagement activities must, by their very nature, remain relatively low-profile if not entirely invisible to the public. Mechanisms for preventive engagement must be designed so as to avoid contributing to the escalation of conflicts. At the very earliest stages of a conflict, for example, such engagement might focus entirely on facilitating the development, by those directly involved, of a process for the peaceful resolution of their conflict, rather than on securing a particular outcome.[52] The activities of the CSCE high commissioner on national minorities are a good example of activities focused on the process of conflict resolution.

Preventive engagement might also involve assisting states to overcome the dilemma of the permanent minority. Sharing extensive Western expertise in the conduct of elections and parliamentary procedures may facilitate attempts by local leaders to increase the political rewards for peaceful, conciliatory behavior and construct institutional safeguards for minority interests while avoiding the dangers of an unrestricted veto. Thus, preventive engagement efforts may involve not only facilitating the process of negotiation, but also assistance in designing political institutions that will in the short term contribute to the resolution of conflicts and, over the longer term, contribute to the democratization process.

Low-key involvement by representatives of multilateral Euro-Atlantic organizations and nongovernmental organizations must have as its ultimate goal bringing states into compliance with the human rights standards articulated in the CSCE framework. It is essential that the international community develop the capacity to increase the intensity and scope of its involvement in a dispute as the threat to peace arising out of it escalates. Informal, nonbinding, advisory participation may be carried out before a conflict threatens to destabilize an existing political regime or before it has turned violent. But the onset of violent incidents of the kind usually associated with interethnic conflicts requires more direct engagement to prevent their escalation. Thus, a series of differentiated or graduated forms of engagement must be created so that the scope and character of international involvement may be appropriately defined in terms of the characteristics of the conflict itself.

The direct involvement of international civilian police, investigatory, and judicial personnel, for example, offers a potentially important means of preventing the escalation of violence in the wake of isolated ethnic incidents by ensuring impartiality in the effort to identify and punish the perpetrators of such incidents and prevent retaliatory attacks on civilian populations. The primary goal of any preventive engagement by the international community must be to preserve the peace. But such engagement can also help advance the democratic values, principles, and practices that contribute to international peace and security.[53] The involvement of international personnel or advisors in the establishment of democratic procedures for the administration of justice may help accelerate the institutionalization of democratic political culture in post-communist states.

In the case of newly emerging states or states in transition from a discredited and collapsed old order to a democratic new one, the scope of the international engagement necessary to stabilize the country and support its transition to democracy may require the establishment of new institutions or authorities staffed by both international and local personnel.[54] Such transitional arrangements could play an especially important role in cases of ethnic conflict by allowing each group to avoid having to submit to the rule of the other, thereby contributing to the de-escalation of the conflict. In the short run, such de-escalation is by itself an important achievement. But the primary longer-term goal of transitional arrangements must be to foster the emergence of an autonomous democratic system.

If such arrangements are to succeed, they must avoid substituting rule by international actors for the consolidation of democratic self-rule. While international personnel may necessarily be centrally involved in the resolution of extremely sensitive issues, they must encourage and rely on self-administration by the local population across a broad range of governmental functions, especially those that transcend the local ethnic communities and integrate them with neighboring states and the broader international community. This will permit the emergence of multiple interests and the identities they create. In combination with economic development policies that foster the emergence of pluralistic patterns of ethnic cooperation in the pursuit of self-interest, the establishment of transitional authorities might allow the same integrative forces that transformed the West European states into the European Community to begin to compete with the disintegrative forces of nationalism. In this way, preventive engagement offers the means by which the international community may engage in genuine and lasting "peacemaking," and ethnic communities may avoid the human tragedy and destruction of war.

The pluralization of interests in society is a critical component of any effort to prevent ethnic conflict. The contrasting roles of the media in Czechoslovakia and Yugoslavia suggest that actions to ensure the openness of newspapers and television to competing views represent an especially important means by which to encourage popular support for democratic government and oppose the efforts of nationalist leaders to impose political homogeneity on ethnic populations. Western governments should make every effort not only to encourage privatization of the media, including the creation of independent—even if still state-owned—television broadcasting, and the multiplication of publishing/broadcast opportunities in the post-communist states, but also to ensure that journalists have access to training and information that increase their understanding of and sympathy for democracy. These efforts require not only financial, technical, and training assistance, but also political support, in the form of resolute opposition on the part of Western governments to efforts by post-communist leaders to muzzle their opposition.

The Yugoslav experience also reinforces and extends lessons about the role of the military in transitions from authoritarian rule learned from recent Latin American history.[55] The direct and indirect participation of the military and the application of war-making capacities against civilian populations and militias have been characteristic of each of the ethnic wars in the post-communist states. Preventive engagement may help establish a stronger barrier against such use of force. Intensive efforts to resocialize the professional military officer corps to democratic principles and civilian control, especially nonintervention in civilian politics, represent an especially important means of encouraging restraint and limiting the destructive consequences of internal conflict. Efforts to extend Western expertise in this area to Eastern Europe, train new military officers in Western military academies, and retrain established military officers and civilian military experts from Eastern Europe in civilian and military academic institutions in the West are already under way and should be expanded.

The Yugoslav experience further underscores the importance of opposing the formation and operation of nationalist militias and terrorist groups. International actors may be able to enlist the professional military of a disintegrating state in the task of controlling violence by appealing to and supporting the military professionalism of the officer corps, and by reinforcing its commitment to the defense of the civilian population. But this cannot be done unless international actors are sensitive to the special dilemmas of a military caught in such circumstances.

Ethnic conflict calls into question the legitimacy of the existing military and its mission to protect the state. The threat of dissolution threatens the very survival of that military.[56] Any effort to prevent an ethnic crisis from turning violent, therefore, must include measures to help the military adapt to new conditions. In the face of the dissolution of a state, provisions must be made for the peaceful division of military resources, the articulation of military-political relationships between successor organizations that take into account the legacies of their former unified existence, and the institution of confidence-building measures among the successor militaries and their civilian leaders.

When a single ethnic group has dominated the military, as the Serbs dominated the Yugoslav military or the Russians the Soviet military, special attention must be paid to the disproportionate advantages and burdens associated with ethnically based allocation of manpower and resources to the successor states. Opposition to nationalist militias cannot be allowed to assume the character of attack by one ethnic group in the military on another group. Similarly, demilitarization efforts must be balanced so as to reduce the perceived threat to all groups simultaneously. In all instances, the natural resistance of professional officers to involvement in combat against the civilian population must be encouraged and supported, and civilian leaders must be deterred from drawing the military into such combat.

NATO's extensive network of military and civilian experts represents a ready resource for assisting in the transformation of formerly communist militaries. The NATO network can also make important contributions to the creation of a new civilian network of conflict-management experts and organizations to carry out the tasks of preventive engagement within the framework of strengthened CSCE institutions. Military personnel released from service as part of the downsizing of Western military establishments associated with the end of the Cold War represent an important pool of candidates for specialized training for such missions. Preventive engagement personnel are likely to have to interact extensively with local military and security forces in tense situations. They can therefore benefit from past military experience. Civilians entering such service can benefit from the enhanced understanding of military organization and culture to be gained from contact with NATO personnel and training in NATO institutions.

Preventive engagement must remain contingent on circumstances. Where there is ethnic conflict, the legitimacy of a regime often is in question. International engagement must be carefully focused on supporting democratic principles and fostering democratic institutions and practices, rather than supporting incumbent regimes. International assistance in resolving incidents and reforming electoral politics may not even be acceptable to an incumbent leadership. That leadership may be seeking to escalate rather than resolve tensions in order to establish a nationalist, authoritarian regime rather than a democratic one. By establishing an international capacity to provide such assistance, however, democratic states of the international community will create the capacity to subject leaderships and governments to a nonthreatening test of their commitment to the agreed-upon principles of the Euro-Atlantic community. American and Western support for the economic transformation of states should be made contingent on evidence of this commitment.

Democratic regimes deserve support, as do governments making good-faith efforts to democratize. But preventive engagement should not be allowed to become an instrument for defending the status quo when governments fail to conform to Euro-Atlantic standards. Preventive engagement efforts thus serve two distinct purposes simultaneously: they help preserve the peace and they foster democratization. Preventive engagement should not, however, be seen as a means of achieving the rapid transformation of a regime. Rather, it must be seen as part of a long-term strategy that requires an extensive, sustained commitment by the United States and other stable democracies of the Euro-Atlantic community to the democratic development of individual states.

Preventive engagement thus represents a means by which the Western democracies may address some of the most immediate security concerns of the post-communist states in a manner supportive of their democratic political development. It does not represent a substitute for deeper military-security integration into an enlarged NATO community. It represents instead a means by which to address conflicts for which military intervention is an inappropriate response and for which NATO remains ill prepared. A strategy of preventive engagement must be seen as an effort to resolve conflict through the establishment of democratic political institutions and procedures that may, in the longer term, contribute to the political demobilization of ethnic identities and the development of civic or democratic political cultures. With the resolution of domestic and interstate ethnic conflicts, the establishment of democratic political institutions, and the convergence of East European political cultures around democratic norms, the bases for the successful military-security and political-economic integration of these states into the West will have been established.

MULTILATERALISM AND AMERICAN LEADERSHIP

The United States cannot achieve these goals alone. The scale of the economic, political, and human resources that are needed to support democratization in the former communist countries and to construct new mechanisms to secure international peace exceeds the capacity of any single actor. Ethnic conflicts that overlap borders cannot be resolved through the actions of a single state. No stable peace can be established in Bosnia-Herzegovina if the status of the other territories in the former Yugoslavia is not addressed. Some of these situations cannot be resolved without the involvement of neighboring states.[57] The challenges of successfully securing and integrating the Hungarian populations of Slovakia and Romania into their host states, for example, cannot be met without the participation of both the host governments and Hungary. Moreover, any attempt to redress the contradictions between the principles of self-determination, sovereignty, and territorial integrity by establishing new norms that enjoy widespread support can be carried out only through multilateral institutions.

Multilateral organizations offer obvious advantages for the mobilization of resources and for efforts to encourage the establishment of new norms. But the inability of the United Nations, the CSCE, or NATO to respond effectively to the Yugoslav crisis highlights some of the obvious disadvantages of multilateral institutions. These disadvantages may be characterized as the problem of "the lowest common denominator." Multilateral organizations, like all collective decisionmaking bodies, will respond to the positions of their most recalcitrant members. Deference to the reservations of individual members is at the core of the multilateral deliberative process. It contributes to the formulation of carefully considered, well-informed policies. But such deference cannot be allowed to paralyze international efforts to resolve conflicts. The divisive effects of conflicting national interests among the great powers that have been evident throughout the course of the Yugoslav conflict underscore the importance of continuing American leadership for securing effective multilateral action in support of human rights and democratic principles.

As the dominant power in the Western alliance, the United States is uniquely positioned to pursue innovative solutions to the challenges of constructing a new framework for international security. The United States brings enormous moral authority to human rights issues, particularly issues of democratic development. In the Yugoslav case, however, the United States failed to identify and pursue political solutions to the underlying issues. The turmoil in U.S. policy toward Bosnia suggests that neither the Bush nor the Clinton administration ever perceived that vital interests were at stake in Bosnia. Policies were thus constantly up for grabs by advocates of one or another general principle or interpretation of the conflict. This failure was primarily a function of the rapidly changing international environment and the inability of policymakers to perceive that the Yugoslav crisis represented only the most dramatic example of the kind of conflict most likely to lead to violence and destabilize international relations in Europe and other areas of the world in the post-communist era.

The abdication of leadership by the United States explains, in part, German assertiveness in the Yugoslav case. A political alliance, like nature, abhors a vacuum. NATO, and American leadership of it, performed the important function of embedding the military capacities of the postwar Federal Republic of Germany in a multinational structure and wedding them to an agreed-upon set of principles. Active American leadership within multilateral political institutions can in the future provide a corresponding framework for German foreign policy, the foreign policies of other alliance states, and the emerging military-security and foreign policies of the post-communist states.

The cohesion that characterized NATO for the first forty-five years of its existence reflected the American commitment to leadership of the alliance, the clarity of its purpose, and the creation of institutional resources to carry out its role. The conflicting policies that have been advanced by Germany, the United States, and other members of the alliance at various times during the Yugoslav crisis reflect the absence of accepted guidelines for action in such situations, the weakness of common institutions, and the absence of American leadership. No effort to secure international peace can work in the absence of coordinated national policies among the major Western democracies. They have the greatest resources to bring to bear on any issue, as well as the greatest stake in a stable international environment.

Paradoxically, the virtues of democratic government that contribute to the prevention of interstate violence at the same time make it more difficult for democratic leaders to commit resources to the pursuit of long-term foreign policy goals. A strategy of preventive engagement requires precisely the kind of long-term commitment of attention, as well as human and material resources, likely to meet with public and therefore domestic political resistance just when it may matter most, that is, before a conflict has turned violent and captured the attention of the news media and the public. Indeed, a survey of American elites conducted in July and August 1993 revealed substantial skepticism that promoting democracy, human rights, and free markets should be the primary foreign policy goals of the United States, as well as outright opposition to doing so if it risked creating anti-American governments. A survey of popular opinion conducted in September 1993 revealed that the American public was even less supportive of these goals.[58]

If the United States is to lead Euro-Atlantic efforts to establish preventive engagement mechanisms, it will not be enough for policymakers to substitute "enlargement of the world's free community of market democracies" for "containment" in outlining America's foreign policy goals. American policymakers must make certain that the American electorate understands the nationalist challenge to liberal democratic principles and supports the need for direct and effective responses to it. In order to do so, policymakers must articulate the ways in which support for democratization and markets may be expected to ameliorate nationalist conflict, contribute to international security, and secure important American interests. They must also identify appropriate policies and actions to achieve these goals and rally public support for them. These are difficult tasks. The failure of successive administrations to understand the importance of the Yugoslav crisis for the principles of international security, as well as the failure to explain this to the American people effectively and propose appropriate solutions to the crisis, ensured that domestic opposition to involvement in the former Yugoslavia would severely limit the options available to American policymakers. Their failure should remind future policymakers that the American public, as well as citizens of other democratic states, is more easily persuaded of the virtues of preventive engagement than of the wisdom of intervening militarily in a conflict that has already turned violent.

If American leadership is to be effective, American leaders must eschew traditional diplomatic ambiguity for clarity. The realities of the post-Cold War era require the United States to recognize that ethnonationalism and the political authoritarianism it breeds represent a direct threat to democratization in the post-communist states and are therefore a threat to international peace in the wider Euro-

Atlantic community. Not only does nationalist authoritarianism lead to war between immediate neighbors, it also represents an ideological threat to the stability of democratic regimes; the international community can oppose this threat only by articulating and upholding principles of human rights and democracy and creating new capacities for preventive engagement in defense of these principles. Neither is possible without the participation of the United States.

Even with the establishment of a new security framework, national actors will continue to differ over specific responses to particular circumstances. If such differences are not to paralyze efforts to secure the peace, as they did in Yugoslavia, the United States must sustain its commitment to international leadership and resist calls for a retreat to isolationism.

NOTES

NOTES TO INTRODUCTION

1. The Ossetian threat is reported in *RFE/RL Research Report* 1, no. 25 (June 19, 1992): 69; the Azerbaijani threat is reported in U.S. Commission on Security and Cooperation in Europe (hereafter cited as U.S. Commission), *Human Rights and Democratization in the Newly Independent States of the Former Soviet Union* (Washington, DC: U.S. Commission, 1993), 117–18; for a denial of the threat, see Foreign Broadcast Information Service (hereafter cited as FBIS), *Daily Report: Central Eurasia,* November 12, 1992, 90.

2. As quoted in *New York Times,* June 26, 1993, 5.

3. Data from the UN High Commissioner for Refugees, Branch Office for the United States of America (Washington, DC), personal communication.

4. Vaclav Havel, "On Home," *New York Review of Books,* December 5, 1991, 49.

5. For widely cited examples of such arguments, see Barry R. Posen, "The Security Dilemma and Ethnic Conflict," in *Ethnic Conflict and International Security,* ed. Michael E. Brown (Princeton: Princeton University Press, 1993), 103–24; and John J. Mearsheimer and Robert A. Pape, "The Answer: A Partition Plan for Bosnia," *New Republic,* June 14, 1993, 22–28; the so-called lift and strike proposal put forward by the United States in May 1993 is another example.

NOTES TO CHAPTER 1

1. These changing values were reflected in the findings of surveys conducted in the Soviet Union in the 1970s and reported in widely read publications of prominent Soviet researchers in the 1980s. See, for example, Iu. V. Arutiunian and L. M. Drobizheva, *Mnogoobrazie kul'turnoi zhizni narodov SSSR* (The diversity of the cultural life of the peoples of the USSR) (Moscow: Mysl', 1987), 189–93. I explored this phenomenon in greater detail in Steven L. Burg, *Multi-Nationality and Political Change in the Soviet Union,* Report to the National Council for Soviet and East European Research, Contract No. 903–02, December 1989. They were not unlike a similar, more pronounced value change taking place in the West in the same period. See Ronald Inglehart, *The Silent Revolution* (Princeton: Princeton University Press, 1977); and idem, *Culture Shift in Advanced Industrial Society* (Princeton: Princeton University Press, 1990).

2. See Robert A. Kann, *The Multinational Empire: Nationalism and National Reform in the Habsburg Monarchy, 1848–1918,* 2 vols. (New York: Octagon Books, 1977).

3. See Francis Fukuyama, "The End of History?" *National Interest* 16 (1989): 3–18.

4. On this difference, see David Easton, "A Re-assessment of the Concept of Political Support," *British Journal of Political Science* 5 (1975): 437, 444–45.

5. Easton, "A Re-assessment."

6. FBIS, *Daily Report: Eastern Europe,* June 4, 1990, 42.

7. Donald S. Kellermann et al., *The Pulse of Europe: A Survey of Political and Social Values and Attitudes* (Washington, DC: Times Mirror Center for the People and the Press, 1991), 149.

8. Kellermann et al., *The Pulse of Europe,* 209.

9. As reported in Michael Shafir, "Preliminary Results of the 1992 Romanian Census," *RFE/RL Research Report* 1, no. 30 (July 24, 1992): 62–68.

10. "Weekly Review," *RFE/RL Research Report* 1, no. 50 (December 18, 1992): 75.

11. Michael Shafir, "Romania's Elections: More Change Than Meets the Eye," *RFE/RL Research Report* 1, no. 44 (November 6, 1992): 1–8; and Tom Gallagher, "Electoral Breakthrough for Romanian Nationalists," *RFE/RL Research Report* 1, no. 45 (November 13, 1992): 15–20.

12. Michael Shafir and Dan Ionescu, "The Tangled Path toward Democracy," *Transition* 1, no. 1 (January 30, 1995): 49–54; and Michael Shafir, "Ruling Party Formalizes Relations with Extremists," *Transition* 1, no. 5 (April 14, 1995): 42–46.

13. Tom Gallagher, "The Rise of the Party of Romanian National Unity," *RFE/RL Research Report* 3, no. 11 (March 18, 1994): 25–32.

14. Michael Shafir, "Ethnic Tensions Run High in Romania," *RFE/RL Research Report* 3, no. 32 (August 19, 1994): 24–32; and Tom Gallagher, "Controversy in Cluj," *Transition* 1, no. 15 (August 25, 1995): 58–61.

15. Gallagher, "Controversy in Cluj."

16. Edith Oltay, "Hungarians in Slovakia Organize to Press for Ethnic Rights," *Report on Eastern Europe* 1, no. 22 (June 1, 1990): 21–27.

17. Kellermann et al., *The Pulse of Europe,* 149.

18. Jiri Pehe, "Czechoslovak Political Balance Sheet, 1990 to 1992," *RFE/RL Research Report* 1, no. 25 (June 19, 1992): 24–31.

19. John Fitzmaurice, "The Slovak Election of September 1994," *Electoral Studies* 14, no. 2 (June 1995): 203–6; Sharon Fisher, "Tottering in the Aftermath of Elections," *Transition* 1, no. 4 (March 29, 1995): 20–25; and idem, "Enforcing a True Picture of Slovakia," *Transition* 1, no. 6 (April 28, 1995): 10–15.

20. "Slovakia: A New State One Year Later," Woodrow Wilson Center, East European Studies Program *Meeting Report,* no. 93 (May-June 1994), 2.

21. *Balkan News and East European Report,* March 26–April 1, 1995, 42; and Sharon Fisher, "Treaty Fails to End Squabbles over Hungarian Relations," *Transition* 1, no. 9 (June 9, 1995): 2–7.

22. For a summary of developments up to January 1993, see U.S. Commission, *Human Rights and Democratization in the Newly Independent States of the Former Soviet Union* (Washington, DC: U.S. Commission, 1993).

23. For the 1959 statistics, see Tsentral'noe statisticheskoe upravlenie SSSR, *Itogi Vsesoiuznoi perepisi naselenia 1959* Azerbaidzhanskaia SSR (Results of the All-Union Census of the population 1959 Azerbaidzhan SSR) (Moscow: Gostatizdat, 1963), 140; for 1989, see Gosudarstvennyi komitet SSSR po statistike, *Natsional'nyi sostav naseleniia SSSR* (National Composition of the Population of the USSR) (Moscow: Finansy i statistika, 1991), 120.

24. See Elizabeth Fuller, "Nagorno-Karabakh: Internal Conflict Becomes International," *RFE/RL Research Report* 1, no. 11 (March 13, 1992): 1–5; and "Weekly Review," *RFE/RL Research Report* 1, no. 36 (September 11, 1992): 75–76. For a summary of attempts to negotiate the several conflicts in the Caucasus, see Elizabeth Fuller, "Mediators for Transcaucasia's Conflicts," *World Today* 49, no. 5 (May 1993): 89–92.

25. Thomas Goltz, "Letter from Eurasia: The Hidden Russian Hand," *Foreign Policy* 92 (fall 1993): 92–106, esp. 98–104.

26. See, for example, Mark Saroyan, "The 'Karabakh Syndrome' and Azerbaijani Politics," *Problems of Communism* 39, no. 5 (September-October 1990): 14–29; and United States Institute of Peace, "Conference Summary: Armenia, Azerbaijan and Nagorno-Karabakh: State Sovereignty vs. Self-Determination," *In Brief . . .*, no. 42 (September 1992). The clash of principles in this instance has been acknowledged by the U.S. Commission for Security and Cooperation in Europe. See U.S. Commission, *Human Rights and Democratization in the Newly Independent States of the Former Soviet Union,* 123.

27. For useful summaries of the situation in the Caucasus, see Elizabeth Fuller, "Georgia, Abkhazia, and Checheno-Ingushetia," *RFE/RL Research Report* 1, no. 6 (February 7, 1992): 3–7; and idem, "Transcaucasia: Ethnic Strife Threatens Democratization," *RFE/RL Research Report* 2, no. 1 (January 1, 1993): 17–24.

28. For a summary of events in Georgia, see Richard Clogg, "War in the Caucasus?" *World Today* 48, no. 12 (December 1992): 214–15.

29. Elizabeth Fuller, "The South Ossetian Campaign for Unification," and Vera Tolz, "The USSR This Week," *Report on the USSR* 1, no. 49 (December 8, 1989): 17–20, 21.

30. For historical background and a narrative of events, see Edward Kline, "The Conflict in Chechnya: A Briefing Paper" (March 24, 1995, mimeo).

31. Edward W. Walker, "The Crisis in Chechnya," *Analysis of Current Events* 6, no. 6 (February 1995): 3–6; and Ian Bremmer, "Spilling Blood over Oil:

Russian Domination in Chechnya and Azerbaijan," *Analysis of Current Events* 6, no. 8 (April 1995): 1–4.

32. Bruce Allyn, "Some Observations on Conflict Management Efforts in Chechnya," *Analysis of Current Events* 6, no. 6 (February 1995): 9–12.

33. Igor Torbakov, "The 'Statists' and the Ideology of Russian Imperial Nationalism," *RFE/RL Research Report* 1, no. 49 (December 11, 1992): 10–16; see also Paul A. Goble, "Russia and Its Neighbors," *Foreign Policy* 90 (spring 1993): 79–88.

34. *RFE/RL Research Report* 1, no. 25 (June 19, 1992): 68. For reports of similar statements, see *New York Times,* June 22, 1992, A3.

35. *RFE/RL Daily Report,* no. 221 (November 18, 1993).

36. Bruce Russett, *Grasping the Democratic Peace* (Princeton: Princeton University Press, 1993). For a useful survey of the empirical literature and a critique of the neorealist argument, see Georg Sorensen, *Democracy and Democratization* (Boulder: Westview, 1993), 91–117; and William J. Dixon, "Democracy and the Management of International Conflict," *Journal of Conflict Resolution* 37 (March 1993): 42–68.

37. Larry Diamond, Juan Linz, and Seymour Martin Lipset, preface to *Democracy in Developing Countries,* vol. 4, *Latin America,* ed. Larry Diamond et al. (Boulder: Lynne Rienner, 1989), vxi.

38. The concept of pluralism has been developed most comprehensively in a series of works by Robert A. Dahl; among them, see *Pluralist Democracy in the United States: Conflict and Consensus* (Chicago: Rand McNally, 1967); *Polyarchy: Participation and Opposition* (New Haven: Yale University Press, 1972); and *Dilemmas of Pluralist Democracy* (New Haven: Yale University Press, 1982).

39. U.S. Commission, *Concluding Document of the Vienna Follow-Up Meeting* (Washington, DC: U.S. Commission, 1989); *Report of the CSCE Meeting of Experts on National Minorities* (Geneva, 1991); and U.S. Commission, *From Vienna to Helsinki: Reports on the Inter-Sessional Meetings of the CSCE Process* (Washington, DC: U.S. Commission, 1992).

40. U.S. Commission, *From Vienna to Helsinki,* 87.

41. *Report of the CSCE Meeting of Experts on National Minorities,* art. 2, par. 3.

42. *Document of the Moscow Meeting of the Conference on the Human Dimension of the CSCE,* par. 9.

43. Boyd Shafer, *Faces of Nationalism: New Realities and Old Myths* (New York: Harcourt Brace Jovanovich, 1972), 68.

44. Kann, *Multinational Empire,* vol. 2, 88 ff.

45. For a fuller discussion, see John Breuilly, *Nationalism and the State* (Chicago: University of Chicago Press, 1985), 3 ff.

46. For an interesting exploration of the interaction between cultural, eco-

nomic, and political forces in the rise of national consciousness, see Benedict Anderson, *Imagined Communities: Reflections on the Origin and Spread of Nationalism* (London: Verso, 1983).

47. See Sidney Tarrow, "'Aiming at a Moving Target': Social Science and the Recent Rebellions in Eastern Europe," *PS: Political Science and Politics* 24, no. 1 (March 1991): 12–20.

48. For discussion of the relative importance of primordial and other factors, see Clifford Geertz, "The Integrative Revolution: Primordial Sentiments and Civil Politics in the New States," in *The Interpretation of Cultures* (New York: Basic Books, 1973), 255–310; Robert Bates, "Modernization, Ethnic Competition, and the Rationality of Politics in Contemporary Africa," in *Ethnicity, State Coherence, and Public Policy: African Dilemmas*, ed. D. Rothchild and V. Olorunsola (Boulder: Westview, 1983), 152–71; and Leo A. Despres, "Toward a Theory of Ethnic Phenomena," in *Ethnicity and Resource Competition in Plural Societies*, ed. Leo A. Despres (Hague: Mouton, 1975), 187–207.

49. Daniel H. Levine, "Paradigm Lost: Dependence to Democracy," *World Politics* 40 (April 1988): 385.

50. Levine, "Paradigm Lost," 385–86.

51. Toomas Ilves, "The Congress of Estonia," and Riina Kionka, "The Congress Convenes," *Report on the USSR* 2, no. 12 (March 23, 1990): 31–32, 32–35; and Nils Muiznieks, "The Committee of Latvia: An Alternative Parliament?" *Report on the USSR* 2, no. 29 (July 20, 1990): 28–31.

52. For an assessment of local politics in Narva, see *Boston Globe*, August 5, 1992; and Philip Hanson, "Estonia's Narva Problem, Narva's Estonian Problem," *RFE/RL Research Report* 2, no. 18 (April 30, 1993): 17–23.

53. *Izvestiia*, July 20, 1993, as trans. in *Current Digest of the Post-Soviet Press* 45, no. 29 (August 18, 1993): 21 (henceforth cited as *CDPSP*).

54. Philip John Davies and Andrejs Valdis Ozolins, "The Latvian Parliamentary Election of 1993," *Electoral Studies* 13, no. 1 (March 1994): 83–86.

55. Open Media Research Institute, *Daily Digest*, no. 191, part 2 (October 2, 1995); and no. 193, part 2 (October 4, 1995).

56. *New York Times*, July 7, 1994, A1.

57. For a discussion of the role of political tolerance in American democracy and its implications for democratic theory, see John L. Sullivan, James Piereson, and George E. Marcus, *Political Tolerance and American Democracy* (Chicago: University of Chicago Press, 1982), 2–23, 254–63.

58. Alfred A. Reisch, "Transcarpathia's Hungarian Minority and the Autonomy Issue," *RFE/RL Research Report* 1, no. 6 (February 7, 1992): 15–23.

59. Andrew Wilson, "The Growing Challenge to Kiev from the Donbas," *RFE/RL Research Report* 2, no. 33 (August 20, 1993): 8–13.

60. On the transformation of German political culture, see Sidney Verba,

"Germany: The Remaking of Political Culture," in *Political Culture and Political Development,* ed. Lucien Pye and Sidney Verba (Princeton: Princeton University Press, 1965), 130–70; David P. Conradt, "Changing German Political Culture," in *The Civic Culture Revisited,* ed. Gabriel A. Almond and Sidney Verba (Boston: Little, Brown, 1980), 212–72; and K. D. Baker et al., *Germany Transformed: Political Culture and the New Politics* (Cambridge: Harvard University Press, 1981).

61. Terry Lynn Karl, "Dilemmas of Democratization in Latin America," in *Comparative Political Dynamics,* ed. Dankwart A. Rustow and Kenneth Paul Erickson (New York: HarperCollins, 1991), 168.

NOTES TO CHAPTER 2

1. Phil Williams, "Old Mechanisms and New Problems," in *Avoiding War: Problems of Crisis Management,* ed. Alexander George (Boulder: Westview, 1991), 500–518.

2. Conference on Security and Co-operation in Europe, *Final Act* (Helsinki: CSCE, 1975).

3. For background on the CSCE, see Vojtech Mastny, *Helsinki, Human Rights and European Security* (Durham: Duke University Press, 1986); Michael R. Lucas, "The Conference on Security and Cooperation in Europe and the Future of U.S. Foreign Policy," in *The New Europe Asserts Itself,* ed. Beverly Crawford and Peter W. Schulze, IIS Research Series, no. 77 (Berkeley: University of California, 1990), 45–83; and U.S. Commission, *The Conference on Security and Cooperation in Europe: An Overview of the CSCE Process, Recent Meetings and Institutional Development* (Washington, DC: U.S. Commission, 1992), 2–3.

4. U.S. Commission, *Concluding Document of the Vienna Follow-Up Meeting* (Washington, DC: U.S. Commission, 1989), 3–10, 34.

5. *Report of the CSCE Meeting of Experts on National Minorities* (Geneva, 1991), art. 2, par. 3.

6. *Document of the Moscow Meeting of the Conference on the Human Dimension of the CSCE,* par. 9.

7. U.S. Commission, *From Vienna to Helsinki: Reports on the Inter-Sessional Meetings of the CSCE Process* (Washington, DC: U.S. Commission, 1992), 87, 88, 92.

8. U.S. Commission, *From Vienna to Helsinki,* 140–43.

9. U.S. Commission, *From Vienna to Helsinki,* 144, 148.

10. For a discussion of the intellectual muddle surrounding the problem of intervention in support of self-determination, see Stanley Hoffmann, "The Problem of Intervention," in *Intervention in World Politics,* ed. Hedley Bull (Oxford: Clarendon Press, 1984), 7–28.

11. *Report of the CSCE Meeting of Experts on Peaceful Settlement of Disputes,* sections VI-XII.

12. For a useful collection of essays analyzing the present status of the European Union as a distinct political actor, see Robert O. Keohane and Stanley Hoffmann, eds., *The New European Community* (Boulder: Westview, 1991), especially the essay by Wolfgang Wessels, "The EC Council: The Community's Decisionmaking Center," 133–54.

13. The following discussion is based on A. H. Robertson, ed., *Human Rights in Europe* (Manchester: Manchester University Press, 1977); and J. G. Merrills, *The Development of International Law by the European Court of Human Rights* (Manchester: Manchester University Press, 1988).

14. For discussion of peacekeeping operations, see Indar Jit Rikhye, *The Theory and Practice of Peacekeeping* (London: C. Hurst, 1984); Alan James, *Peacekeeping in International Politics* (London: Macmillan, 1990); Indar Jit Rikhye and Kjell Skjelsbaek, eds., *The United Nations and Peacekeeping: Results, Limitations and Prospects: The Lessons of Forty Years of Experience* (London: Macmillan, 1991); and Marrack Goulding, "The Evolution of United Nations Peacekeeping," *International Affairs* 69, no. 3 (July 1993): 451–64.

15. On the evolution and operation of this system, see Steven L. Burg, *Conflict and Cohesion in Socialist Yugoslavia* (Princeton: Princeton University Press, 1983).

16. See Bogdan Denitch, *The Legitimation of a Revolution: The Yugoslav Case* (New Haven: Yale University Press, 1976).

17. For an analysis of the data on "Yugoslav" identity, see Steven L. Burg and Michael L. Berbaum, "Community, Integration, and Stability in Multi-National Yugoslavia," *American Political Science Review* 83 (June 1989): 535–54. See also Dusko Sekulic et al., "Who Were the Yugoslavs? Failed Sources of a Common Identity in the Former Yugoslavia," *American Sociological Review* 59 (February 1994): 83–97.

18. On the resurgence of nationality issues and political divisions in the leadership in the 1980s, see Steven L. Burg, "Elite Conflict in Post-Tito Yugoslavia," *Soviet Studies* 38, no. 2 (April 1986): 170–93; and Christopher Cviic, "The Background and Implications of the Domestic Scene in Yugoslavia," in *Problems of Balkan Security,* ed. Paul S. Shoup (Washington, DC: Wilson Center Press, 1990), 89–119.

19. See, for example, Arend Lijphart, *Democracy in Plural Societies* (New Haven: Yale University Press, 1977).

20. I have traced this process in detail in "Elite Conflict in Post-Tito Yugoslavia."

21. See Dusan Janjic, "Bosna i Hercegovina: Otvoreno pitanje drzavnopolitickog identiteta multietnicke i multikonfesionalne zajednice" (Bosnia and Her-

zegovina: The open question of the state-political identity of a multiethnic and multiconfessional community), in *Bosna i Hercegovina izmedu rata i mira* (Bosnia and Herzegovina between war and peace), ed. Srdjan Bogosavljevic et al. (Belgrade and Sarajevo: n.p., 1992), 7–23.

22. Peter Jambrek, "Political Landscape of a Communist Nation in Transition: Slovenia 1988–1989" (paper prepared for the Colloquium on Social Structure and Social Change in Yugoslavia, Center for Russian and East European Studies, University of Pittsburgh, April 27–29, 1989); and Tomaz Mastnak, "Civil Society in Slovenia: From Opposition to Power," *Studies in Comparative Communism* 23 (autumn-winter 1990): 305–17, esp. 313–14.

23. For a full accounting of these events, see Dennison Rusinow, *The Yugoslav Experiment, 1948–1974* (Berkeley: University of California Press, 1977), chaps. 7 and 8.

24. Louis Zanga, "The Question of Kosovar Sovereignty," *RFE/RL Research Report* 1, no. 43 (October 30, 1992): 21–26.

25. For an insightful account of the unrest among Serbs of the Krajina, see Misha Glenny, *The Fall of Yugoslavia* (London: Penguin Books, 1992), 12–14.

26. *New York Times*, November 28, 1990, A7.

27. *Bulletin of the European Communities* 5 (1991): 63 (emphasis added) (henceforth cited as *Bull. EC*).

28. Marc Weller, "The International Response to the Dissolution of the Socialist Federal Republic of Yugoslavia," *American Journal of International Law* 86 (July 1992): 570–71.

29. U.S. Department of State, *Dispatch* 2, no. 22 (June 3, 1991): 395–96 (emphasis added).

30. U.S. Department of State, *Dispatch* 2, no. 26 (July 1, 1991): 463, 468.

31. U.S. Commission, *The Conference on Security and Cooperation in Europe: An Overview of the CSCE Process, Recent Meetings and Institutional Development,* 22, 28.

32. *New York Times,* July 6, 1991, 4.

33. *New York Times,* July 6, 1991, 4.

34. Nikola Tietze, "German Reactions to the Crisis in Yugoslavia" (research paper, Department of Politics, Brandeis University, spring 1993).

35. *Süddeutsche Zeitung,* February 22, 1991, as cited in Tietze, "German Reactions to the Crisis in Yugoslavia."

36. Tietze, "German Reactions to the Crisis in Yugoslavia."

37. *Bull. EC* 7–8 (1991): 107–8.

38. *New York Times,* July 7, 1991, 6; and July 8, 1991, A1. The difficulty of these negotiations was confirmed in private discussions with participants on both the European and Yugoslav sides.

39. *New York Times,* July 11, 1991.

40. See *Delo,* December 4, 1993.

41. FBIS, *Daily Report: Eastern Europe,* January 25, 1991, 70.

42. FBIS, *Daily Report: Eastern Europe,* July 8, 1991, 56–57.

43. *Pravda,* June 29, 1991, as trans. in *Current Digest of the Soviet Press* 43, no. 26 (July 31, 1991): 19 (henceforth cited as *CDSP*).

44. *Izvestiia,* August 7, 1991, as trans. in *CDSP* 43, no. 32 (September 11, 1991): 19.

45. See *Bull. EC* 7–8 (1991): 115–16; and 9 (1991): 63.

46. Much of the account of the Conference on Yugoslavia that follows is based on public reports given by Lord Carrington at the tenth plenary session of the conference, March 9, 1992, at the London meeting of the International Conference of the Former Yugoslavia, August 26–27, 1992, and on separate interviews with two senior members of the EC negotiating team, conducted in March 1992 and June 1993.

47. *Times* (London), August 16, 1991, 8; *Sunday Times* (London), September 1, 1991, 6; *New York Times,* July 5, 1992, 6.

48. See, for example, Miodrag Ivanovic, "The Fate of the Yugoslav Military Industry," *Jane's Intelligence Review* 5, no. 3 (March 1993): 164–65; Milan Vego, "The New Yugoslav Defence Industry," parts 1 and 2, *Jane's Intelligence Review* 5, no. 11 (November 1993): 502–5; no. 12 (December 1993): 541–46; idem, "The Muslim Defence Industry in Bosnia and Herzegovina," *Jane's Intelligence Review* 6, no. 5 (May 1994): 213–14.

49. U.S. Department of State, *Dispatch* 2, no. 39 (September 30, 1991): 723; see also *New York Times,* September 27, 1991, A6.

50. *Bull. EC* 11 (1991): 70–72, 91.

51. UN Security Council documents S/23239 (November 24, 1991), S/23280 (December 11, 1991), and S/23592 (February 15, 1992).

52. The provision not to prejudge the outcome is contained in UN Security Council document S/23280 (December 11, 1991), Annex III, 15. For a report on German opposition, see *Times* (London), November 16, 1991, 11.

53. John Newhouse, "The Diplomatic Round: Dodging the Problem," *New Yorker,* August 24, 1992, 65; cf. John Zametica, *The Yugoslav Conflict,* Adelphi Paper 270 (London: Brassey's for the International Institute for Strategic Studies, 1992), 65.

54. Complete text in *Bull. EC* 12 (1991): 119–20.

55. EC Conference on Yugoslavia, Arbitration Commission, *Opinion No. 4 on International Recognition of the Socialist Republic of Bosnia-Hercegovina by the European Community and its Member States,* January 11, 1992, as translated by the services of the Commission of the European Communities.

56. Newhouse, "Diplomatic Round," 65.

57. Lord Carrington suggested as much in his comments at the London

Conference in August 1992, and both he and Secretary Vance are quoted to this effect in Newhouse, "Diplomatic Round," 66.

58. The text of the agreement can be found in FBIS, *Daily Report: Eastern Europe,* March 19, 1992, 21–22. Later information was secured from EC Conference on Yugoslavia, *Background Documents Pack* (mimeo).

59. FBIS, *Daily Report: Western Europe,* April 23, 1992, 2.

60. For an account by the then U.S. ambassador of his advice to the Bosnians, see *New York Times,* August 29, 1993, 10.

61. According to the testimony of Lt. Gen. Barry R. McCaffrey, assistant to the chairman of the Joint Chiefs of Staff before the Senate Armed Services Committee on August 11, 1992, the Bosnian Serb army then consisted of thirty-five thousand former JNA troops and several hundred armored vehicles and artillery. Serb and Croatian irregular forces also each numbered about thirty-five thousand men, but they were less well armed. The Muslim-led Bosnian government forces numbered about fifty thousand poorly armed troops. General McCaffrey estimated that up to fifteen thousand regular Croatian troops were operating in Bosnia at the time, concentrated in the north (Bosanska Posavina) and in the south (western Herzegovina).

62. James Gow, "Belgrade and Bosnia: An Assessment of the Yugoslav Military," *Jane's Intelligence Review* 5, no. 6 (June 1993): 246.

63. *Izvestiia,* June 8, 1992, as trans. in *CDPSP* 44, no. 22 (July 1, 1992): 5–6.

64. UN Security Council, Resolution 777 (September 19, 1992).

65. By the end of July 1992, the UN high commissioner for refugees estimated that some 2.25 million refugees had fled. Croatia was caring for some 628,500 refugees, who had fled from the fighting in Croatia itself, as well as from the conflict in neighboring Bosnia-Herzegovina. Slovenia was sheltering 66,000 refugees. Hungary had received 60,000 and Austria 50,000. Each then placed tighter restrictions on entry, as had several other European states. Germany had accepted 200,000 refugees. Sweden, which had taken in some 44,000 refugees, began to consider their deportation. *New York Times,* July 21, 1992, A6; and July 24, 1992, A1.

66. *New York Times,* May 14, 1992, A1.

67. *New York Times,* May 5, 1992, A10.

68. *Washington Post,* May 13, 1992, A28.

69. *New York Times,* May 23, 1992, A1.

70. *Washington Post,* May 8, 1992, A17; see map, A19.

71. *Washington Post,* May 20, 1992, A24.

72. *Washington Post,* June 27, 1992, A1.

73. *New York Times,* June 29, 1992, A13.

74. *Nezavisimaia gazeta,* June 9, 1992, as trans. in *CDPSP* 44, no. 23 (July 8, 1992): 19.

75. For examples of such criticism in *Pravda, Sovetskaia Rossiia,* and *Izvestiia,* see *CDPSP* 44, no. 22 (July 1, 1992): 2–5.

76. *Izvestiia,* June 8, 1992, as trans. in *CDPSP* 44, no. 22 (July 1, 1992): 6.

77. *Izvestiia,* June 27 and 29, 1992, as trans. in *CDPSP* 44, no. 26 (July 29, 1992): 24–25.

78. This warning came in Kozyrev's provocative, mock speech to the Stockholm meeting of CSCE foreign ministers. *Izvestiia,* December 15, 1992, as trans. in *CDPSP* 44, no. 50 (January 13, 1993): 120.

79. *Washington Post,* July 9, 1992, A19.

80. *New York Times,* June 19, 1992, A6.

81. *New York Times,* July 16, 1992, A8.

82. *New York Times,* July 18, 1992, 4.

83. *Washington Post,* August 6, 1992, A1.

84. *New York Times,* August 9, 1992, 1.

85. *New York Times,* August 12, 1992, A8; and August 14, 1992, A6.

86. The discussion below is based on the verbatim record, printed as International Conference on the Former Socialist Federal Republic of Yugoslavia, *The London Conference, 26–27 August 1992* (mimeo).

87. UN Security Council document S/24795 (November 11, 1992).

88. *New York Times,* October 30, 1992, 1.

89. UN Security Council document S/25015 (December 24, 1992).

90. E.g., Arend Lijphart, "The Power-Sharing Approach," in *Conflict and Peacemaking in Multiethnic Societies,* ed. Joseph V. Montville (Lexington, MA: Lexington Books, 1990), 491–509.

91. Published as Annex VII of S/24795.

92. UN Security Council document S/25015 (December 24, 1992), 6–8.

93. *New York Times,* January 7, 1993, A23; and January 8, 1993, A25.

94. Steven L. Burg and Paul S. Shoup, *A Workshop on Peace in Bosnia-Hercegovina: Co-Chairs' Report* (Washington, DC: International Research and Exchanges Board and Woodrow Wilson International Center for Scholars, 1993).

95. *New York Times,* September 28, 1992, A1.

96. *New York Times,* September 28, 1992, A1.

97. *New York Times,* January 22, 1993, A1.

98. *New York Times,* January 28, 1993, A7.

99. U.S. Department of State, *Statement by U.S. Secretary of State Warren Christopher,* February 10, 1993, 4.

100. *New York Times,* March 11, 1993, A1.

101. *Washington Post,* May 23, 1993, A1.

102. *New York Times,* June 16, 1993, A13.

103. *Boston Globe,* December 5, 1993, 1.

104. UN Security Council document S/26233 (August 3, 1993), 7.

105. UN Security Council document S/26260 (August 6, 1993), 8.

106. UN Security Council documents S/26337 (August 20, 1993), S/26337/ Add.1 (August 23, 1993), and S/26337/Add.2 (August 23, 1993).

107. For reports of these splits, see *New York Times,* June 23, 1993, A1; June 25, 1993, A3; June 30, 1993, A6; and August 1, 1993, 14.

108. *New York Times,* August 28, 1993, 4; and August 29, 1993, 10.

109. On U.S. efforts, see *New York Times,* August 1, 1993, 15; August 3, 1993, A1; August 4, 1993, A1; and August 6, 1993, A8. On distortions in media coverage and their effect on policymakers, see Nik Gowing, "Real-Time Television Coverage of Armed Conflicts and Diplomatic Crises: Does It Pressure or Distort Foreign Policy Decisions?" *Working Paper Series,* no. 94–1 (Joan Shorenstein Barone Center on the Press, Politics and Public Policy, John F. Kennedy School of Government, Harvard University, June 1994), 59–66.

110. For the articulation of these positions, see comments by Haris Silajdzic, reported in *New York Times,* August 25, 1993, A6.

111. UN Security Council document S/26395 (September 1, 1993), 2–5.

112. *New York Times,* September 8, 1993, A3; and September 10, 1993, A3.

113. UN Security Council document S/26486 (September 23, 1993).

114. *New York Times,* October 3, 1993, 10; September 22, 1993, A12; September 29, 1993, A3; and September 30, 1993, A1.

115. *New York Times,* September 30, 1993, A1.

116. UN Security Council document S/26922 (December 29, 1993).

117. UN Security Council document S/1994/64 (January 21, 1994): appendix 1.

118. *New York Times,* January 31, 1994, A9; and February 1, 1994, A8; *Boston Globe,* February 1, 1994, 8.

119. *New York Times,* February 14, 1994, A6.

120. On these differences, see *New York Times,* January 22, 1994, 4; January 24, 1994, A5; and January 28, 1994, A6.

121. *New York Times,* January 6, 1994, A8.

122. Gowing, "Real-Time Television Coverage," 69–76; and *New York Times,* February 6, 1994, 13; February 7, 1994, A1; and February 8, 1994, A1. For an informative retrospective account of U.S. decisionmaking, see *New York Times,* February 14, 1994, A6.

123. *New York Times,* February 14, 1994, A6.

124. *New York Times,* April 26, 1994, A6; and April 30, 1994, 3.

125. See, for example, *New York Times,* February 12, 1994, 5; and March 13, 1994, 10.

126. For a detailed examination of the American view, see *New York Times,* March 13, 1994, 10.

127. *New York Times,* April 8, 1994, A1.

128. *Balkan News and East European Report,* March 27, 1994, 14.

129. *New York Times,* February 11, 1994, A6; and February 13, 1994, 12.

130. *New York Times,* March 18, 1994, A1.

131. *New York Times,* October 11, 1993, A1.

132. On the meeting of diplomats, see *New York Times,* February 23, 1994, A8. On the reduced role of the ICFY, see UN Security Council document S/1994/811 (July 8, 1994), 13–16.

133. UN Security Council document S/1994/1081 (September 21, 1994).

134. *New York Times,* July 7, 1994, A1.

135. *Izvestiia,* August 3, 1994, as trans. in *CDPSP* 46, no. 31 (August 31, 1994): 21.

136. *New York Times,* November 26, 1994, 7.

137. *New York Times,* March 1, 1995, A5.

138. For an extensive review of the evidence, see *Washington Post,* July 28, 1995, A1.

139. *Washington Post,* April 14, 1995, A1. See also *New York Times,* April 15, 1995, 3.

140. *New York Times,* July 20, 1995, A1.

141. *New York Times,* July 12, 1995, A6; July 13, 1995, A1, A6; and July 18, 1995, A1.

142. *New York Times,* July 18, 1995, A1; July 21, 1995, A1; July 22, 1995, 1; and July 23, 1995, 1. On the domestic political forces shaping administration actions, see *New York Times,* August 19, 1995, 1.

143. *New York Times,* August 13, 1995, 1.

144. *New York Times,* August 9, 1995, A7.

145. *New York Times,* August 16, 1995, A8; and August 18, 1995, A4.

146. *New York Times,* August 26, 1995, 2; and August 28, 1995, 1.

147. *New York Times,* August 29, 1995, A10.

148. *New Europe,* September 3–9, 1995, 3, 25; and September 10–16, 1995, 27.

149. For a report of the attack, see *New York Times,* August 29, 1995, A1. For the dispute over its origins, see *Boston Globe,* September 3, 1995, 1.

150. *New York Times,* September 9, 1995, 1.

151. The BBC reported on January 5, 1993, for example, that Izetbegovic challenged Karadzic by agreeing to the political agreement and demanding that the Serbs say yes to the principle that provinces could not secede, thereby throwing the onus for any failure to reach agreement onto the Serbs.

152. *New York Times,* January 23, 1993, 5; and February 3, 1993, A8.

153. *New York Times,* April 29, 1993, A1; and *Washington Post,* April 29, 1993, A35.

154. *New York Times,* April 29, 1993, A1; and May 1, 1993, 5.

155. *New York Times,* May 2, 1993, 1.

156. Compare the NATO statement reported in *New York Times,* August 4, 1993, A8, and the briefing by an unnamed administration official in *New York Times,* August 6, 1993, A8.

157. *New York Times,* August 11, 1993, A3.

158. *Prague Document on Further Development of CSCE Institutions and Structures,* January 30, 1992 (mimeo), paras. 16, 22.

NOTES TO CHAPTER 3

1. Gabriel A. Almond and Sidney Verba, *The Civic Culture* (Princeton: Princeton University Press, 1963).

2. Robert D. Putnam, *Making Democracy Work: Civic Traditions in Modern Italy* (Princeton: Princeton University Press, 1993).

3. Terry Lynn Karl, "Dilemmas of Democratization in Latin America," in *Comparative Political Dynamics,* ed. Dankwart A. Rustow and Kenneth Paul Erickson (New York: HarperCollins, 1991), 163–91, esp. 168. Edward N. Muller and Mitchell A. Seligson, "Civic Culture and Democracy: The Question of Causal Relationships," *American Political Science Review* 88, no. 3 (September 1994): 635–52. John Rawls, "The Idea of an Overlapping Consensus," in *Political Liberalism* (New York: Columbia University Press, 1993), 133–72.

4. On the transformation of German political culture, see Sidney Verba, "Germany: The Remaking of Political Culture," in *Political Culture and Political Development,* ed. Lucien Pye and Sidney Verba (Princeton: Princeton University Press, 1965), 130–70; and David P. Conradt, "Changing German Political Culture," in *The Civic Culture Revisited,* ed. Gabriel A. Almond and Sidney Verba (Boston: Little, Brown, 1980), 212–72.

5. Beate Sissenich, "Transforming Political Culture in Unified Germany" (research paper, Department of Politics, Brandeis University, April 1994), 6–11.

6. David Easton, "A Re-assessment of the Concept of Political Support," *British Journal of Political Science* 5 (1975): 435–57. See also Edward Muller and Thomas Jukam, "On the Meaning of Political Support," *American Political Science Review* 71, no. 4 (December 1977): 1561–95.

7. In 1921, ethnic Germans constituted 30.6 percent of the population of the Czech lands. By 1970, Germans constituted less than 1 percent of the population. Alice Teichova, *The Czechoslovak Economy, 1918–1980* (London: Routledge, 1988), 7.

8. Stephan M. Horak, *Eastern European National Minorities, 1919–1980* (Littleton, CO: Libraries Unlimited, 1985), 120.

9. See, for example, *New York Times,* March 15, 1991, A3; and March 16, 1991, 3.

10. H. Gordon Skilling, *Czechoslovakia's Interrupted Revolution* (Princeton: Princeton University Press, 1976), 16–19.

11. Carol Skalnik Leff, *National Conflict in Czechoslovakia* (Princeton: Princeton University Press, 1988), 148–77.

12. See, for example, Gary K. Bertsch, "A Cross-National Analysis of the Community-Building Process in Yugoslavia," *Comparative Political Studies* 4, no. 4 (January 1972): 438–60.

13. Misha Glenny, *The Fall of Yugoslavia* (London: Penguin Books, 1992), 6–7.

14. See Michael Hechter, *Internal Colonialism: The Celtic Fringe in British National Development, 1536–1966* (London: Routledge and Kegan Paul, 1975); and idem, "Group Formation and the Cultural Division of Labor," *American Journal of Sociology* 82 (September 1978): 296–301.

15. See Jiri Musil, "Czech and Slovak Society: Outline of a Comparative Study," reprinted in English from *Czech Sociological Review* 1 (1993).

16. Peter Martin, "Rising Unemployment in Czechoslovakia," *RFE/RL Research Report* 1, no. 3 (January 17, 1992): 39; and Kamil Janacek, "Recent Czechoslovak Trends Offer a Mixed Picture," *RFE/RL Research Report* 1, no. 32 (August 14, 1992): 58.

17. The political economy of interregional conflict and its effect on ethnic relations in Yugoslavia is presented in detail in Steven L. Burg, *Conflict and Cohesion in Socialist Yugoslavia* (Princeton: Princeton University Press, 1983); and idem, "Elite Conflict in Post-Tito Yugoslavia," *Soviet Studies* 38, no. 2 (April 1986): 170–93; and in Dijana Plestina, *Regional Development in Communist Yugoslavia: Success, Failure, and Consequences* (Boulder: Westview, 1992).

18. Income ratios were calculated on the basis of national income data in *Statisticki godisnjak SFRJ 1963* (Statistical Yearbook SFRY 1963) (Belgrade: SZS, 1963), 360; *Statisticki godisnjak Jugoslavije 1973* (Statistical yearbook of Yugoslavia 1973), 385 (henceforth cited as *SGJ*); *SGJ 1983*, 464; and *SGJ 1990*, 477; population data in Savezni savod za statistiku (SZS), "Popis stanovnistva, domacinstva i stanova 1981. godini: Nacionalni sastav stanovnistva po opstinama" (Census of the population, households, and apartments, 1981: National composition of the population by counties), *Statisticki bilten 1295* (Belgrade: SZS, 1982), 9–17; and the population estimate for 1988 in *SGJ 1990*, 437.

19. Milica Zarkovic Bookman, "The Economic Basis of Regional Autarchy in Yugoslavia," *Soviet Studies* 42, no. 1 (January 1990): 93–109.

20. *Prague Post*, October 1–7, 1991, 12.

21. Marek Boguszak, "Nationalism, Democracy, and Economic Reform in Czechoslovakia: 1990–1992," in *Bound to Change: Consolidating Democracy in East Central Europe*, ed. Peter M. E. Volten (New York: Institute for East-West Studies, 1992), 233–34.

22. FBIS, *Daily Report: Eastern Europe,* January 30, 1992, 8.

23. See Martin O. Heisler, "Ethnicity and Ethnic Relations in the Modern West," and Milton J. Esman, "Political and Psychological Factors in Ethnic Conflict," in *Conflict and Peacemaking in Multiethnic Societies,* ed. Joseph V. Montville (Lexington, MA: Lexington Books, 1990), 21–64.

24. James Gow, "One Year of War in Bosnia and Hercegovina," *RFE/RL Research Reports* 2, no. 23 (June 4, 1993): 1–13.

25. John J. Mearsheimer and Robert A. Pape, "The Answer: A Partition Plan for Bosnia," *New Republic,* June 14, 1993, 22–28.

26. See *Prague Post,* June 9–15, 1993, 1, 2.

27. Fabian Schmidt, "Has the Kosovo Crisis Been Internationalized?" *RFE/RL Research Report* 2, no. 44 (November 5, 1993): 36.

28. *Bull. EC* 6 (1993): 12.

29. On EU decisionmaking formulas, see *Economist,* October 16–22, 1993, 51. On the more general dilemmas of East European accession, see Alexis Galinos, "Central Europe and the EU: Prospects for Closer Integration," *RFE/RL Research Report* 3, no. 29 (July 22, 1994): 19–25.

30. *Bull. EC* 6 (1993): 13.

31. This definition is adapted from Philippe C. Schmitter, "Modes of Interest Intermediation and Models of Societal Change in Western Europe," *Comparative Political Studies* 1 (April 1977): 9.

32. Seymour Martin Lipset, *Political Man* (Garden City, NY: Doubleday, 1963), 70 ff; Arend Lijphart, "Consociational Democracy," in *Consociational Democracy,* ed. Kenneth McRae (Toronto: McClelland and Stewart, 1974), 70–74; and idem, *The Politics of Accommodation,* 2d rev. ed. (Berkeley: University of California Press, 1975), 1–15.

33. Gabriel A. Almond, "Comparative Political Systems," *Journal of Politics* 18 (August 1956): 391–409. See also Alvin Rabushka and Kenneth A. Shepsle, *Politics in Plural Societies: A Theory of Democratic Instability* (Columbus, OH: Charles E. Merrill, 1972).

34. Daniel J. Elazar, "International and Comparative Federalism," *PS: Political Science and Politics* 26, no. 3 (June 1993): 194.

35. Val R. Lorwin, "Segmented Pluralism: Ideological Cleavages and Political Cohesion in the Smaller European Democracies," in *Consociational Democracy,* ed. McRae, 33.

36. Eric Nordlinger, *Conflict Regulation in Divided Societies,* Occasional Papers in International Affairs, no. 29 (Cambridge: Center for International Affairs, Harvard University, 1972).

37. Lijphart, "Consociational Democracy," 76.

38. Brian Barry, "Political Accommodation and Consociational Democracy," *British Journal of Political Science* 5 (October 1975): 477–505, esp. 502–3.

39. I have examined these in detail in *Conflict and Cohesion.*

40. See Burg, "Elite Conflict in Post-Tito Yugoslavia" for a detailed narrative and analysis.

41. Vladimir V. Kusin, "Czechs and Slovaks: The Road to the Current Debate," *Report on Eastern Europe* 1, no. 40 (October 5, 1990): 6; see also the polling data reported in *Prague Post,* October 1–7, 1991, 1.

42. FBIS, *Daily Report: Eastern Europe,* September 24, 1991, 13.

43. Dzintra Bungs, Saulius Girnius, and Riina Kionka, "Citizenship Legislation in the Baltic States," *RFE/RL Research Report* 1, no. 50 (December 18, 1992): 38–40. For a useful summary of the debates over constitutional reforms in the Baltic states, see articles by the same authors, *RFE/RL Research Report* 1, no. 27, July 3, 1992, 57–69.

44. Ann Sheehy, "The Estonian Law on Aliens," *RFE/RL Research Report* 2, no. 38 (September 4, 1993): 7–11.

45. Richard J. Krickus, "Latvia's 'Russian Question,' " *RFE/RL Research Report* 2, no. 18 (April 30, 1993): 29–34.

46. FBIS, *Daily Report: Eastern Europe,* October 30, 1990, 14–15.

47. Jan Obrman, "Language Law Stirs Controversy in Slovakia," *Report on Eastern Europe* 1, no. 46 (November 16, 1990): 13–17.

48. Pavel Mates, "The New Slovak Constitution," and Alfred Reisch, "Meciar and Slovakia's Hungarian Minority," *RFE/RL Research Report* 1, no. 43 (October 30, 1992): 39–42, 13–20.

49. These are ably surveyed in Robert M. Hayden, "Constitutional Nationalism in the Formerly Yugoslav Republics," *Slavic Review* 51, no. 4 (winter 1992): 654–73.

50. "[Croatian] Law on Citizenship," in *Constitutions of the Countries of the World,* ed. Albert P. Blaustein and Gisbert H. Flanz (Dobbs Ferry, NY: Oceana Publications, 1993), article 9, 127.

51. FBIS, *Daily Report: Soviet Union,* November 1, 1989, 92–93; and November 5, 1991, 63–64.

52. Susan Stewart, "Ukraine's Policy toward Its Ethnic Minorities," *RFE/RL Research Report* 2, no. 36 (September 10, 1993): 55–62.

53. John Allcock, "Yugoslavia," in *New Political Parties of Eastern Europe and the Soviet Union,* ed. Bogdan Szajkowski (Essex: Longman Group UK, 1991), 312–19.

54. For a compendium of views on proportional representation systems, see Arend Lijphart, "Constitutional Choices for New Democracies," Guy Lardeyret, "The Problem with PR," Quentin L. Quade, "PR and Democratic Statecraft," and Arend Lijphart, "Double-Checking the Evidence," in *The Global Resurgence of Democracy,* ed. Larry Diamond and Marc F. Plattner (Baltimore: Johns Hopkins University Press, 1993), 146–77.

55. Donald Horowitz, *A Democratic South Africa?* (Berkeley: University of California Press, 1991), 175.

56. Horowitz, *A Democratic South Africa?* 172–93.

57. Horowitz, *A Democratic South Africa?* 190.

58. Horowitz, *A Democratic South Africa?* 197.

59. James Coleman, "Democracy in Permanently Divided Systems," *American Behavioral Scientist* 35, nos. 4–5 (March-June 1992): 363–74.

60. Coleman, "Democracy in Permanently Divided Systems," 373.

61. Milan Andrejevich, "Elections in Slovenia Maintain the Status Quo," *RFE/RL Research Report* 1, no. 50 (December 18, 1992): 28–31.

62. *RFE/RL News Briefs,* January 25–29, 1993, 11.

63. Stan Markotich, "Stable Support for Extremism?" *Transition* 1, no. 4 (March 29, 1995): 31–32, 63.

64. Saulius Girnius, "The Parliamentary Elections in Lithuania," *RFE/RL Research Report* 1, no. 48 (December 4, 1992): 6–12.

65. Saulius Girnius, "Lithuanian Politics Seven Months after the Elections," *RFE/RL Research Report* 2, no. 27 (July 2, 1993): 16–21.

66. Riina Kionka, "Free-Market Coalition Assumes Power in Estonia," *RFE/RL Research Report* 1, no. 46 (November 20, 1992): 6–11.

67. *New York Times,* November 12, 1993, A6; and *Nezavisimaia gazeta,* October 21, 1993, as trans. in *CDPSP* 45, no. 42 (November 17, 1993): 22–23.

68. Saulius Girnius, "A Tilt to the Left," *Transition* 1, no. 9 (June 9, 1995): 38–40.

69. Milan Andrejevich, "Croatia between Stability and Civil War," parts 1 and 2, *Report on Eastern Europe* 1, no. 37 (September 14, 1990): 38–44; no. 39 (September 28, 1990): 38–44.

70. U.S. Commission, *Parliamentary and Presidential Elections in an Independent Croatia* (Washington, DC: U.S. Commission, 1992).

71. *New York Times,* August 5, 1993, A10.

72. T. J. Pempel, "Introduction: Uncommon Democracies: The One-Party Dominant Regimes," in *Uncommon Democracies: The One-Party Dominant Regimes,* ed. T. J. Pempel (Ithaca, NY: Cornell University Press, 1990), 7.

73. See the collection of articles under the heading "Regime Transitions, Elites, and Bureaucracies in Eastern Europe," edited by Hans-Ulrich Derlien and George J. Szablowski, in a special issue of *Governance* 6, no. 3 (July 1993).

74. Karoly Okolicsanyi, "Hungary Sets Limits on State Ownership," *RFE/RL Research Report* 1, no. 44 (November 6, 1992): 40–45.

75. Okolicsanyi, "Hungary Sets Limits," 43.

76. Tamas L. Fellegi, "Regime Transformation and the Mid-Level Bureaucratic Forces in Hungary," in *Bound to Change,* ed. Volten, 119–50.

77. FBIS, *Daily Report: Eastern Europe,* April 12, 1995, 13; and *Budapest Sun,* September 7–13, 1995, 1.

78. *New York Times,* February 21, 1995, D2.

79. Wolfgang Wessels, "The EC Council: The Community's Decisionmaking Center," in *The New European Community,* ed. Robert O. Keohane and Stanley Hoffman (Boulder: Westview, 1991), 136.

80. Easton, "A Re-assessment."

NOTES TO CHAPTER 4

1. For an example of the clash between narrowly economic and more broadly social perspectives on political change in the post-communist states, see the argument of Jeffrey Sachs, the leading proponent of "shock therapy," in "Post-communist Parties and the Politics of Entitlements," *Transition: The Newsletter about Reforming Economies* 6, no. 3 (March 1995): 1–4; and the critical response by Polish economists Mieczyslaw Kabaj and Tadeusz Kowalik, "Who Is Responsible for Postcommunist Successes in Eastern Europe?" (letter), *Transition: The Newsletter about Reforming Economies* 6, nos. 7–8 (July-August 1995): 7–8.

2. Jozef M. van Brabant, *Remaking Eastern Europe: On the Political Economy of Transition* (Dordrecht: Kluwer Academic Publishers, 1990), 107–9.

3. Alessandro Giustiniani, Francesco Papadia, and Daniela Porciani, "Growth and Catch-Up in Central and Eastern Europe: Macroeconomic Effects on Western Countries," *Essays in International Finance,* no. 186 (Princeton: International Finance Section, Department of Economics, Princeton University, April 1992), 16–21, esp. table 7, p. 18.

4. Giustiniani et al., "Growth and Catch-Up," 22.

5. Amartya Sen, "What Did You Learn in the World Today?" *American Behavioral Scientist* 34, no. 5 (May-June 1991): 530–48.

6. Sen, "What Did You Learn in the World Today?" 544–45.

7. Larry Diamond, "Economic Development and Democracy Reconsidered," *American Behavioral Scientist* 35, nos. 4–5 (March-June 1992): 486.

8. Diamond, "Economic Development and Democracy Reconsidered," 488.

9. Adam Przeworski, *Democracy and the Market: Political and Economic Reforms in Eastern Europe and Latin America* (Cambridge: Cambridge University Press, 1991), 186–87.

10. Van Brabant, *Remaking Eastern Europe,* 117.

11. See A. E. Dick Howard, *Democracy's Dawn: A Directory of American Initiatives on Constitutionalism, Democracy, and the Rule of Law in Central and Eastern Europe* (Charlottesville: University of Virginia Press for the United States Institute of Peace, 1991).

12. See Bilahari Kausikan, "Asia's Different Standard," *Foreign Policy* 92 (fall 1993): 24–41.

13. Aryieh Neier, "Asia's Unacceptable Standard," *Foreign Policy* 92 (fall 1993): 42–51.

14. John Zametica, *The Yugoslav Conflict,* Adelphi Paper 270 (London: Brassey's for the International Institute for Strategic Studies, 1992), 78.

15. Steven L. Burg, "Avoiding Ethnic War: Lessons of the Yugoslav Crisis," *Twentieth Century Fund Newsletter* 2, no. 3 (fall 1992): 1, 4, 11.

16. United States Institute of Peace, "Armenia, Azerbaijan and Nagorno-Karabakh: State Sovereignty vs. Self-Determination," *In Brief...,* no. 42 (September 1992): 5.

17. Robert A. Dahl, *Dilemmas of Pluralist Democracy* (New Haven: Yale University Press, 1982), 85 ff.

18. Kumar Rupesinghe, *Conflict Resolution: Current Options and New Mechanisms* (International Alert, London, March 1993, mimeo), 9.

19. Rupesinghe, *Conflict Resolution,* 10–11.

20. Florence Benoit-Rohmer and Hilde Hardeman, *The Minority Question in Europe: Towards the Creation of a Coherent European Regime,* CEPS Paper no. 55 (Brussels: Center for European Policy Studies, 1994), 22–37.

21. For discussion of the American institutional approach versus a European cultural approach to rights, see Michael J. Lacey and Knud Haakonssen, eds., *A Culture of Rights: The Bill of Rights in Philosophy, Politics and Law, 1791 and 1991* (Cambridge: Cambridge University Press, 1991).

22. See Andre Molitor, "The Reform of the Belgian Constitution," in *Conflict and Coexistence in Belgium,* ed. Arend Lijphart, Institute of International Studies Research Series, no. 46 (Berkeley: University of California, Institute of International Studies, 1981), 139–53. For a more detailed treatment, see Kenneth D. McRae, *Conflict and Compromise in Multilingual Societies,* vol. 2, *Belgium* (Waterloo, Ont.: Wilfrid Laurier University Press, 1986).

23. See William Zimmerman, *Open Borders, Nonalignment, and the Political Evolution of Yugoslavia* (Princeton: Princeton University Press, 1987), 107–24.

24. Pal Dunay, "Stability in East Central Europe," *Journal of Peace Research* 29, no. 1 (February 1992): 3

25. David J. Scheffer, "Challenges Confronting Collective Security: Humanitarian Intervention," in United States Institute of Peace, *Three Views on the Issue of Humanitarian Intervention* (Washington, DC: United States Institute of Peace, 1992), 4.

26. As quoted in Scheffer, "Challenges Confronting Collective Security," 4.

27. For reports on the Rome Summit and the new NATO strategy, as well as the text of the Rome Declaration, see *NATO Review* 6 (December 1991).

28. Alfred A. Reisch, "Central and East Europe's Quest for NATO Membership," *RFE/RL Research Report* 2, no. 28 (July 9, 1993): 33–47.

29. Press conference, October 21, 1993, Travemünde, Germany.

30. See Joshua B. Spero, "Central European Security," *Problems of Communism* 40, no. 6 (November-December 1991); and idem, "The Warsaw-Prague-Budapest Triangle: Central European Security after the Visegrad Summit," Polish Institute of International Affairs, *Occasional Papers,* no. 31 (1992).

31. See his op-ed essay in *New York Times,* October 17, 1993, IV:17.

32. Harold Brown and Charles Kupchan, *Should Nato Expand? Report of an Independent Task Force* (New York: Council on Foreign Relations, 1995).

33. Brown and Kupchan, *Should Nato Expand?* 15.

34. *New York Times,* November 26, 1993, A11.

35. Alfred A. Reisch, "Slovakia's Minority Policy under International Scrutiny," *RFE/RL Research Report* 2, no. 49 (December 10, 1993): 35–42.

36. *Balkan News and East European Report,* March 26–April 1, 1995, 42.

37. John Kriendler, "NATO's Changing Role: Opportunities and Constraints for Peacekeeping," *NATO Review* 3 (June 1993): 17–18. For the NACC texts, see *NATO Review* 1 (February 1993): 28 ff.

38. *New York Times,* September 9, 1995, 1.

39. *NATO Review* 4 (August 1993): 30–35.

40. *An Agenda for Peace: Preventive Diplomacy, Peacemaking, and Peacekeeping,* United Nations document A/47/277 (June 17, 1992).

41. The mandate of the high commissioner is defined in section 2 of the Helsinki Summit Declaration, reprinted in *CSCE Helsinki Document 1992: The Challenges of Change* (Washington, DC: U.S. Commission, 1992).

42. "Key-Note Speech of Mr. Max van der Stoel, High Commissioner on National Minorities," *CSCE ODHIR Bulletin* 2, no. 2 (spring-summer 1994): 7–13.

43. "High Commissioner on National Minorities," *CSCE ODHIR Bulletin* 2, no. 2 (spring-summer 1994): 52–53; "High Commissioner on National Minorities," *CSCE ODHIR Bulletin* 3, no. 2 (spring 1995): 56–57; and Wilhelm Hoynck, "New Challenges on the OSCE Conflict Resolution Agenda," *CSCE ODHIR Bulletin* 3, no. 2 (spring 1995): 1–8.

44. For an overview of CSCE discussions of peacekeeping, see U.S. Commission, *The Helsinki Follow-Up Meeting of the Conference on Security and Cooperation in Europe, March 24–July 8, 1992* (Washington, DC: U.S. Commission, 1992), 18–20.

45. Provisions for CSCE peacekeeping are to be found in paragraphs 17 to 56 of section 3 of *CSCE Helsinki Document 1992: The Challenges of Change.*

46. U.S. Commission, *Helsinki Follow-Up Meeting,* 41–42.

47. This interpretation is based on the account contained in Victor-Yves Ghebali, "The CSCE Forum for Security Cooperation: Opening Gambits," *NATO Review* 3 (June 1993): 26–27; and the final text contained in "CSCE: Budapest Document 1994: Towards a Genuine Partnership in a New Era" (mimeo).

48. U.S. Commission, *Human Rights and Democratization in Croatia* (Washington, DC: U.S. Commission, 1993); idem, *Human Rights and Democratization in Slovakia* (Washington, DC: U.S. Commission, 1993); idem, *Human Rights and Democratization in Estonia* (Washington, DC: U.S. Commission, 1993); and idem, *Human Rights and Democratization in Latvia* (Washington, DC: U.S. Commission, 1993).

49. For a report on U.S. opposition to this proposal, see U.S. Commission, *Update on Peaceful Settlements of Disputes in the CSCE Process* (Washington, DC: U.S. Commission, 1993).

50. Anthony Lake, "From Containment to Enlargement" (address given at Johns Hopkins University, September 21, 1993; text distributed by U.S. Department of State, Bureau of Public Affairs, Office of Public Communications).

51. U.S. Commission, *CSCE's High Commissioner on National Minorities* (Washington, DC: U.S. Commission, 1993); and Konrad J. Huber, "The CSCE and Ethnic Conflict in the East," *RFE/RL Research Report* 2, no. 31 (July 30, 1993): 30–36.

52. Conflict Management Group, *Conflict Prevention and Early Warning* (Cambridge, MA: Conflict Management Group, 1992), 3.

53. This distinction is suggested in Conflict Management Group and Harvard Negotiation Project, *Early Warning and Preventive Action in the CSCE: Defining the Role of the High Commissioner on National Minorities* (Cambridge, MA: CMG and HNP, 1992).

54. For a similar suggestion, see John Chipman, "Managing the Politics of Parochialism," *Survival* 35, no. 1 (spring 1993): 163–65.

55. Guillermo O'Donnell and Philippe C. Schmitter, *Transitions from Authoritarian Rule: Tentative Conclusions about Uncertain Democracies* (Baltimore: Johns Hopkins University Press, 1986), 32–34; and Samuel P. Huntington, *The Third Wave: Democratization in the Late Twentieth Century* (Norman: University of Oklahoma Press, 1991), 231 ff.

56. For an exploration of this issue, see James Gow, *Legitimacy and the Military: The Yugoslav Crisis* (London: Pinter, 1992).

57. Chipman makes a similar argument for the Caucasus in "Managing the Politics of Parochialism," 158.

58. Robert C. Toth, *America's Place in the World: An Investigation of the Attitudes of American Opinion Leaders and the American Public about International Affairs* (Washington, DC: Times Mirror Center for the People and the Press, 1993), 65–68, 90–91.

INDEX